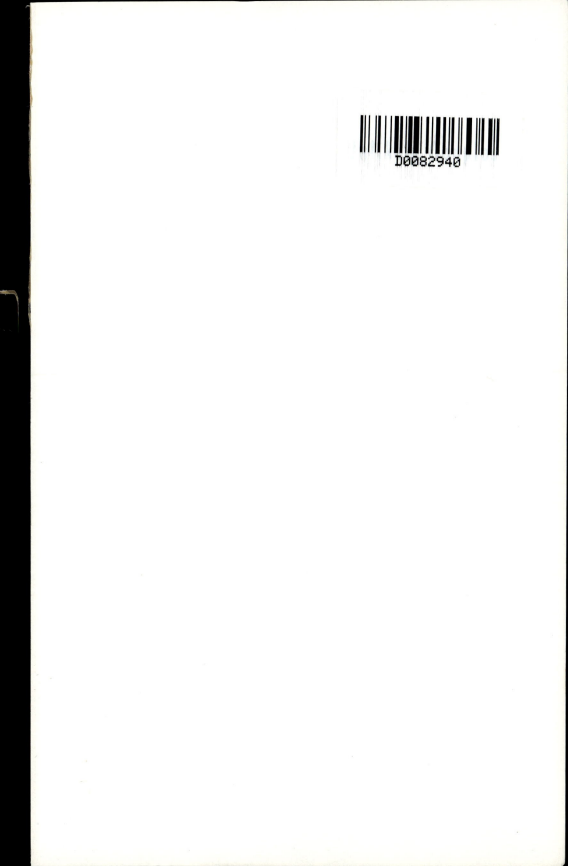

D0082940

Thinking Through Cinema

Thomas E. Wartenberg, Series Editor

Unlikely Couples: Movie Romance as Social Criticism,
Thomas E. Wartenberg

*What Is Non-Fiction Cinema? On the Very Idea of
Motion Picture Communication,* Trevor Ponech

FORTHCOMING

Visions of Virtue in Popular Film, Joseph H. Kupfer

*The Naked and the Undead: Evil and the Appeal of
Horror,* Cynthia A. Freeland

*Reel Racism: Confronting Hollywood's Construction of
Afro-American Culture,* Vincent Rocchio

UNLIKELY COUPLES

COUPLES

Movie Romance as Social Criticism

Thomas E. Wartenberg

Westview Press
A Member of the Perseus Books Group

Thinking Through Cinema

Copyright © 1999 by Westview Press, A Member of the Perseus Books Group

Published in 1999 in the United States of America by Westview Press, 5500 Central Avenue, Boulder, Colorado 80301-2877, and in the United Kingdom by Westview Press, 12 Hid's Copse Road, Cumnor Hill, Oxford OX2 9JJ

Find us on the World Wide Web at www.westviewpress.com

Library of Congress Cataloging-in-Publication Data
Wartenberg, Thomas E.
  Unlikely couples : movie romance as social criticism / Thomas E. Wartenberg.
    p.   cm. — (Thinking through cinema : 2)
  Includes bibliographical references and index.
  ISBN 0-8133-3438-1 (hc).—ISBN 0-8133-3439-X (pbk.)
  1. Love in motion pictures.   I. Title.   II. Series.
PN1995.9.L6W37   1999
791.43'6543—dc21   99-20238
                                                        CIP

The paper used in this publication meets the requirements of the American National Standard for Permanence of Paper for Printed Library Materials Z39.48-1984.

10   9   8   7   6   5   4   3   2

For Wendy

Contents

Part 2
Race

Part 3
Sexual Orientation

Illustrations

Filmography

The photo stills used in the text were taken from the following films (photo numbers are in parentheses):

Some Like It Hot, Billy Wilder, 1959 (1.1)

King Kong, Merian C. Cooper and Ernest B. Schoedsack, 1933 (1.2)

Pygmalion, Anthony Asquith and Leslie Howard, 1938 (2.1 and 2.2)

It Happened One Night, Frank Capra, 1934 (3.1 and 3.2)

Pretty Woman, Gary Marshall, 1990 (4.1, 4.2, and 4.3)

White Palace, Luis Mandoki, 1990 (5.1 and 5.2)

Guess Who's Coming to Dinner, Stanley Kramer, 1967 (6.1 and 6.2)

Jungle Fever, Spike Lee, 1991 (7.1 and 7.2)

Mississippi Masala, Mira Nair, 1991 (8.1 and 8.2)

Angst essen Seele auf (*Ali: Fear Eats the Soul*), Rainer Werner Fassbinder, 1974 (9.1 and 9.2)

Desert Hearts, Donna Deitch, 1986 (10.1 and 10.2)

The Crying Game, Neil Jordan, 1992 (11.1, 11.2, and 11.3)

Preface

Like many American couples, before my wife and I had our son, we would often go to a movie on a Saturday night. One particular Saturday in the winter of 1991, we found ourselves in Cambridge, Massachusetts, and after some discussion—I had been put off by ads for *White Palace* (1990) that featured James Spader crushing Susan Sarandon's bosom—I agreed to see the film anyway. Afterward, Wendy and I found ourselves disagreeing. The central bone of contention between us—I am Jewish, she is not—was whether the film was anti-Semitic: The ending, especially, had angered me.

As I sat down to work the following Monday morning, I could not get our disagreement out of my mind. If I had been able to express my position more clearly, I was sure I could have convinced my wife that I was right. So I sat down—this was seven years ago—to work out my intuitions about the film and, after many false starts and changes of mind, began to write the essay that contained the seeds of this book.

In writing about *White Palace,* I decided I wanted to do two things. First, could I justify devoting so much time to worrying about this film? I did not share the assumption of many who write about popular films that elaborating on their shortcomings is sufficient justification for the effort. *My* preoccupation with this film stemmed instead from a sense that its shortcomings detracted from its interest, that they trivialized the important perception that lay at its heart. As my reflections expanded into a book-length project, I have maintained my commitment to the idea that popular film, a mass art form, can be a locus for reflection on the sorts of issues that have traditionally been the domain of philosophy. Thus, a first aim of this study is to vindicate popular narrative film as a philosophic medium.

But the more I thought about *White Palace,* the more I began to see it as one of a perennial type, a genre that I came to call "the unlikely couple film." All instances of the genre, as I came to conceive it, explore the predicament of two individuals whose efforts to be a romantic couple transgress a social norm regulating appropriate partnering choice. For me, a central question became: Why do so many popular films fit this basic pattern and must they necessarily suffer from flaws similar to those that I had detected in *White Palace?* If so, I decided to try to understand the significance of that fact. This became my second aim in writing about film.

As intimated, my interest in romantic relationships between unlikely partners is more than simply academic. I am the elder son of German-Jewish Holocaust survivors; my wife is the youngest daughter of parents of German-Lutheran heritage. My grandparents belonged to the wealthy Jewish community in Berlin; my wife's paternal grandfather was a mail carrier, and her maternal one, a Lutheran missionary in India. The differences in our religious and, to a lesser extent, class backgrounds qualify us as an unlikely couple, even if not, in this society, highly so. In part, my attraction to films about unlikely couples stems from my realization that the very differences between my wife and me that make our union unlikely have been and continue to be a source of enrichment for both our lives.

It seems to me, and may have already struck the reader, that there is another "unlikely couple" implicated here, the couple consisting of philosophy and film. The unlikeliness of *this* couple is constituted by the fact that philosophy is supposed to be concerned with eternal truths whereas film is the most evanescent of media, one whose very substance is fleeting. Indeed, Plato's condemnation of art for concerning itself with images rather than "the Real" seems particularly apropos for "the reel." So, then, what constitutes the rationale for a philosophic study of popular film?

One claim made by film theorists, although challenged with increasing frequency particularly by those influenced by cultural studies, is that film creates passive spectators. But this seems to me less a claim about the inherent nature of the medium than about the social practice of film viewing that has developed in mainstream American culture. My practice owes as much to its origin in the collegiate culture of the late 1960s, when I first became a passionate consumer of films, as it does to my professional status as a philosopher. When I began seriously watching films, as well as watching serious films—I am thinking here of, for example, the French new wave and Bergman—this was not simply a way of passing an entertaining evening, it was an occasion for serious, often heated, discussion. Far from being passive consumers, my college friends and I used the occasion of the screening—of *Persona,* say, or *Pierrot le fou*—as a jumping-off point for discussions of war and peace, anomie and solidarity, and other pressing issues.

Although we would not have put it this way then, I now see us as having created a practice of active film viewing. We were simply unwilling to allow a film, its images, and its sounds to wash over our consciousnesses, only to be forgotten as we left the theater. Films were works demanding critical intervention rather than acquiescence. In this way, we opened a space between our reception of films and their attempt to position us as viewers.

The lines on these pages may seem distant, indeed, from the sometimes intense give-and-take that accompanies a postflick espresso, but my hope is that the critical practice they embody retains the traces of its origin in those late-night sessions of long ago. To help shape that type of critical practice in my readers is my hope for this book.

The cultivation of a critical practice is, not coincidentally, my understanding of the aim of philosophy, too. Despite a repeated tendency among philosophers to conceive their discipline as a body of knowledge, a science, or even a science of the sciences, I see it as the practice of critique. Socrates did not seek so much to convince his followers to accept a body of doctrine that could be associated with his name—there is, *pace* Nietzsche, no Socratism to compete with Platonism or Cartesianism—as to cultivate in his followers the desire to challenge those platitudes of the age everyone else in fifth-century Athens took for the truth.

So if there is a spirit guiding this work, it is not that of Minerva, the goddess of wisdom, raptly staring at the screen. It is rather that of Socrates, that garrulous old man, seated in a coffeehouse pushing his friends to defend their analyses of the movie they have just seen. I will be satisfied if in the chapters that follow, I manage to convey some sense of what *that* would be like.

Finally, it is not just the cultivation of critical capacities directed toward film for their own sake that concerns me. In developing the interpretations set out in this book, I have focused my attention on four categories central to understanding our social world: class, race, gender, and sexual orientation. (One section, each, is devoted to issues of class, race, and sexual orientation; gender issues recur throughout.) The critical awareness that I hope to model for readers of this text is one that identifies corresponding structures and practices of hierarchy. The four terms thus function as shorthand for some of the profoundest ways in which, in our society, human beings are shaped—and oppressed, demeaned, exploited, and stunted. In interpreting the unlikely couple films treated in this book, I mean to show how a truly critical practice can concern itself with questions that go to the very heart of how we imagine a life worth living. If Socrates were alive today, his agora might very well be the food court outside the multiplex at the mall.

Thomas E. Wartenberg
Lower Highland Lake
Goshen, Massachusetts

Acknowledgments

I have found working on film to be a genuinely communal experience. Whenever I have mentioned what I was writing about, people have joined in with an enthusiasm different from anything I had previously experienced in my scholarly life. Not all of the spontaneous suggestions about unlikely couple films that have helped with the writing of this book remain in my memory, so I cannot explicitly thank each and every person for his or her contribution. Let me just say that I have welcomed the enthusiasm with which friends, colleagues, and acquaintances have joined me in reflecting on these films. Not only were their suggestions useful for my understanding of the films, the interest they showed in this project encouraged me to pursue it.

A number of people have provided significant help as I have worked on this book. First and foremost, I want to thank Alan Schiffmann, whose detailed editing and critical comments have helped shape every chapter of this book. Without his efforts, this book would have lacked whatever style and rigor it now has. More generally, I have taken inspiration from the example Alan set of someone for whom ideas mattered in a genuine and nonselfish manner. I cannot adequately express how important it has been for me to have Alan as a friend and intellectual companion.

Angela Curran and Julie Inness—both now members of the Mount Holyoke College Philosophy Department—provided important support during my writing of this book. At different times, each helped me see my way more clearly as I tried to articulate precisely what I was trying to say.

Ed Royce deserves credit for various efforts in support of my undertaking. His wide knowledge and critical acumen were constant sources of assistance. Cynthia Freeland provided insightful comments on parts of the manuscript. Our parallel philosophic development also gave me a sense that the changes in my philosophic interests were not completely idiosyncratic. Stephen Davies read an earlier version of this manuscript and gave me detailed comments that were of great help in refining my thinking.

Robert Gooding-Williams read parts of this manuscript and helped me think more clearly about some of the racial issues involved, as did Awam Amkpa in regard to postcolonial ones.

I want to express my appreciation to a group of friends and colleagues who over the years have given me a sense of a philosophic audience: the members of SOFPHIA, the Socialist-Feminist Philosophers Association. Without their repeated support, I would not have a sense of myself as writing philosophy for a group of readers who share my political and philosophic orientation. Over the past ten years, Sandra Bartky, Dion Farquhar, Ann Ferguson, Alison Jaggar, Bill McBride, Linda Nicholson, Richard Schmitt, Karsten Struhl, and Iris Young have all helped me as friends, colleagues, and critics. They, together with all the others too numerous to mention, have made it possible for me to experience philosophy as a genuine path of intellectual investigation rather than display.

My colleagues at Mount Holyoke College, and in the Valley more generally, have been very supportive of my efforts to move beyond the traditional boundaries of philosophy as a discipline. Early on, a writing seminar organized by Rebecca Fairy, who is unfortunately no longer at the college, allowed me to try out my first tentative gropings. At a later stage, the Five-College Women's Research Center offered me a more formal opportunity to present the fruits of my research. The Pew Faculty Seminar on Film Theory, subsequently the Film Studies Program, has been a continuing source of inspiration and critical dialogue. The Five-College Oppositional Attitudes Task Force has also been a supportive environment for my work.

I was able to complete substantial portions of the manuscript during both parental and sabbatical leaves from Mount Holyoke College. The members of the Philosophy Department of the University of Auckland generously provided me with a hospitable and stimulating home during my sabbatical in 1994–1995.

I have been fortunate to be able to read drafts of various portions of this manuscript in a variety of different settings. Pieranna Garavaso arranged for a visit to the University of Minnesota at Morris. I spent a wonderful two days there and left encouraged by the response my work had received. I want to thank my commentator at a meeting of the Eastern Division of the American Society for Aesthetics, Karen Evans, for both her sympathetic criticisms and her excellent suggestions about films to consider. Morris Kaplan's commentary at a meeting of the Pacific Division of the American Society for Aesthetics helped me think about issues of sexual orientation more competently, as did Ed Stein's comments. The Society for the Study of the Contemporary Visual Arts also provided an opportunity to discuss my ideas.

During my sabbatical in New Zealand, I presented papers at the University of Auckland, New England University in Armidale, the Australian National University, Victoria University at Wellington, Canterbury University in Christchurch, and Otago University in Dunedin. At all of these places, the comments and criticisms made by members of the audience contributed to this project.

A number of people have helped with the preparation of the final manuscript. Stephanie T. Hoppe did an admirable job of copyediting. Lee Bouse spent innumerable hours helping prepare the illustrations for this book. Matthew Mattingly provided some last-minute assistance with the capturing of the images. I thank all of them for their assistance with this project.

Earlier versions of some chapters were published in *Radical Philosophy: Tradition, Counter-Tradition, Politics,* edited by Roger Gottlieb (Philadelphia: Temple University Press, 1993); the *Journal of Social Philosophy;* and *Philosophy and Film,* edited by Cynthia A. Freeland and Thomas E. Wartenberg (New York and London: Routledge, 1995). All have been radically revised for inclusion in this volume.

This is a book about unlikely couples. My acknowledgments would be incomplete were I not to recognize the support of my own unlikely partner, Wendy Berg, who has always been there for me during the writing of this book. While writing about how a couple can aid its partners' self-development, I have always had our relationship in mind. Finally, a word to my son, Jake. Although he is not ready to read what I have written, he has given my life a joy I had not thought possible. I hope that this book will someday be one he treasures.

T. E. W.

1
The Subversive Potential of the Unlikely Couple Film

In the final sequence of Billy Wilder's 1959 comedy, *Some Like It Hot*, two couples are seated in a motor launch (see Photo 1.1). The pair in the stern appears to be lesbian, the one in the bow heterosexual. According to the terms used in this book, the former couple seems *unlikely*, transgressive of the social norm specifying that romantic couples must be composed of a man and a woman, a norm to which, by contrast, the latter couple appears to conform.

Things are not that simple, however, for two of the three "women" in the launch are actually men in drag. The situation, then, is really the opposite of what it seems: The truly unlikely couple is the apparently heterosexual but actually homosexual one seated in the bow, whereas the genuinely *likely* couple is the apparently homosexual but actually heterosexual one seated astern. The image of these two contrasting couples, taken together with the inversion of their apparent and real natures, anticipates a number of important themes that will emerge in this study of a genre I call "the unlikely couple film."

Let us look more carefully at the "lesbian" couple, composed of Sugar Cane (Marilyn Monroe), a nightclub singer, and Joe (Tony Curtis), a womanizing saxophone player who is disguised as Josephine: Apparently unlikely, the only really improbable element in this relationship is that Joe—a cad of the sort for whom the unfortunate Sugar has repeatedly fallen—has himself fallen for her. As a result, instead of pursuing his seduction, he now feels compelled to confess his love.

Photo 1.1 Two couples—one likely and one unlikely

The inversion of appearance and reality this seemingly unlikely pair embodies provides one key to understanding the structure of the unlikely couple film, for it is predicated on a conflict between two approaches to the featured couple. From one point of view, which I shall call the *social perspective,* an unlikely couple is inappropriate because its composition violates a social norm regulating romance. The image of Joe-in-drag with Sugar is as striking and delightful a visual representation of unlikeliness as the movies offer—and one that immediately registers the couple's (apparently) transgressive character.

The contrasting point of view, which might be called the *romantic perspective,* and which is usually, but not always, that of the filmmaker, deems the transgressive couple appropriate—*likely,* I shall say—setting the love the two partners share above the conventions it violates. Because Joe loves Sugar, the audience understands that the two really do belong together, regardless of how they look. Of course, since this couple's unlikeliness is the result of Joe's dissembling, their unorthodox appearance does not signify a real obstacle to their relationship.

The situation is quite different in the ten films discussed in the chapters that follow, for all feature couples genuinely violative of the gender, class, racial, and/or sexual norms governing socially permitted romance. Hence, the conflict between romantic love and societal norm represented in the narrative figure of the unlikely couple cannot be resolved in these films, as it is with Sugar and Joe, with the simple revelation that its unlikeliness is merely apparent.[1]

Shifting our attention now to the pair seated in the bow of the launch, we see another couple whose appearance belies its reality. This apparently heterosexual, but actually homosexual, couple is composed of Osgood Fielding (Joe E. Brown), the eccentric millionaire at the helm, and Gerry (Jack Lemmon), who, to give his friend, Joe, time to seduce Sugar, has himself inflamed Fielding by masquerading as Daphne.[2] When Daphne/Gerry admits to really being a man in hopes of cooling Osgood's passion, Osgood does not respond with the outrage and disgust that Daphne/Gerry expects but deadpans one of the most famous tag lines in film, "Nobody's perfect."

Osgood's response to Daphne/Gerry's revelation elicits our startled laughter because it treats the sex of a romantic partner as just a minor matter—a "detail," to quote *The Crying Game,* a film I discuss in Chapter 11—rather than the major problem we know it to be. But if, as it should, our laughter prompts us to reflect on why Osgood's response is so startling, the subversion of heterosexuality's normative status has been initiated.

The ending of *Some Like It Hot* thus gestures toward a crucial feature of the genre—transgressive romance as a vehicle for social critique. By focusing attention on the social norms governing romantic attachments, these films confront very basic questions about social hierarchy, for the norms reflect fundamental societal assumptions about the differential worth of human beings. The interpretations presented in this book emphasize how the very structure of the unlikely couple film entails this possibility: Since the narratives of such films must mediate the conflict between the romantic love that binds the unlikely partners and the social norms it violates, they can mobilize sympathy for the couple for purposes of critique.

My attribution of socially critical ambitions to popular narrative films like *Some Like It Hot* may strike readers as odd, for such films do not present themselves as vehicles for serious social analysis. *Some Like It Hot* can stand as a metaphor for my response to this challenge: Sugar, the stereotypical "dumb blonde" the womanizing Joe targets for seduction, invites easy condescension, but the more he comes to know her—as Josephine, he plays at being a sympathetic woman friend while actually acquiring the information necessary to bed her—the more difficult he finds it to reduce the totality of her being to her appealing surface.

Joe's initial attitude toward Sugar resembles the perspective dominant in academic film studies: Too often, the "sexy" production values of narrative films, especially Hollywood films, are taken as a license for condescension.[3] Although this attitude has not gone unchallenged, the reigning assumption has been that popular narrative films are necessarily complicit with dominant social interests.[4] Since many of those who write about film see themselves as hostile to such interests, they have been correspondingly suspicious of box office success. Assuming a posture of superiority, these writers contemptuously dismiss such fare as superficial.

The stance adopted in this study is reminiscent instead of a chastened Joe's at the end of *Some Like It Hot:* Just as he no longer reads Sugar's attractions as evidence of her superficiality, I refuse the reflexive condescension that popular narrative film often evokes. To repeat, a central goal of this book is to demonstrate that unlikely couple films include important social criticism even as their audiences find them entertaining and appealing. To the extent that my interpretations succeed in showing that instances of the genre mount sophisticated challenges to hierarchy—whether of class, race, gender, or sexual orientation—they also illustrate how empathetic yet critical readings of these films reveal more about their structure and effects than the hypertheoretical dismissal so prevalent in the academic study of film.

Although I emphasize the socially critical, hence subversive, potential of the unlikely couple film, I recognize that not every, or even any, individual film fully and consistently realizes that potential. Works of art, like other cultural products, bear traces of the contradictions of their societies. A film that seeks to subvert the hold of one mode of social domination may inadvertently support that of another. Alternatively, a film that attacks, say, one stereotype may employ others, equally demeaning.[5] Films do not live up to the ideal of consistency any more than do their human makers.

More problematic for my argument are those unlikely couple films with narratives that support dominant social interests. The act of criticism required by these films is complex, calling for an analysis of how they mute the genre's critical potential. So, for example, my interpretation of *Pretty Woman* (1990), in Chapter 5, shows how the film uses specific narrative and representational strategies to contain the critique of class and gender privilege that it initially promises.

The body of this book, then, comprises detailed interpretations of the narrative and representational strategies of ten unlikely couple films and focuses on the ways in which those strategies both articulate and contain the critical potential inherent in the genre. Such detailed interpretations are necessary, for only through them does it become possible to demonstrate how a particular aspect of a film either subverts or supports a given social interest. All too often, film scholars neglect the context in which an image appears, taking its mere presence to establish a film's politics—so that, for example, the presence of a heterosexual couple at the end of a film is taken as evidence of the film's support of patriarchy.[6] But as my readings demonstrate, nothing follows simply from the presence of an image, for the issue is how the narrative positions it and how it is received by an audience.

A second reason for offering such detailed interpretations is to show that popular films are worthy of the kinds of serious intellectual engagement philosophers have generally reserved for written texts. Because these films question the extent to which hierarchic social relationships are legitimate, they inevitably raise important questions about a wide range of philosophic issues: What role can romantic love play in the lives of human beings? How can individuals transform their lives to bring them more fully into accord with their sense of what is an appropriate life to live? Is education accomplished only through explicit instruction or are there other, perhaps more important, processes through which human beings learn? Why is our finitude—our dependence and mortality—so difficult for human beings to accept and how do we seek to avoid acknowledging it? What is the nature of human desire? What assumptions about gender structure our sexuality? To demonstrate that popular narrative films can actually address such philosophic concerns and elucidate them in their own distinctive way requires that one look at films carefully and in some detail, treating them as texts worthy of serious and sustained attention.

Still, the overriding concern of the unlikely couple film is the legitimacy of social hierarchy. Despite the range of its philosophic concerns, it is in its confrontation with issues surrounding hierarchy—What is so problematic about hierarchy? Why is it such a persistent phenomenon in human life, one so difficult to eradicate?—that the unlikely couple film establishes itself as a truly philosophic genre.

My approach to film owes a great deal to the work of Stanley Cavell. Distinctive of Cavell's approach is the way he places film and philosophy in dialogue, according neither pride of place.[7] Central to both, he argues, is a concern with the difficulties human beings have in acknowledging others as fully and completely real.[8] Through nuanced readings of an impressive variety of works of literature, philosophy, and film, Cavell has demonstrated how important an issue this problem of acknowledgment has been for intellectuals and artists in the modern West.

Cavell has written at length about two groups of Hollywood films from the 1930s and 1940s—"comedies of remarriage" and "melodramas of the unknown woman"—that use romance as a means of addressing the problem of acknowledgment. In justifying his philosophical claims, Cavell shows, in a series of insightful and daring readings, that these films are both vehicles for mass entertainment and genuinely creative works of art.

Despite the sophistication of Cavell's readings, they are beset by a fundamental inadequacy: For him, the ultimate root of the failure to acknowledge is always psychological, explicable in terms of the individual's confrontation with elemental features of "the human situation." As a result, his readings tend to level the social and historical settings of the texts/works he considers. Although he does, at times, admit that regard for social context can be an important consideration in interpreting a film, his analyses of how the struggle for acknowledgment presents itself consistently scant the specific sociohistorical terms through which individuals actually live that struggle.

My focus on the centrality of hierarchy in the unlikely couple film thus significantly departs from Cavell's emphases. Although I do not deny that film tackles issues fundamental to the traditions of Western philosophy— indeed, my interpretations explicitly seek to support Cavell's contention that they do—I insist that those issues not only arise in specific historical and social circumstances but inevitably present themselves to individuals in terms that register those specificities. As a result, the analyses of individual unlikely couple films contained in this volume are obliged to show both that the films are philosophically illuminating and that their philosophical ruminations emerge out of and are marked by these specificities of sociohistorical context.

Destabilizing Hierarchy

The guiding perspective of this study, then, is that through narratives of transgressive romance, the unlikely couple film confronts various forms of social oppression. To see exactly how the genre addresses these issues, we need a more developed understanding of its salient characteristics.

The unlikely couple film traces the difficult course of a romance between two individuals whose social status makes their involvement problematic. The source of this difficulty is the couple's transgressive makeup, its violation of a hierarchic social norm regulating the composition of romantic couples. For example, in the context of the American South in the early decades of the twentieth century—although not only there or only then—a black man and a white woman constituted an unlikely couple because of social norms—and often laws—against miscegenation. Transgressors would often find themselves in dire straits, as the tragic history of lynching attests.[9] Of course, breaching the norms regulating couple formation need not result in tragedy. Indeed, one source of interest in the genre is in the sheer variety of its narrative outcomes. Thus, although tragedy looms as a possible fate for these socially transgressive couples, more often than not the lovers triumph over adversity.

The norms governing romantic relationships are, of course, themselves reflective of more basic assumptions about human beings. Only in a society in which their position in a social hierarchy assigns individuals their human worth would a couple be deemed inappropriate simply because it violated such principles of social ordering. By criticizing restrictive romantic norms, the unlikely couple film questions the division of society into groups of differing social value.

Because hierarchies of class, gender, race, and sexual orientation are so structurally central to our society, I have chosen to examine films that feature problematic romances of a cross-class, interracial, or homosexual character.[10] (The films depicting class and race injustice are heterosexual romances and so raise issues of gender.) All the films I discuss present interesting and, I would argue, unique modes of interrogating the nature of hierarchy, as well as the subtle and not-so-subtle injuries it inflicts.

Because of its reliance on what I call the *narrative figure* of the unlikely couple, a figure constituted by the transgression of a principle of hierarchic ordering, the genre is in a unique position to destabilize categorical distinctions, to provide its audience with experiences that show the limited validity of such categories. More than simply a visual image, the narrative figure includes two conceptual elements at once in tension and potentially in dialogue—an awareness of both the *attraction* between the partners, their desire for one another, and the *transgression* resulting from that attraction, its violation of social norms regulating romantic union. The narrative figure of the unlikely couple, a microcosmic crystallization of that basic conflict, determines the narrative possibilities of the unlikely couple film, its potential to criticize the different positions in the conflict.

The first element, then, of the narrative figure of the unlikely couple is the romantic couple itself. The obviousness of this fact conceals its complexity, for the fact that love makes this a couple has important consequences. In particular, the narrative figure includes what I have called the romantic perspective, according to which the experience of romantic love is one of the principal spurs to human self-development. From this point of view, the love the two partners have for one another allows them to achieve a fuller sense of their possibilities. Hence, the norms that would deny this all-important experience, that stand in the way of the couple, are subject to criticism.

By contrast, the social perspective focuses on the couple's unlikeliness, the second significant element of the narrative figure. Now, the couple's transgression becomes a justification for disapproval, for the social perspective takes such regulation of romantic relationships as essential to the continuity of human social life: The unlikely couple, by contravening a principle of hierarchy, portends social chaos and must either be prevented from forming or sanctioned in some way.

Because these two perspectives coexist in tension in the narrative figure of the unlikely couple, that is, because each perspective denies the other's validity, the basic task for the film's narrative is to somehow resolve the tension between them, to provide a form of narrative development that satisfies the audience. As a result, my discussions of particular films repeatedly recur to what I shall call their *narrative strategies*—the paths mapped out to resolve this tension. For example, in Shakespeare's narrative of tragic love, *Romeo and Juliet*—a significant dramatic forebear of the genre—the deaths of the romantic partners serve to indict the feudal clans for treating clan membership as a significant social difference or principle of hierarchy that marriages should not transgress.[11] The narrative strategy of such a work is to exhibit the deep and unexpected costs exacted by practices endorsed by the social perspective.

To effect their narrative strategies, the films deploy *representational strategies*—specific depictions of character. A straightforward example is D. W. Griffith's portrayal of black men, in his problematic 1915 masterpiece, *Birth of a Nation,* as pathologically desirous of white women, their professions of love veiling their real intent: rape. Griffith's representational strategy here implements his narrative strategy: vindication of Ku Klux Klan vigilantism.

The tensions embodied in the narrative figure of the unlikely couple explain a number of features of the genre, most importantly its critical potential. For a film to fully endorse the romantic perspective, for example, it would have to demonstrate problems with the social one. Most of the films analyzed in this book—from *Pygmalion* (1938) to *Desert Hearts* (1986)—embrace the romantic perspective on the unlikely couple, hence are critical of one or more forms of hierarchy. As we shall see, however, the specific narrative strategies employed differ radically from one another. For example, cross-class romances frequently employ the trope of transformation—one partner's class position being adjusted up—as in *Pretty Woman*—or down—as in *White Palace* (1990)—to accord with the other's.

Films endorsing the social point of view, on the other hand, find a way to defeat the romantic perspective—for example, by denying what the couple is feeling is really love. We see this possibility worked out in *Jungle Fever* (1991), whose title alone implies that the relationship at issue is not an instance of love but rather one incited by sexual stereotypes of the forbidden Other.

The range of the genre's possible narrative strategies is not exhausted by the options of endorsing straightforwardly either one or the other perspective embodied in the couple's narrative figure. A more complex strategy, registering the deepest potential of the genre, is that of destabilizing the hierarchically organized category *both* perspectives employ to articulate themselves. Something like this is going on, for example, in *The Crying Game* (1992), a film less concerned with criticizing the assumption that heterosexuality is the only appropriate sexual orientation than with undermining the very categorical scheme that opposes hetero- and homosexuality as the two mutually exclusive and exhaustive modes of human sexual expression.

King Kong's Critique of "Civilization"

Although *King Kong,* the 1933 classic directed by Merian C. Cooper and Ernest B. Schoedsack, is not an unlikely couple film—the great ape's love is unreciprocated and, anyway, the would-be couple's composition transgresses a biological rather than a social barrier—the structure of its narrative illustrates with exemplary clarity the different narrative strategies that define the genre. For my purposes, then, an extended reading of *King Kong* can illustrate how popular narrative film can be the site for a profound, even philosophic, confrontation with the injustices of hierarchy.

As noted, the King Kong–Ann Darrow (Fay Wray) "couple" is not really a couple at all, for Darrow has absolutely no romantic interest in

Kong, who seems more the rapist than the lover. Taking this point, the couple's violation of the human/animal hierarchy makes it a very improbable couple, one that can serve as a visual marker of the idea of unlikeliness—or, more precisely, the idea that romantic relationships that violate hierarchic assumptions require suppression.[12]

The film's central sequences are each identified with an island—Skull Island, first, and then Manhattan—and each exemplifies one of the two points of view embodied in the narrative figure of the unlikely couple. Because Kong's defeat and Darrow's rescue are presented as a victory for the ideals of "civilization," the Skull Island sequence embodies the social perspective.[13] But once Kong has been humanized by his love for Darrow, his death at the end of the Manhattan sequence is framed as a tragic crime. The film's indictment of Western civilization for its violent suppression of an Other it does not understand illustrates the unlikely couple film's destabilization of hierarchy.[14]

We can see how the film develops the dialectic between these two perspectives by examining first the Skull Island sequence. Because Kong is an animal—and a monstrous one at that—he represents unregulated desire, that is, desire beyond or beneath social control. Before ever laying eyes on him, Carl Denham (Robert Armstrong), Kong's eventual captor, describes the mythical creature in those kitsch-uncanny terms meant to arouse our dread: "Neither beast nor man, something monstrous, still living, still holding that island in the grip of fear."[15] Huge and powerful, Kong overwhelms even the dinosaurs residing on Skull Island.

But Kong's physical size is not the primary reason he poses a threat to society; rather, it is his unbounded sexual desire, requiring frequent and copious offerings of young women by Skull Island's human inhabitants, that makes him an object of terror.[16] Only through this provision is Kong persuaded to honor the barrier that separates him from these natives. When the arrival of Denham and his troupe disrupts a sacrificial ceremony to the great ape, Darrow is captured and offered up instead. Perhaps the gift of this beautiful white virgin will be sufficient propitiation.

The social perspective is represented in the film by Carl Denham, who believes himself capable of controlling Kong's transgressive desire by force, repression. Initially feigning an interest only in capturing Kong's image on film, Denham's real intent is to display the awe-inspiring beast before the fascinated gaze of New York's theater-going public.[17]

In its Skull Island sequence, then, *King Kong* endorses the social perspective, and Darrow's strenuous resistance to Kong confirms its rightness—she must escape Kong's monstrous lust, a point emphasized by her repeated and legendary screams. But it is not just Darrow's terror, or even the fact that Kong has abducted her, that condemns the relationship: Above all, it is the very unnaturalness of such an erotic union that is horrifying.[18] Darrow's rescue is thus doubly welcome, not only because she desires it, but also because it puts an end to the prospect of an unimaginable sexual transgression.

King Kong's Skull Island sequence thus presents Kong's defeat as a vindication of the social perspective. Since the huge ape is a wild beast, his desire is not amenable to civilized restraint: His frustration threatens society, for Kong will smash anything that stands in the way of his gratification. Unregulated desire must be met by social coercion, for in its drive for fulfillment, it spares nothing. *King Kong* here approximates Freud's diagnosis, in *Civilization and Its Discontents,* of society's hostility to the individual's demand for libidinal gratification. Since Kong can be read as unsocialized desire, his defeat affirms society's tragic demand for renunciation.

King Kong would be a far less interesting film, however, without the Manhattan sequence's reversal of perspective, which presents another possibility for the unlikely couple film: an indictment of society for murdering love. Transported from his home to New York and billed by Denham as the Eighth Wonder of the World—a designation the film uses self-referentially in its own title sequence—Kong becomes a tragic hero, trivialized and misunderstood by the "civilized" society that ultimately destroys him.

The events of this sequence of the film are well known: Maddened by popping flashbulbs he believes are threatening Darrow, Kong breaks his chains and escapes Denham's freak show. Wreaking havoc as he goes, Kong searches for, and finally finds, Darrow, although not without killing a great many people in some of the film's most memorable and terrifying footage. With Darrow in his grip, he makes his famous climb up the side of the Empire State Building, mistakenly believing that doing so will bring him to safety. Menaced by fighter planes, Kong protectively sets Darrow down on a ledge, then bravely turns to face them, ready to give his life to defend the one he loves. Ironically, Kong's chivalrous action brings on their attack, for, once the pilots see that Darrow is out of danger, they unleash their weapons against him. His body riddled with bullets, Kong falls 102 stories to the pavement below, to the fascinated horror of the crowd gathered to watch.[19]

Photo 1.2 King Kong caresses his white beauty

Kong remains to the end a monster capable of great violence, yet his love for Darrow has had a civilizing effect. With its emphasis on the significance of his transformation, *King Kong* adumbrates the unlikely couple film's belief in the power of love. Kong's passion for the beautiful, white woman has not only socialized his monstrous desire but brought out the courtly lover submerged within this savage beast, although only in the final scene on the Empire State Building is Kong shown unambiguously transformed by that passion. In a series of remarkable shots in which the camera alternately assumes the place of both Kong and the gunners who kill him, the audience understands that Kong is prepared to die to protect his beloved. Kong's aggression is given an appropriate direction through his love for this beauty.

In a famous set piece in his *Phenomenology of Spirit*, the German philosopher G. W. F. Hegel claims that risking one's life in a struggle to the death is automatically a step in the development of freedom or "civilization": Human beings encounter each other most fundamentally as threats to their self-certainty, so that to confirm his or her own existence, each must seek the other's death. And "it is only through staking one's life that freedom is won."[20]

On Skull Island, Kong engages a variety of prehistoric monsters in just such life-and-death struggles. But so long as these beasts fight simply for their own survival, there is nothing elevating about these struggles. The crucial step occurs when one elects to do battle not out of self-interest but for the sake of another—out of love. Now, the significance of the willingness to risk one's life has been transformed: To choose to risk one's life for the sake of another—as when Kong fights not merely to possess Darrow but to protect her—is humanizing in the sense Hegel describes.

Thus, although Kong's violent rampages in search of Darrow on both Manhattan and Skull Islands involve similar scenes of mayhem, the two sequences make fundamentally different impacts on us because we realize that in Manhattan he searches not simply to gratify his lust but out of a lover's genuine concern. The collateral damage Kong wreaks is only a by-product of his limited understanding of his situation, for he reacts to a threat in the only way he knows—in a violent jungle, only the strongest survive.[21] But now he is no longer simply the savage beast, for his desire has been socialized, indeed "civilized," through his love.

Kong's humanization grounds the film's critique of "civilizing" repression as a means of controlling the Other. First, Denham—Western civilization's emissary to the island—believes he can subdue Kong by force. Later, when the great ape proves too much for Denham, America's machine guns complete the task. But at that point we realize society's violent suppression of its Other ignores an alternative, nonviolent means of subduing nature: beauty. In effect, civilization has been indicted for its exclusive reliance on violence to socialize the savage.

At the end of the film's Manhattan section, then, things appear in a very different light than they did on Skull Island. In the earlier sequence, Kong's defeat had signified the validity of civilization's need to regulate sexual desire. Now, we experience Kong's death as tragic, caused by a hubristic "civilization" quick to violence but blind to beauty.

But although one might take Kong's death to represent the film's endorsement of the romantic perspective, something more profound has transpired: The film has *destabilized* the hierarchic terms on which society's suppression of Kong was based. Thus, although our experience of Kong's death as tragic precludes us from endorsing the social perspective, neither can we support his abduction of Darrow. The very terms in which we conceive of Kong and his actions are rendered inadequate by our experience of the film, for the tragic death of the giant ape destabilizes the human/animal and culture/nature dichotomies. Despite appearing to be the paradigm of animality and unsocialized nature, Kong's susceptibility to Darrow's beauty proves that he exceeds the grasp of these oppositions.

This destabilization of a hierarchic framework operating at the base of our thinking and acting is one of the deepest possibilities for the unlikely couple film: It undermines our faith in our habitual modes of conceptualization.

The dialectic between society's recognition that sexual desire must be regulated and the individual's need for emotional fulfillment is the terrain on which the unlikely couple narratives discussed in this book are worked out. The Kong-Darrow couple shares the opprobrium directed at the socially unlikely couples portrayed in these films. Although Kong's one-sided love for Darrow is never reciprocated, *King Kong* nonetheless presents the same opposition between social prohibition and romantic love inherent in the narrative figure of the unlikely couple.[22]

King Kong touches on another aspect of many unlikely couple films. So far, I have avoided the issue of whether the film is racist or Eurocentric. Clearly, however, there are features of its narrative that call out for critical examination on this score. For example, the film presents a white woman as the epitome of human beauty: Many native women had been sacrificed to Kong, but only Darrow, the white beauty, is fit to become the object of his love. In addition, despite its destabilization of the dichotomy, the film nonetheless operates with an embarrassingly crude opposition between civilization and savagery in its presentation of the natives of Skull Island—all of whom are African American actors made up as "savages"—as ignorant brutes.

I cite these instances of the film's Eurocentrism not so much to show that the film suffers from these flaws but more to use it as an example of how even a film that is critical of Western civilization for resorting to excessive violence can nonetheless unthinkingly rehearse other ugly aspects of Eurocentrism. The following chapters continue this interpretive practice: Although the interpretations of unlikely couple films they contain seek to demonstrate these films' critical potential, they also examine ways in which the films' narrative and representational structures contain or evade that potential.

Outlining the Genre

An index of the usefulness of the idea of the unlikely couple is that as soon as one hears of it, one sees it everywhere, in contexts both expected and surprising. Indeed, the response I most often encounter when discussing these films is for my interlocutors to pause, think for a moment, and then ask me if I have thought of _____, their favorite unlikely couple film. Although this response is gratifying—I like seeing how quickly people warm to the idea that it makes sense to group these films as a genre—the vast range of unlikely couple films raises the question not only of why it is important to study this narrative figure in relation to film but also—and more important—of why I choose to investigate it in relation to *these* films in particular. I defer an answer to the first question to the concluding chapter and turn to the second now.

For reasons part historical and part conceptual, the idea for this book took shape gradually, between the years 1990 and 1992, when I noticed that a number of popular films debuting at that time—*White Palace, Pretty Woman, Jungle Fever, Mississippi Masala* (1992), and *The Crying Game*—employed the same narrative figure. Struck by their similarity—and despite their many, interesting differences from one another—I wondered whether it made sense to think of these as belonging to a genre the socially critical potential of which constituted its attraction to so many filmmakers.

To justify my growing sense that the unlikely couple film was an important, but overlooked, type, I thought it important to provide antecedents to those current films that had first caught my attention. The primary reason for this was that the films themselves often included references to predecessor films, so that I felt I could only understand the recent films by relating them to the earlier ones. A most obvious example is *Jungle Fever:* Unless viewed with *Guess Who's Coming to Dinner* (1967) in mind—the film to which *Jungle Fever* refers in its explicit disparagement of Hollywood's treatment of interracial romance—an important aspect of Spike Lee's agenda would be lost. Similarly, to understand *Pretty Woman*, I found myself going back to *Pygmalion*, its model, viewing that film more closely than I had before.

In this way, nine of the ten films for which I provide interpretations in the body of this book suggested themselves. Five are the films from 1990 to 1992 that represent contemporary instances of the genre; four are earlier films that helped to establish its conventions. That leaves only one to explain: Rainer Werner Fassbinder's 1974 masterpiece, *Ali: Fear Eats the Soul (Angst essen Seele auf)*. *Ali* differs from the other films treated in the book in being neither in the English language nor a popular narrative. Its analysis of the persistence of racism best exemplifies the potential of the genre to extend our understanding of racial injustice, however. This film, which I believe to be truly profound and, I might add, to have been profoundly misread by its many academic critics, completes the "cast" of the ten films through whose interpretations I hope to establish the philosophical significance of the unlikely couple film.

Notes

1. Some unlikely couple films rely on such a revelation, although often their audiences know full well that the unlikeliness is merely apparent. One example is Eddie Murphy's 1988 comedy, *Coming to America,* in which an African prince masquerades as a poor student.

2. I leave to the side the question of what precise figure the cross-dressing Daphne/Gerry represents. For an interesting perspective on cross-dressing that articulates it as a phenomenon distinct from homosexuality, see Marjorie Garber, *Vested Interests: Cross-Dressing and Cultural Anxiety* (New York: Routledge, 1992).

3. The paradigm here is Laura Mulvey's amazingly influential article, "Visual Pleasure and Narrative Cinema," *Screen,* 16:3 (Autumn 1975): pp. 6–18, according to which narrative cinema as a whole is complicit with structures of social domination. I discuss this view more fully in Chapter 12.

4. Many emendations to Mulvey's paradigm have been suggested, not least by Mulvey herself in "Afterthoughts on 'Visual Pleasure and Narrative Cinema' Inspired by *Duel in the Sun* (King Vidor, 1946)," *Framework,* 15–17 (1981): pp. 12–15. Most do not challenge her basic perspective, but for just such a challenge, see Noël Carroll, "The Image of Women on Film: A Defense of a Paradigm," *The Journal of Aesthetics and Art Criticism,* 48:4 (Fall 1990): pp. 349–360.

5. My discussion of *King Kong* (1933) later in this chapter explores this type of inconsistency.

6. Again, *King Kong* furnishes an example, for the context of Kong's death affects the audience's reaction to the presence of the human couple at the film's end.

7. Cavell has written a great deal about film. Three of his books—*The World Viewed: Reflections on the Ontology of Film* (Cambridge, MA: Harvard University Press, 1979), *Pursuits of Happiness: The Hollywood Comedy of Remarriage* (Cambridge, MA: Harvard University Press, 1981), and *Contesting Tears: The Hollywood Melodrama of the Unknown Woman* (Chicago: University of Chicago Press, 1996)—deal exclusively with film, and he has written numerous articles that discuss particular films as well as more general topics in the philosophy of film.

8. Probably the best introduction to Cavell's understanding of this problem is "Knowing and Acknowledging" in *Must We Mean What We Say?* (New York: Charles Scribner's Sons, 1969), pp. 238–266.

9. John Singleton's film *Rosewood* (1987) shows how deeply ingrained this norm was in the South at that time.

10. There are sources of unlikeliness other than those I have been able to include in this study. Differences in age, physical ability, and religion have been

subjects of such interesting films as *Harold and Maude* (1971), *Manhattan* (1979), *Coming Home* (1978), *Children of a Lesser God* (1986), and *A Stranger Among Us* (1994). Incestuous couples are another variation that I have not discussed, although films like *Murmur of the Heart* (1971) and *Sister, My Sister* (1995) provocatively explore this issue. I have also limited this study to sound films, thereby passing over such classic films as *Birth of a Nation* (1915) and *City Lights* (1931). Monster films, especially the many film adaptations of *Dracula*, are another offshoot of the genre, as are "buddy films," such as *Thelma and Louise* (1993) and the *Lethal Weapon* series. All of these deserve attention in their own right.

11. I develop this interpretation in an unpublished manuscript titled, "Romantic Love and the Feudal Household: *Romeo and Juliet* as Social Criticism."

12. Any complete interpretation of *King Kong* needs to take account of the film's identification of Kong with blacks. But it is equally important not to reduce Kong's "Otherness" to that of blacks. For a more extended discussion of the film, see my "Humanizing the Beast: *King Kong* and the Representation of Black Male Sexuality" in *Classic Whiteness,* Daniel Bernardi, ed.(Minneapolis: University of Minnesota Press, forthcoming).

13. My use of "civilization" is meant to echo Freud's in *Civilization [Kultur] and its Discontents,* James Strachey, tr. and ed. (New York: W. W. Norton, 1962). The scare-quotes register my conviction that his usage is Eurocentric.

14. For purposes of my argument, I treat the two sequences as employing two different narrative strategies. Actually, the second sequence transcends the first and represents the film's real view. There are clues to this during the first sequence itself.

15. All quotations from *King Kong* are from my own transcription of the film's sound track. For interesting claims about the anxiety that anomalies present, as well as reflections on the need for order, see Mary Douglas, *Purity and Danger* (New York and Washington, DC: Praeger, 1966).

16. It is worth noting that the very characteristics that make Kong a creature to be feared, and even killed, also make him an object of fascination for Denham and the other members of his expedition. Indeed, their reaction to him mixes fear with attraction, and Denham's plan explicitly recognizes this. We see here an anticipation of the insight that unlikeliness, although based on an interdiction of desire, can also incite that very desire, an idea that appears in a number of unlikely couple films, preeminently *Jungle Fever.*

17. *King Kong* thus self-reflexively posits film as a tool of social violence.

18. When, of course, it is not simply an object of voyeuristic curiosity: How would it work?

19. Because Kong represents African Americans, his love for a white woman triggers racist fears of miscegenation that are only stilled through an act analo-

gous to lynching. For an interesting, if incomplete, account of the film from this point of view, see James Snead, *White Screens: Black Images* (New York and London: Routledge, 1994), pp. 1–36.

20. Hegel makes this claim in the passage "Self-Consciousness" in his *Phenomenology of Spirit,* A. V. Miller, tr. (Oxford, UK: Oxford University Press, 1977), p. 114.

21. In "*King Kong*: Ape and Essence," in *Planks of Reason: Essays on the Horror Film,* Barry Keith Grant, ed. (Metuchen, NJ, and London: The Scarecrow Press, 1984), pp. 215–244, Noël Carroll presents the film as "a popular illustration of Social Darwinist metaphors" (p. 216).

22. Although Darrow does not come to love Kong, the possibilities of love springing from such roots are explored in films like *The Piano* (1994) and *Letter from an Unknown Woman* (1949).

Part One

Class

2
Pygmalion
The Flower Girl and
the Bachelor

Pygmalion, Anthony Asquith's 1938 film adaptation of George Bernard Shaw's famous play, presents two of the central themes of this study of the genre of the unlikely couple film. The first theme is the potential of narratives of transgressive love to undermine assumptions about the legitimacy of social hierarchy. *Pygmalion* is exemplary in this regard, for it critiques such hierarchy along two distinct dimensions. On the one hand, Eliza Doolittle's (Wendy Hiller) transformation from flower girl to "duchess" vindicates Henry Higgins's (Leslie Howard) rejection of the aristocratic pretension that social privilege is a mark of innate worth. And if bearing is the outward expression of social merit, then Eliza's ability to pass as a member of the aristocracy shows that, on the contrary, education, rather than biology, is its basis. *Pygmalion* does not stop with its deflation of the aristocracy, however, but turns its critique back on the critic himself, revealing Higgins's belief in the superiority of the "man of science" to be equally unfounded. This masculinist assumption also keeps Eliza from negotiating a successful relationship with Higgins after their triumph and shows that assumptions about gender are as significant a problem for romance as assumptions about class.

A second theme of this study of the unlikely couple film, as basic in its interest as the genre's critical potential, is its popular appeal as romantic narrative. Film is, after all, a mass medium and, as such, its ability to give pleasure to many millions of moviegoers is a condition of its continued existence. Predictably, this imperative often conflicts with the unlikely couple film's ability to sustain a socially critical perspective. Asquith's *Pygmalion,* for example, succumbs to its audience's expectations by departing from the play's ending. Where Shaw has Eliza walk out on Higgins, pointedly foreclosing the possibility of their romance, the film concludes with her return to Higgins's study, intimating, instead, that a romantic future is available to them. With this upbeat ending, *Pygmalion* obscures its own critical perspective, licensing viewers to experience the film as, finally, an updated variant of the Cinderella story. Of course, *Pygmalion* is not unique in this: Commercial pressures push these mass entertainments toward a kind of narrative and emotional closure that is in tension with the social critical potential of the unlikely couple narrative.

At the outset, one question that needs attending to is the legitimacy of treating *Pygmalion* as an unlikely couple film at all. There are many indications that Higgins and Eliza's relationship will not end in romantic union.[1] For example, when Eliza explains to Higgins her need to be treated with "a little kindness," she is explicit that she does not want him "to make love" to her.[2] Also, by providing Eliza with another romantic possibility, the Freddy Eynsford Hill subplot can be seen as an attempt to preclude romance between Higgins and Eliza.

Nonetheless, there are a number of reasons for treating *Pygmalion* as an instance of the genre. First, audiences clearly experience Higgins and Eliza as a couple, the conventions of romantic comedy having taught them that the more vigorous the denial, the more certain the ultimate triumph of love. *My Fair Lady* (1964), the Lerner and Loewe musical based on the play, explicitly yields to these conventional expectations. And *Pretty Woman* (1990), a film that presents itself as a contemporary *Pygmalion,* makes the romantic relationship between its partners central to its narrative.[3] More tellingly perhaps, the film's own title is an explicit reference to the myth of Pygmalion, the sculptor who falls in love with Galatea, a statue of his own creation. But most important, treating *Pygmalion* as an unlikely couple film illuminates both the film—attributing significance to aspects that might otherwise be passed over—and the genre itself. I therefore take the film to be raising the question of whether Higgins and Eliza can become romantic partners and propose to show that a negative answer is central to an understanding of the narrative.

Establishing Difference

In the unlikely couple film, by definition, the social composition of the featured couple presents an obstacle to the formation of an ongoing romantic relationship between its members. In many such films, the partners' love for one another is unproblematic, opposition to their union coming from others. The archetype here is Shakespeare's tragedy *Romeo and Juliet*, in which the two young lovers are doomed by murderous feuding between their families.

In the four films discussed in this first section of the book, class difference between the partners is a central obstacle to the formation of the couple. These films depart from the Romeo-and-Juliet premise, however, in their depiction of couples for whom this obstacle is not simply socially imposed: In each of the four, at least one partner views the other as completely unsuited for romantic partnership because of his or her differing class position. This device permits a subtler investigation of class difference as a regulator of romantic attraction.

These films begin by establishing a disparity between their audiences' perception of the potential for romantic relationship between the two central characters and the characters' own estimation of that possibility. Typically, the tensions produced by this disparity are resolved through narrative strategies that align the characters' recognition of their suitability for one another with the filmgoers'.

One such strategy has one or both partners make a discovery about the other that allows them to get past the obstacle of class. This revelation, the narrative pivot in the couple's development, disrupts habits of social classification that block recognition of the suitability of the other as love object.

In the simplest form that such a narrative can take, the discovery is made that the social position of one of the two partners is different from what it appears to be. For example, in *A Gay Deception* (1935), the male partner who is working as a bellhop turns out to be a prince. Only after the female partner admits that she cares for him despite his apparent working-class status does the prince reveal his identity, thereby legitimizing this no longer unlikely union.[4] *Coming to America* (1988) also relies on the revelation of a previously concealed identity. In this film, however, the discovery that the male is really an African prince in disguise threatens a couple founded on the assumption that he is instead a lower-class black African. Nor it this narrative strategy limited to films in which the obstacle to love between the two central characters is class difference. Thus, *Desert Hearts*, a film in which two women appear to differ in sexual orientation, turns on the discovery that one of them is mistaken about her sexuality. Once this error has been revealed, the couple's path has been cleared.[5]

In films that invoke class difference, however, it is rare for there simply to be a mistake about a character's class. The more usual narrative involves a *transformation* of one of the partners that eliminates the class difference between them. Such narratives of class relocation can take one of two basic narrative forms. The first depicts the social *ascent* of one of the characters, who thereby comes to share the higher status of the other. Both *Pygmalion* and *Pretty Woman* are examples. By contrast, narratives of *descent*—of which *It Happened One Night* (1934) and *White Palace* (1990) are instances—feature characters who give up their privilege to share the lower-class position of their partner. Whether the trajectory is up or down, this strategy of class repositioning allows the two characters to finally recognize one another as at least potential romantic partners, something the audience has long since understood.

One take on narratives of class transformation is to see in them the denial of the significance of class difference. This is the view, for example, of Benjamin DeMott, who argues that a great deal of American popular culture is directed at obscuring the reality of class division in American society. Using the unlikely couple films of John Hughes (such as *Some Kind of Wonderful* [1987]) as evidence, DeMott claims, "The message is unvarying: The surface of things may look structured [by class differences], and some members of society may talk themselves into believing that escape from fixed levels is impossible, but actually where we place ourselves is up to us; whenever we wish to, we can upend the folks on the hill."[6] For DeMott, such films contribute to Americans' failure to understand the social significance of class, presenting individuals' class positions as a matter of choice. Transformation narratives are thus but one example of the tendency of popular film to deny that class represents a barrier to individual aspiration, for one can simply transform one's class at will.

DeMott's view calls attention to the transformation narrative's apparent erasure of the socially transgressive character of the cross-class couple. Because, finally, the partners no longer possess different class identities, they no longer transgress norms regulating romantic attraction. But where DeMott condemns this narrative strategy as part of the general failure to acknowledge the class character of American society, I argue that the transformation narrative is capable not only of acknowledging the reality of class but of indicting its effect on people's lives. As we shall see, representing class identity as capable of radical transformation endows the unlikely couple film with the potential to criticize basic assumptions about class, such as, for example, that class status is an expression of genetic capital. Admittedly, not all unlikely couple films exploit this critical potential. Indeed, I will show that some struggle to contain it, thereby contributing to the very erasure of class that DeMott sees as characteristic of popular culture as a whole.

Class as Obstacle

Pygmalion wastes no time showing that the unlikeliness of the Higgins-Eliza couple is obvious to the two principals. Their difference in class, and, less centrally, age, places each of them outside the other's circle of eligible romantic partners. This gentleman scholar's interest in a common flower girl extends only as far as her accent, which presents an opportunity for scientific investigation. In fact, Eliza's Cockney speech makes her particularly repulsive to him, for this linguist sees command of language as an alternative basis for social ranking. Ultimately, the film is critical of Higgins for regarding others solely as objects of scientific curiosity, but that point of view emerges only gradually.

When he first meets Eliza in the portico of St. Paul's Church during a rainstorm, Higgins treats her with utmost contempt. To Eliza's insistence that she has as much right as he to shelter there, Higgins responds that her deplorable accent belies her claim:

> A woman who utters such depressing and disgusting sounds has no right to be anywhere. Remember that you are a human being with a soul and the divine gift of articulate speech, and that your native language is the language of Shakespeare and Milton and the Bible; and don't sit there crooning like a bilious pigeon. (*Collected Screenplays*, p. 231)

Although one has to be wary of taking Higgins's sarcasm at face value, the film contains ample evidence that he views Eliza as less than fully human. For to him, language is sacred, a divine gift that Eliza desecrates whenever she opens her mouth.

I shall have more to say about Higgins's view of class, but here I simply emphasize that both Eliza's class position and her linguistic improprieties make unlikely any sort of ongoing relationship with Higgins, much less a romantic one. Indeed, to Higgins class differences appear as much a matter of linguistic skills as of economic privilege. Eliza's mangling of English so infuriates him that in an outburst following closely on the heels of the one just quoted, the upper-class linguist views the subproletarian Cockney with unbridled contempt: "You squashed cabbage leaf, you disgrace to the noble architecture of these columns, you incarnate insult to the English language" (*Collected Screenplays*, p. 231). Once the weather has cleared and they are free to go their separate ways, the great gulf of class should preclude any further dealings.

Soon after, however, Eliza shows up at Higgins's door requesting speech lessons. She is interested in learning to speak properly so that she can get a decent job and not have to sell flowers on the street. She explains all this to Colonel Pickering (Scott Sunderland), whom Higgins has invited into his home: "I want to be a lady in a flower shop. But they won't take me unless I can talk more genteel. He [Higgins] said he could teach me" (*Collected Screenplays*, p. 235). Eliza wishes a more respectable form of employment than selling flowers on the street to passersby, an activity problematic not least for its associations with prostitution. (Hence Eliza's repeated claim to being "a good girl.") But Eliza is barred from pursuing her dream because of her accent. In class-conscious England, the upper-class patrons of a flower shop expect a salesperson to conform to their manners and not betray her vulgar origins.

Eliza sees in Higgins the means to pursue her dreams. During the film's initial scene, Higgins boasted to Pickering that his skills as a linguist were such that "in three months I could pass that girl off as a duchess at an ambassador's garden party" (*Collected Screenplays*, p. 231). Now, taking to heart Higgins's claim to be able to teach her to speak correctly, Eliza appears at his doorstep, offering to pay him to do so.

Higgins is himself taken with the idea of teaching Eliza proper English, but not simply to provide her with the skills necessary to a suitable employment. His central motivation for undertaking what he terms an experiment is scientific: If he is able to provide Eliza with the skills necessary to pass as a duchess, he will show the vacuity of the pretension that aristocratic privilege is based on an inherent biological superiority. Eliza's masquerade, if successful, will show that anyone, even a lowly "guttersnipe," can be trained to act like an aristocrat, thereby establishing that class is a matter of training rather than breeding. At the heart of this experiment is Higgins's desire to prove the superiority of his scientific worldview—with its embrace of a hierarchy based on knowledge—to that of the nobility—with its faith in heredity.

Although he claims to be motivated by purely scientific considerations, Higgins is also revealed to be moved by a desire to demonstrate his own skill. Should this experiment prove successful in "mak[ing] a duchess of this draggletailed guttersnipe" (*Collected Screenplays*, p. 236), it will estab-

Photo 2.1 Higgins towers over Eliza as Pickering watches

lish Higgins as a linguist without peer. As they lay a wager on the outcome of this experiment, Pickering assures Higgins that he will "say you're the greatest teacher alive if you make that good [i.e., get Eliza to pass at the ambassador's party]" (*Collected Screenplays*, p. 236).

Eliza's desire to better herself and Higgins's interest in scientifically confirming his understanding of class provide the rationale for continuing their relationship. Explicitly, the connection is purely instrumental: Each has something to gain from an arrangement into which he or she enters for reasons of his or her own. Eliza stands to benefit from learning to speak "proper" English, whereas Higgins has a chance to prove the validity of his own scientific theories. Although the audience suspects (hopes?) that there is more to their desires than they acknowledge, the film attempts to foreclose the possibility of a sexual or romantic relationship between them.

Eliza, for her part, repeatedly rejects what she takes to be sexual advances. For example, when Higgins peremptorily directs his housekeeper, Mrs. Pearce (Jean Cadell), to burn all of Eliza's old clothes and to "wrap her in brown paper till they [new clothes] come," Eliza protests her virtue, rejecting any possible sexual implications in Higgins's orders: "You're no gentleman, you're not, to talk of such things. I'm a good girl, I am; and I know what the likes of you are, I do" (*Collected Screenplays*, p. 236).

The film also addresses this question of sexual motivation when Pickering asks Higgins not to take advantage of Eliza's position. Higgins is adamant that his interest in Eliza is purely "scientific," and, in any case, he has no desire for romantic involvement, let alone "that thing": "I find that the moment a woman makes friends with me, she becomes jealous, exacting, and a confounded nuisance. So I'm a confirmed bachelor, and likely to remain so."[7] We shall see that Higgins's attachment to his bachelorhood will become an important factor in his relationship with Eliza. For the moment, we need only acknowledge that Higgins's misogynist sentiments rule out a sexual interest in Eliza. (He later confides to his mother, "Oh, I can't waste my time with young women. They're all such idiots anyhow.")[8] This scientific investigator clearly enjoys the company of fellow male investigators like Pickering much more than he does that of women.[9] As a result, the audience is meant to be reassured that Higgins is not the familiar upper-class rake, seeking to take advantage of an innocent and impressionable young woman.

Were there still lingering concern about Higgins's designs, they are finally banished when Alfred Doolittle, Eliza's father, appears. Doolittle, a dustman (garbage collector), assumes that Higgins's interest in Eliza is sexual and as her father comes to request the payment he is due. Although there are a number of important aspects to this scene, what is significant here is how Doolittle's misplaced assumption serves to establish that Higgins's attitude toward Eliza is nonsexual.

The very terms of Higgins and Eliza's relationship, then, seem to preclude their becoming a couple. As in many films employing the trope of class ascent, however, there is an ironic structure to *Pygmalion*'s plot: The very terms of their relationship that seem to rule out love require Higgins to transform Eliza into an eligible candidate for romantic partnership. A serious obstacle to their union—the great barrier of class difference—will have been hurdled.

Transforming Eliza

In showing that a common flower girl can acquire the skills and bearing of a duchess, *Pygmalion* subverts class hierarchy by denying aristocratic privilege a rational basis. To understand how the film develops this critique, we need to consider carefully the process of Eliza's transformation.

There are two scenes in which Eliza is shown attempting to "pass." The first, at an at home hosted by Higgins's mother, allows the audience to see both the distance Eliza has traveled under Higgins's tutelage and how far she still has to go. The second is the reception at the ambassador's where Eliza triumphs and Higgins wins his bet. I consider each in turn.

The scene of Mrs. Higgins's at home, a comic masterpiece, follows a montage in which Higgins is shown struggling to teach Eliza. Despite her progress, Eliza is not yet ready to pass as a duchess. Indeed, following this scene Pickering even suggests that Higgins admit the experiment has failed.

The most important guests at the at-home are the Eynsford Hills, whose presence makes this scene a sort of replay of the film's opening encounter between Higgins and Eliza—the Eynsford Hills, too, had sought shelter from the rain in the portico of St. Paul's. Their failure to recognize Eliza provides a specific marker of how far she has come, even as her conduct shows that she needs to accomplish a great deal more before Higgins can win his bet.

Eliza's transformed appearance is one reason the Eynsford Hills do not recognize her for who she is (or was). Despite Higgins's reminder that they had all met previously, his concern that Eliza will be remembered as the flower girl they had encountered earlier is misplaced. She thoroughly charms the entire family—especially Freddy, the doltish son who becomes her admirer—even though her conversation actually betrays her social class. When the macabre story of her suspicion that her aunt was murdered threatens to give her away, Higgins saves the day by assuring the guests that the expressions Eliza uses are part of "the new small talk" (*Collected Screenplays,* p. 250). The scene ends with Mrs. Hill regretting her inability to use such language.

Although the film is here satirizing the attempts of the English upper class to keep their speech abreast of the latest linguistic fads—specifically their use of vulgarity as a way of proving themselves au courant—the audience gets its first look at the partially transformed Eliza. Her speech has changed a great deal, but its artificiality and her slips make her still appear something less than a real lady. Higgins remains undeterred, however, and decides that he will take Eliza to a reception at the Transylvanian Embassy to which he has been invited. This will be the true test of the experiment.

To ready Eliza, Higgins subjects her to another round of brutal instruction, again presented in montage. The two montage sequences together serve to demonstrate how much training has gone into refining Eliza, a process that has exhausted both Higgins and his pupil. And their exhaustion shows us the lengths that Higgins is willing to go to confirm his views.

By the time of the reception at the Transylvanian Embassy, Higgins has managed to complete Eliza's transformation. Physically, she has come a long way from the dirty young woman first encountered in the portico of St. Paul's. With the aid of a team of beauticians and dressmakers, Eliza now possesses a truly aristocratic appearance. The scene begins with an extended sequence in which, as she ascends the embassy staircase, her regal bearing creates a sensation (see Photo 2.2).

There follow a number of incidents detailing Eliza's triumph. The most humorous involves a former student of Higgins's, Aristide Karpathy,[10] a sort of Higgins run amok, who uses his skills as a linguist for crass self-aggrandizement. Although the film drops the play's suggestion that Karpathy actually blackmails people who wish to conceal their humble origins, he remains a vulgarian. The experiment receives its most serious test when he is asked to determine Eliza's real origins.

Despite some anxious moments, Karpathy does not penetrate the facade that Higgins has created for Eliza. After talking with her, Karpathy proclaims her to be a fake—she is, he announces, really a Hungarian royal. When Higgins asks whether he tried speaking to Eliza in Hungarian, this nemesis reveals himself to be a fool for not trusting what he hears:

> I did. She was very clever. She said, "Please speak to me in English: I do not understand French." French! She pretends not to know the difference between Hungarian and French. Nonsense: she knows both. . . . She's a princess. (*Collected Screenplays*, p. 256)

Even when Higgins reveals the truth about Eliza—that she is "an ordinary London girl out of the gutter and taught to speak by an expert"— neither Karpathy, the scientist less interested in truth than in financial gain, nor the hostess, the genuine aristocrat, believes him. The truth cannot be discerned by people such as these, taken in as they are by Eliza.

If the reception scene emphasizes Eliza's linguistic transformation, her physical metamorphosis, which has made her an appropriate object of desire for the assembled male aristocrats, is equally celebrated. Here, then, the film recalls the story of Cinderella, another dirty young woman who

Photo 2.2 Eliza enters the ball under the gaze of Higgins and Pickering

achieves great success at a ball. Central to both narratives is a transformation in appearance that reveals the radiant young woman beneath the grime. But if Cinderella is thereby restored to her rightful social position, Eliza's appropriate social location has been thrown into question.

Higgins's experiment is successful. Eliza has taken in the ball-goers. He has proved himself the master linguist and she has become an alluring young woman. It seems that all that remains to complete the fairy tale is for this obtuse Prince Charming to fall in love with his Cinderella.

Before considering the obstacles that remain in the way of this storybook ending, we need to reflect on what Eliza's successful passing has accomplished. From a narrative point of view, a significant barrier to the formation of this unlikely couple has been removed. Eliza is now an attractive woman whose transformed bearing makes her a socially appropriate companion for Higgins. Her class background no longer precludes her from being seen by Higgins as a possible romantic partner. The future, if any, of their relationship is now on the agenda.

At the same time, Eliza's triumph vindicates Higgins's criticism of the castelike character of England's class structure. One justification for aristocratic privilege alleges that class differences are simply a reflection of natural distinctions among human beings. Rather than treating class as a specifically social phenomenon, this view grounds hierarchy in biology, making it difficult to see how the class structure of society could be changed.

The story of Eliza's transformation and successful passing denies this innatist view, arguing instead that class differences are the result of the unequal access people have to various social goods. Although dress and hygiene are shown to play a role in the creation of class difference, the film presents language and, more generally, education as the most important factors in constituting class identity.

In *Pygmalion*'s England, class dialect is foremost among the means used to register and enforce elite cultural dominance. For wealthy parvenus to achieve a social status commensurate with their economic power, they must master elite speech patterns. Higgins, the scientific researcher, is also a teacher who can offer his status-anxious clients the linguistic makeover they require.

The film, and Shaw's play on which it is based, indict innatist defenses of class privilege, emphasizing instead the fundamental roles in individual development of education and training. The works are concerned not so much with the economic determinants of class as with what might be called its moral dimensions. Viewed from above, the lower orders behave in ways the upper classes find inappropriate, if not reprehensible. For example, respectable young women do not earn their living by accosting strangers in the streets.

Eliza is a flower girl, however, not through a choice of her own, but because she lacks the linguistic polish required of a shop assistant. As becomes clear when her father appears, she has had no chance of receiving the sort of parenting or education that would have made her capable of holding such a position. By giving her the sort of instruction she ought to have received and that society should have ensured her, Higgins offers Eliza a sort of alternate parenting.[11] And once adequately instructed, not only is she fit for respectable employment, but her bearing proves her at least the equal of those who view themselves as her betters. The film thus demonstrates that society itself produces the deficits that keep people like Eliza in subjection.

Higgins's experiment has proved that even a "guttersnipe" can learn to pass as an aristocrat. We have been shown that in a highly stratified society those who occupy superior social positions do so not so much as a result of superior moral virtue, but simply because the circumstances of their birth guarantee them the necessary socialization. To cure the ills of poverty, the film implies, the poor require the sort of instruction that Higgins provides Eliza.

Rather than obscuring the nature of class division, as DeMott would have it, this ascent narrative argues the reality and hurtfulness of class. If, with appropriate training and grooming, Eliza is made to pass for royalty, then class differences must be the result of society's differential treatment of human beings, not a reflection of inherent differences among them. As a result, the "vices" associated with poverty do not show that the poor are destined to be worse than the rich—in fact, Alfred Doolittle, the play's example of a character who lacks the standard moral virtues, is also its only creative moralist—but that they have been stunted by a denial of social resources. If society committed those resources in the way that Higgins commits his energies to Eliza, the poor would be "elevated," that is, their behavior would be indistinguishable from that of the rich.

Eliza's transformation, then, has not only articulated a critique of aristocratic self-understanding, it has cleared the way for a romantic relationship between Eliza and Higgins. The reasons that this romance fails to develop lie in Higgins's character and approach to life.

The Ethics of Bachelorhood

Instead of bringing Higgins closer to Eliza, the success of his experiment drives them apart. Ignored by Higgins and Pickering at the very moment of her triumph, Eliza flees from them. Higgins tracks her down at his mother's home, but the attempted reconciliation fails and Eliza bids him goodbye once more. Unlike the play, the film ends with a short scene in which Eliza returns to Higgins's laboratory. The significance of this departure from Shaw's text is considered in the next section. Here, I am interested in how gender overtakes class as the principal obstacle to romantic union.

That a particular variant of the traditional male gender role, the figure of the confirmed bachelor, creates a new and more profound barrier to romance becomes clear once Eliza's transformation has mooted the issue of class. Eliza has passed as a duchess and Higgins has won his bet, yet his condescension persists. Higgins's continued refusal to treat Eliza as an equal suggests that that condescension has had multiple determinants.

Higgins's dismissive attitude toward Eliza first becomes an issue as a result of the discussion that takes place between him and Pickering when the three return to Wimpole Street immediately after the reception. Ecstatic that Eliza has passed as an aristocrat, the two men converse as if Eliza herself played no part in the success of their experiment. Higgins tells Pickering how happy he is that the entire enterprise is over, for it has come to weigh him down:

> Thank God it's over. . . . It was interesting enough at first, while we were at the phonetics; but after that I got deadly sick of it. . . . It was a silly notion: the whole thing has been a bore. . . . I tell you, Pickering, never again for me. No more artificial duchesses. The whole thing has been simple purgatory. (*Collected Screenplays*, p. 257–258)

What is startling about these comments is not that Higgins expresses such negative feelings about the experiment, but that he speaks without acknowledging that Eliza is in the room and might be hurt by his comments. The two confirmed bachelors talk as if alone, entirely ignoring the young woman. Such an erasure of presence occurs among the very wealthy, who are as accustomed to their domestic servants as they are to their furniture and often treat them similarly. Indeed, during the course of her instruction, Eliza becomes something of a domestic in Higgins's household. Early in the film, Higgins denies that Eliza has any feelings about which he needs to be concerned (*Collected Screenplays*, p. 237), but that was before he had gotten to know her. Now, even after all those months of arduous instruction, she remains for him an object on which to exercise his talents and a servant to be ordered about.

Eliza is so outraged at being ignored precisely at this moment of triumph that when Higgins asks where his slippers are she hurls them at him. Caught totally off guard, Higgins ingenuously asks if anything is wrong.

> ELIZA [breathless]: Nothing wrong—with you. I've won your bet for you haven't I? That's enough for you. *I* don't matter, I suppose.
> HIGGINS: You won my bet! You! Presumptuous insect! *I* won it.
> (*Collected Screenplays*, p. 258)

Higgins's response reveals that flaw in his character that dooms any prospect of romance and that the film will now explore. Eliza reacts angrily to Higgins's relief that their lessons are ended, accusing him of overlooking her. But what Higgins responds to is not that accusation but her assumption that she had won the bet for him. He is irked that Eliza claims some responsibility for the victory, for this challenges his assumption that his skills as a linguist and scientist have alone brought it about. As a result, he is deaf to her complaint that he shows no concern for her fate. Instead of reacting with empathy, Higgins narcissistically upbraids Eliza for presuming to think of herself as a full participant in the experiment.

This exchange illustrates Higgins's inability to acknowledge Eliza as a human being whose needs and desires are as worthy of respect as his own. His self-conception as bachelor man of science legitimates a narcissism that denies that other people, Eliza most centrally, are both important to him and have legitimate claims on him.

But what of Higgins's belief that the credit for the victory is his alone? Surely, Higgins's superior expertise justifies his authority as Eliza's teacher, but she too has made important contributions to the experiment's success. By hogging the victory for himself, Higgins/Pygmalion reduces his Galatea to inert matter, a cipher who requires the form-giving power of his own knowledge and skills, thus reflecting his acceptance of a hierarchy based on these qualities rather than on blood.

Of course, for Higgins's teaching to have had any effect at all, Eliza has had to be a willing and active participant in the experiment. Higgins and Pickering themselves are effusive in their praise of Eliza's talent and effort when talking to Mrs. Higgins prior to her at home. Each of them speaks over the other in his enthusiasm to enumerate Eliza's accomplishments. Higgins, for example, praises Eliza's "most extraordinary quickness of ear," which allows her to pick up accents that "it took me years to get hold of," and Pickering assures Mrs. Higgins that "that girl is a genius" who "can play the piano quite beautifully" (*Collected Screenplays*, p. 252). At this point, both Higgins and Pickering are clear about Eliza's own contribution to her progress. Both see her as a talented and eager student, able to accomplish the tasks that they set her because of her abilities as well as their guidance. Just as important—although neither recognizes it—is Eliza's desire to please them, to do what they ask to the best of her ability because it is they who ask. This understanding of Eliza as equal partner to the experiment is forgotten after the episode at the embassy because it challenges these males' faith in a social hierarchy based on superior knowledge.[12]

Higgins's refusal to concede Eliza's autonomy continues throughout their interaction after returning from the ambassador's. When she cries out to him for some acknowledgment that he has developed affection for her, Higgins nitpicks once more. Eliza reproaches him: "You don't care. I know you don't care. You wouldn't care if I was dead. I'm nothing to you—not so much as them slippers" (*Collected Screenplays*, p. 259). To which Higgins, ever ready to reassert his linguistic and epistemic superiority by reminding Eliza of her deficiencies, snaps, "Those slippers." Higgins here chooses to deflect attention from Eliza's concerns, reacting instead to an incidental lapse. But this callous attempt to contain her plea for mutuality misfires—this Galatea's transformation has been more complete that Higgins realizes.

The issue of the extent to which Eliza is Higgins's creation is underscored by the irony of Shaw's title. Ovid's story "Pygmalion and Galatea" concerns a great sculptor who falls so deeply in love with the statue he has created that he asks the gods to give it life.[13] The intensity of Pygmalion's love persuades the gods to grant his request. One interpretation of this myth would have it that men desire women who are simple projections of their own desires, lacking independent being. The cultural role of this myth, on such a reading, is to teach that women need to accommodate themselves to this economy of male desire.

The film's use of the Pygmalion myth, however, is ironic, for it invokes the myth only to dispel it. Higgins may conceive of himself as a latter-day Pygmalion, shaping a mere "block" into a lady—indeed, he appropriates the power of the gods as well, claiming responsibility for giving her a more fully human life—but the film mocks these pretensions. In particular, Higgins's failure to acknowledge the role that Eliza has played in her own transformation diminishes him. Like Pygmalion, Higgins can only see the transformed Eliza as his own creation, the object of his intellectualized desire. But unlike Galatea, Eliza was already human prior to her encounter with her artist-teacher, even if, as he continually reminds her, only a lowly flower girl. The satisfaction of Higgins's masculinist desire is threatened by this woman's insistence on both her power and her need for reciprocity.

A further irony introduced by the film's title is that although Higgins and Pygmalion are both masters of their professions, Pygmalion's distinction is the intensity of his love. But this is precisely what Higgins cannot acknowledge about himself: that he really cares for Eliza. To do so would be to admit that he is more than the dispassionate scientific investigator and that his fulfillment depends on more than his own efforts. Higgins's inability to concede Eliza's significance for him thwarts the possibility of their love.

Inevitably, Higgins's refusal alters our attitude toward him. Where previously we might have been willing to discount his quirky manner and dismissive style, we now see this brilliant and witty linguist in a harsher light. Because we admire Eliza's achievements, we fault Higgins for his failure to acknowledge them. By the end of this sequence, the audience is firmly on Eliza's side as she faces up to her former mentor.

Their final confrontation, which takes place on the morning after Eliza has bolted from Higgins's laboratory, probes more deeply into the ethical failing at the root of his character. Desperately searching for Eliza, who has fled to his mother's home for help, Higgins finds her there but then only continues to denigrate her achievements. For example, after Eliza has angered him by putting on her best manners in a way that parodies her performance at the at home, he rebukes his mother for taking up Eliza's cause:

> Let her speak for herself. There isn't an idea that I haven't put into her head. I tell you I have created this thing out of the squashed cabbage leaves of Covent Garden; and now she pretends to play the fine lady with me. (*Collected Screenplays*, p. 267)

Eliza responds to this diatribe by explaining that she has a different view of things. Turning to Colonel Pickering, Eliza coolly and calmly tells him that *he* was responsible for teaching her good manners, which are what really count. When Pickering reminds her that Higgins was the one who taught her to speak, Eliza gives her own, deflationary account of Higgins's contribution to her education—and, along with it, his faith in knowledge as justifying hierarchy:

> It was just like learning to dance in the fashionable way: there was nothing more than that in it. But do you know what began my real education?. . . Your calling me Miss Doolittle that day when I first came to Wimpole Street. That was the beginning of self-respect for me. You see, the difference between a lady and a flowergirl is not how she behaves, it's how she's treated. I know I shall always be a flowergirl to Professor Higgins, because he always treats me as a flowergirl, and always will. . . . But I know I can be a lady to you, because you always treat me as a lady, and always will. (*Collected Screenplays*, pp. 267–268)

The distinction that Eliza makes here is both subtle and far-reaching. She sees Higgins's contribution to her education as essentially technical, equipping her with forms of conduct necessary to acting the lady.

Pickering, on the other hand, has taught her a very different lesson, namely to see herself as someone as worthy of respect as anyone else. This insight is not one that can be conveyed as one teaches a skill, but it is central to her transformation into a lady. For this reason, Eliza values it more highly.

Eliza's ability to articulate such a distinction proves her independence, for now she can think things out for herself. She does not see language as sacred, as does Higgins, but as simply one skill among others that she has acquired in learning to pass as a duchess. What *is* sacred to her is her own self-respect, something that Higgins is unable to foster. Because he continues to treat her as the grimy Cockney flower girl, that is, with contempt, Eliza will not accept a relationship with him on those terms.

Now, Higgins protests that Eliza does not understand him at all. She does not see why, from his point of view, the issue is not having the appropriate sort of manners, for these are, he agrees, just a set of customs that can be taught. What is important, according to Higgins, is treating everyone in the same way.

> HIGGINS: My manners are exactly the same as Colonel Pickering's.
> ELIZA: That's not true. He treats a flowergirl as if she were a duchess.
> HIGGINS: And I treat a duchess as if she was a flowergirl. The question is not whether I treat you rudely, but whether you ever heard me treat anyone else better. (*Collected Screenplays,* pp. 269–270)

Thus, beneath Higgins's facile egalitarianism is an attitude of nearly universal contempt. This linguist approaches others as if they were mere bearers of accents to be studied, objects for scientific investigation. He can treat all equally because he treats everyone as inferior to himself.[14] His attainments as *the* man of science authorize his leveling disdain for others for their lack of scientific knowledge.

This exchange establishes that the real obstacle to the Higgins-Eliza couple is Higgins's *bachelorhood,* a term that he uses to characterize his way of being-in-the-world and that I adopt to signify the ethic of conduct exemplified by his relationship with Eliza. A bachelor in this sense is a man committed to living free of significant intimate relationships. Although Higgins has repeatedly and proudly asserted his allegiance to this form of life, only now does the audience understand how impoverishing a choice this is.

By using the term "bachelorhood" to characterize Higgins's way of life, I intend to connect the concerns of this film with what Stanley Cavell has called the problem of skepticism. For Cavell, the skeptic is one who denies the reality of others, who fails to acknowledge that their humanity is as significant as one's own. Cavell sees this as a perennial human temptation, one that philosophy continually seeks to keep at bay. He also identifies its overcoming as a crucial concern of the Hollywood comedies of remarriage that form the subject of his study, *Pursuits of Happiness*.[15]

Higgins's way of being-in-the-world, his bachelorhood, is related to what Cavell terms skepticism because Higgins cannot fully credit the reality of other human beings. This authorizes his contempt and his reduction of others to objects for his scientific investigation. And it also keeps him from acknowledging that he has so come to care for Eliza, that his happiness depends on his deepening their connection.

Pygmalion does not present this failure to acknowledge others as a human failing, as Cavell's analysis would have it, but as a specifically masculine one.[16] Hence, the aptness of the term "bachelorhood." According to the film, Higgins's bachelorhood enacts the masculinist fantasy that he is complete and self-sufficient, not a finite human being with needs and desires that only others can satisfy.

This temptation to deny the implications of our finitude, the vulnerability of our well-being to factors beyond our control, has motivated philosophers at least as far back as Plato in his *Symposium*. That dialogue portrays the steps by which human beings may transcend their attachment to the merely finite and come to love only the infinite—for Plato, the Form of the Beautiful. *Pygmalion* counters that to attempt to shed one's attachment to the finite is to deny the work of weaving other human beings and their autonomous projects into the fabric of our own fulfillment.

Being in a couple, being in love, is only possible for those who admit their need for another, but this is an admission Higgins cannot make, that he uses his bachelorhood—and his commitment to science—to forestall. The film shows that Higgins's vaunted self-sufficiency is really an evasion of his own finitude. He is unwilling, unable to admit his dependence on Eliza, to admit that he, like all of us, needs other people, that his happiness depends on others.

Thus, when Higgins tells Eliza that "she will relapse into the gutter in three weeks without me at her elbow" (*Collected Screenplays*, p. 268), Eliza insists, "I can do without you. Don't think I can't." Higgins counters, has she ever asked herself whether he can do without her, implying that he is, indeed, vulnerable, that he really does need her. But Eliza's firm response that he will have to learn to do without her pushes Higgins into retreat:

> I can do without anybody. I have my own soul: my own spark of divine fire. But I shall miss you, Eliza. I confess that humbly and gratefully. I have grown accustomed to your voice and appearance. I like them, rather.[17]

He *will* miss Eliza, but he does not really need her. As a man of science, he avers, "Once for all, understand that I go my way and do my work without caring twopence what happens to either of us." Hardly the sort of reassurance that Eliza has asked for and needs, but what his subordination of subjectivity to the demands of scientific investigation requires.

Eliza, on the other hand, presents her commitment to their experiment in very different terms. For her, it was all about her relationship with Higgins:

> I want a little kindness. I know I'm only a common ignorant girl; but I'm not dirt under your feet. What I done—what I did was not for the dresses and the taxis: but because we were pleasant together and I come—came—to care for you; and not forgetting the differences between us and not wanting you to make love to me, but more friendly like.[18]

The difference between their motivations could not be clearer: Higgins uses his commitment to science to support his sense of superiority, which allows him to avoid human entanglement, but Eliza sticks with the experiment because she cares for him and wants to make him happy.

Higgins's equivocal response to Eliza's confession emphasizes his difficulty in admitting emotion. Initially, he reciprocates, "Of course, Eliza, that's exactly how I feel." But after a pause, he adds, "and how Pickering feels," once again distancing himself from his attachment to her. Then, as if exasperated by her need to know what he feels, he concludes, "Eliza, you're a fool!"[19] As he passes from personal avowal to evasive generality to, finally, angry displacement, Higgins is a man who cannot accept the power of his own feelings to move him.

The final break between Higgins and Eliza occurs when she begins to appreciate that she now has more resources in her situation than she previously understood. The first inkling of this fact comes after she threatens to marry Freddy and Higgins responds with anger: "Woman: do you not understand that I have made you a consort for a king?" (*Collected Screenplays*, p. 270). As the conversation progresses, Eliza issues a second threat, this time to use the very skill that she has acquired as a result of Higgins's teaching: her ability to speak properly. She can ally herself with Karpathy, Eliza announces triumphantly:

> Now I know how to deal with you. What a fool I was not to think of it before! You can't take away the knowledge you gave me. You said I had a finer ear than you. And I can be civil and kind to people, which is more than you can! (*Collected Screenplays*, p. 270)

With Higgins's reaction to this threat, Eliza finally understands that she can, in fact, live independently of Higgins. This development parallels that of Ibsen's Nora, another woman who realizes that she can live newly glimpsed possibilities only by rejecting the man who stifles her.

In *A Doll's House* by Henrik Ibsen—a playwright much admired by Shaw—a woman faces the realization that her marriage has infantilized her, made her into a doll. Through her growing disillusionment with her husband, Helmer, Nora comes to see that to become the woman she is, she needs to separate from him. The play ends literally with a bang, as Nora slams the door on her home and her marriage.[20]

In a similar way, Eliza has discovered that she must separate from Higgins to live her own life. His refusal to accord her the respect she now realizes she deserves means that she too must slam the door on a relationship that requires her subordination. Because the newly transformed woman at the end of *Pygmalion* requires more than her male mentor can give her, she must leave him so she can lead the life that he has equipped her to live. Higgins is not the hypocrite that Helmer is, yet Eliza can no more live under his freely acknowledged masculinist regime than Nora can under Helmer's unavowed practice of domination.

For this reason, Eliza must remain without a partner at the end of the film. Despite Shaw's attempt to insinuate Freddy as a plausible lover (something the film wisely drops), there is no male character equal to the challenge of being Eliza's partner. *Pygmalion*'s men are either bachelors or dolts, so that Eliza is left without the possibility of genuine intimacy.[21] Contributing to her desperation is her awareness that having become a woman for whom no man is a suitable partner, at least in the world of this film, she also has no social location to which to return. Unlike Nora, however, Eliza is now a woman of significant accomplishment. She realizes that she can use the linguistic skills that Higgins has given her—as well as her own talent—to train others to speak proper English. As the figure of Karpathy suggests, this is a prestigious and lucrative profession. So even though Higgins's intervention in her life has compelled Eliza to give up whatever aspirations a Cockney flower girl might have had, she is not bereft. She has become a professional woman, with all the advantages and disadvantages of that newly created social role.

In this sequence, then, *Pygmalion* gives a bleak assessment of the situation of feminist women. England's men are simply not fit partners for independent women like Eliza. The Higginses of this world, comfortably constrained by their own bachelorhood, are not able to give such women the respect they deserve, and the Freddies, despite their blind adoration, lack the substance that would make them interesting. The film concludes that gender roles so constituted offer no hope for genuinely reciprocal romantic relationships. Heterosexual love can find a place in the world only if men, too, are changed by feminism.

On the other hand, the film offers women the possibility of striking out on their own. The cultural possibilities created by feminism allow women to secure their own fortunes with skills acquired through education. Although this may not be everything, the film shows us that it is also not nothing. As she walks out on Higgins, Eliza knows that she can live a life of possibilities unimaginable to the flower girl Higgins first encountered in the portico of St. Paul's.

The Problem of an Ending

I conclude this discussion of *Pygmalion* with a brief consideration of how its final scene undercuts the critique of masculinism that follows Eliza's triumph at the ball. After Eliza walks out on him at his mother's home, Higgins retreats to his laboratory and listens wistfully to his recordings of Eliza's voice. We see that Higgins misses her. Unbeknownst to him, Eliza enters, turns off the recording, and continues the dialogue in her own voice. When Higgins realizes that she is back, his expression changes and once again assuming his posture of superiority, he orders her to fetch his slippers. Eliza has returned and apparently accepted Higgins's terms for continuing their relationship.[22]

This breezy negation of the film's sustained critique of bachelorhood is deeply problematic. Simply providing an ending that supposedly allows the audience to leave the theater with their fantasies fulfilled is an aesthetic as well as an ethical lapse. This film must show that the weighty issues raised by the crisis between Eliza and Higgins have at least been respected. Eliza's unmotivated acceptance of Higgins's terms, a plot maneuver Shaw repeatedly denounced, undercuts her, and *Pygmalion*'s, point of view.

Pygmalion's filmmakers impute to their audiences so powerful a desire for romance between Higgins and Eliza that their breakup cannot be allowed. And perhaps they are right: To the average filmgoer, Shaw's liberatory yet depressing message might have seemed out of tune with what had promised to be merely an amusing story. But satisfying this desire means dismissing the narrative's claims about heterosexual relationships: that independent women cannot accept the assumption of justified male dominance. *Pygmalion* thus distorts its own message. Even as the film presses its critique of class privilege, it retreats from its demonstration of the destructiveness of traditional masculinist postures.

The argument of this chapter has been that *Pygmalion* exemplifies two of the central themes of this study of the unlikely couple film. First, I have established that this narrative of transgressive love has made an important set of criticisms of oppressive social structures. By interrogating both class and gender relationships, *Pygmalion* illustrates the critical bite available to the figure of the unlikely couple. In its final submission to cliché, however, the film also shows how the pressure to satisfy the expectations of a mass audience can compromise both the aesthetic and the moral integrity of this genre of filmmaking.

Notes

1. Most of the criticism of Shaw's play concerns the question of whether Higgins and Eliza will have a romantic relationship. In *Shaw's Daughters: Dramatic and Narrative Constructions of Gender* (Ann Arbor: University of Michigan Press, 1991), J. Ellen Gainor focuses on gender issues raised by the play. Unfortunately, her reading of the play as a variant of the fairy tale "Snow White" gives *Pygmalion* a much more sinister atmosphere than is warranted. In addition, she fails to interrogate the play's view of class.

2. Neither the screenplay nor the text of the play give an accurate transcript of the film. Parenthetical citations refer to the text of the screenplay of *Pygmalion* in *The Collected Screenplays of Bernard Shaw*, Bernard F. Dukore, ed. (Athens: University of Georgia Press, 1980). I have amended my quotations from the screenplay to bring them into accordance with the actual film. Citations to lines in the film that do not appear in the published screenplay are footnoted. In the present case, the line is actually from the play: See George Bernard Shaw, *Pygmalion* (London: Penguin Books, 1957), p. 130.

3. I discuss *Pretty Woman* and its relationship to *Pygmalion* in Chapter 4.

4. *A Gay Deception* is unusual because the final couple is a cross-class one. In this sense, the discovery is less that the couple is not unlikely than that the female partner is not a superficial gold digger, thereby establishing her as a worthy candidate for social elevation.

5. I discuss *Desert Hearts* in Chapter 10.

6. Benjamin DeMott, *The Imperial Middle: Why Americans Cannot Think Straight About Class* (New York: William Morrow and Co., 1990), p. 66.

7. These lines actually reverse the claim of the play, where Higgins blames himself for becoming "selfish and tyrannical." See Shaw, *Pygmalion,* pp. 49–50.

8. The first sentence is on page 247 of the screenplay. The second sentence is an addition to it.

9. Higgins's dormant sexuality provides a possible narrative avenue that the film eschews. In comedies such as *Bringing Up Baby* (1938), the possibility of a woman awakening a man's sexuality balances the male's ability to provide something for the woman. It is also possible that Higgins's latent homosexuality would make him prefer Pickering as a partner, although this is another possibility not envisioned by the film.

10. The film changes this character's name. In the *Collected Screenplays,* Dukore suggests that it is to make him sound more Hungarian. In the play, he is referred to as "Nepommuck," a Czech name.

11. Shaw's discomfort at suggestions of romance between Eliza and Higgins is due, in part, to a desire to avoid having this parenting relationship be seen as sexual.

12. The film here presents the relation of teacher to student as a noncoercive form of power. For a fuller discussion of power in this context, see my *The Forms of Power: From Domination to Transformation* (Philadelphia: Temple University Press, 1990).

13. Ovid, *Metamorphoses,* Rolfe Humphries, tr. (Bloomington: Indiana University Press, 1955), pp. 241–243.

14. Actually, Higgins does not treat Pickering with the same contempt he bestows on others, such as Mrs. Hill. This is because Pickering, like Higgins, is a man of science. Higgins's unself-conscious elitism is based on his elevated view of science.

15. Stanley Cavell, *Pursuits of Happiness: The Hollywood Comedy of Remarriage* (Cambridge, MA: Harvard University Press, 1981).

16. "Masculine" in this context should not be read as an essentialist reference to biological maleness. I intend it to refer to a gender role that is usually enacted by men. In *Contesting Tears: The Hollywood Melodrama of the Unknown Woman* (Chicago: University of Chicago Press, 1996), Cavell does explore the issue of skepticism as gendered.

17. Although not in the screenplay, this speech, as well as the next, are taken directly from the play, with some omissions. See Shaw, *Pygmalion,* p. 127.

18. Shaw, *Pygmalion,* p. 130.

19. Shaw, *Pygmalion*, p. 131.

20. Cavell uses Ibsen's *A Doll's House,* Michael Meyer, tr. (London: Methuen, 1985) to introduce the idea of the comedy of remarriage in *Pursuits of Happiness.*

21. In this respect, *Pygmalion* resembles the films that Cavell calls "melodramas of the unknown woman," the subject of *Contesting Tears.*

22. In the final analysis, it remains unclear whether the two of them will ever have a full romantic relationship. It appears that Higgins offers Eliza only a return to the status quo ante.

3
It Happened One Night
An Education in Humility

In the previous chapter, I traced *Pygmalion*'s critique of two forms of social hierarchy: the class hierarchy that privileges the British aristocracy and the gender hierarchy that privileges males. In this chapter, I argue that *It Happened One Night,* Frank Capra's 1934 romantic comedy, delivers parallel criticisms of class and gender hierarchy, but articulated now in the more broadly democratic context of American society. Wealth and masculinist assumptions of superiority based on expertise are represented as forms of pride inimical to the democratic values the film endorses.

It Happened One Night tells the story of Ellie Andrews (Claudette Colbert), the pampered, strong-willed daughter of a Wall Street tycoon. Ellie's desire to escape from her overbearing father has led her to marry King Westley (Jameson Thomas), an upper-class aviator whom Daddy regards as a fake and something of a joke. The film's plot centers on Ellie's attempt to rejoin her husband after her father has kidnapped her to prevent the consummation of her marriage. Her journey brings her into contact with Peter Warne (Clark Gable), a newspaper reporter, who decides to help her, banking that an exclusive account of her travels will help him regain his job. On their way to New York, Ellie and Peter fall in love, but a misunderstanding between them on the eve of their arrival threatens to drive Ellie back into her marriage to Westley. The film ends happily, however, with Ellie and Peter embarked on matrimony, Ellie's marriage to Westley having been annulled.

A great deal of critical attention has been directed at *It Happened One Night*. For academic film theory, it has served as an example of how Hollywood narratives misrepresent and legitimize relationships of social domination. For example, in their book *Popular Film and Television Comedy*,[1] Steve Neale and Frank Krutnik offer an interpretation that adopts this approach. They cite *It Happened One Night* as a paradigm in their analysis of the 1930s screwball comedy, arguing that although premised on a violation of gender norms, these films ultimately served to redeem patriarchal practice in general and traditional marriage in particular. More broadly, they claim that the genre as a whole functioned to normalize anxieties caused by the Great Depression.

Neale and Krutnik emphasize that by the end of *It Happened One Night*, the once-rebellious Ellie has been taught "acceptance of the authority of the male and a rejection of the woman's economic independence" (Neale and Krutnik, p. 154). The dangers to good order posed by the economic and social independence of women are evoked only to be trivialized—these threats to the patriarchy can be contained. Finally, Neale and Krutnik assert, the film's critique of class domination is not serious, for it makes "no attempt to challenge the *status quo* in regard to the class hierarchy" (Neale and Krutnik, p. 155).

In presenting their view, Neale and Krutnik rely on Stanley Cavell's interpretation of both *It Happened One Night* and the genre that Cavell calls the comedy of remarriage. This is ironic because Cavell's assessment of these films is diametrically opposed to theirs, a fact they apparently fail to notice. For Cavell, these are major works of art, "trac[ing] the progress from narcissism and incestuous privacy to objectivity and the acknowledgment of otherness as the path and goal of human happiness; and since this happiness is expressed as marriage, we understand it as simultaneously an individual and social achievement."[2] That is, Cavell views these narratives as explorations of the development of genuine mutuality. Although he acknowledges that the sociohistorical context of their production is implicated in their interpretations of human existence, Cavell denies that these films are simply meant to persuade the oppressed to consent to their oppression, the very position that Neale and Krutnik endorse.

In my view, both approaches to the film suffer from significant deficits. Cavell's demonstration that the film addresses inescapable issues of human life and conduct shows that *It Happened One Night* cannot be dismissed as mere ideology. On the other hand, his reading underplays the narrative weight of class in the film to the point that he is precluded from seeing how vital to its intentions is its critique of class hierarchy. One symptom of this blindness is that although Cavell does notice that the film, like all comedies of remarriage, is set among the wealthy, he denies that it is concerned with wealth per se or that wealth is even an issue for it. Instead, its social location is justified by its real subject, conversation, a luxury only the wealthy can afford.[3] This surprising claim suggests how the metaphysical framework Cavell uses to think about this film—and the other comedies of remarriage—excludes serious consideration of class.

My analysis of *It Happened One Night* shares Cavell's respect for this film as a serious intellectual product, deserving of the careful analysis usually accorded to works of philosophy, but with an approach to its central dilemmas that is socially critical rather than metaphysical. Like *Pygmalion, It Happened One Night* indicts both wealth and masculine self-assurance, but it does so on different grounds: as forms of *pride* that inhibit genuinely democratic relationships. To these forms of pride, the film counterposes "using strategy," a form of conduct that we can construe as living by one's wits, by improvisation. At a personal level, the film's brief for this mode of being-in-the-world is that it makes happiness attainable; at the social level, to live by one's wits implies that openness to the stream of experience that a democratic order requires.

A Brat and a Lout

From the outset, *It Happened One Night* presents class and gender as obstacles to romance between Peter and Ellie. As in *Pygmalion,* these obstacles are understood as such by both principals, who initially react to one another as representatives of objectionable social types. For Ellie, Peter is an impudent young man on the make. To keep him in his place, she takes the haughty line the wealthy reserve for their social inferiors. On the other hand, Peter registers Ellie as a spoiled, upper-class brat, a young woman ignorant of life. Because Peter sees himself as a man of the world, someone who knows his way around—a stance authorized by a masculinist inflation of his own capabilities—he has nothing but contempt for her. These two could hardly be less suited to one another—although, of course, from the titles on, everyone in the theater knows better.

The film's initial scenes establish Ellie's position as the scion of a superrich American family. When we first see her, she is captive aboard her father's yacht. Alexander Andrews (Walter Connolly), a Wall Street tycoon, has kidnapped his daughter because he thinks she rushed headlong into a foolish marriage. The plush surroundings on the yacht, as well as the presence of a large crew, establish Andrews's wealth and power.

His high-handed response to Ellie's choice of husband shows that Andrews's wealth has accustomed him to getting his way. Ellie has grown up in these opulent, yet because she is female, isolating circumstances. As a result, her social position—at once privileged and inexperienced—dictates her approach to life.

There are a number of reasons why, by contrast, describing the precise way in which the film establishes Peter's class position is difficult. The first is that he writes for a newspaper. Because reporters earn a wage by writing at the command of an editor, they can stand for the mass of Americans who live by wage labor. In the 1930s, the financial circumstances of newspaper reporters were sufficiently modest that their way of life resembled that of other workers. But journalism is not a typical working-class occupation, for reporters make their living manipulating language rather than brute matter.

It is worth noting that the figure of the newspaper reporter was a staple of the Hollywood comedies of the 1930s. Because many of the scriptwriters lured to Hollywood by its glamour and good money had been newspaper people, the figure of the cynical and hard-boiled reporter became a means of commenting on their own situation. Like reporters, scriptwriters are generally not free to choose their subjects but produce to meet the demands of a paymaster. Writers working under the Hollywood studio system of the 1930s were employed to work on pictures in which the studio moguls were interested. Thus, as Pauline Kael has remarked, the reporter functions as a stand-in for the Hollywood scriptwriter: "The new heroes of the screen were created in the image of their authors: They were fast-talking newspaper reporters."[4] By heroizing the reporter, scriptwriters were able to assert their own superiority to the circumstances in which they worked.

A second difficulty in precisely determining Peter's class position is that, unlike *Pygmalion*, *It Happened One Night* deploys a populist rhetoric of representation that denies the existence of rigid class divisions in America. Although the film acknowledges that the rich constitute a class apart, it treats all the rest as simply members of an amorphous "American people." As a result, Peter cannot be identified as a worker in the Marxian sense; he is instead an everyman, that contentless abstraction that in American eyes brings together all but the very wealthiest. Despite the ambiguities of Peter's class position, however, there is a vast gulf between his status and Ellie's.

Peter and Ellie first meet on a bus. Having escaped from her father's yacht, Ellie makes her way to a bus station, anxious to travel back to her husband in New York. Peter is on the same New York–bound bus, hoping to reclaim the job from which he has just been fired. They meet when she takes the seat he has just cleared of a pile of newspapers. While he argues with the driver, who is upset that he has simply tossed the papers out the bus window, she blithely walks by and takes his seat, as if it had been prepared for her. When Peter challenges her, she asks the driver if the seats are reserved and he replies that they are not, happy to put Peter in his place or, rather, to keep him out of it. Irritated by this turn of events and not wanting to allow Ellie to best him, Peter demands to know whether the seats are meant for one occupant or for two. When the driver reluctantly allows that they are for two, Peter gruffly assumes the seat next to Ellie.

A scene that takes place soon after serves to emphasize how difficult it will be for the two of them to get past this sort of sparring. At the first rest stop, in a long shot taken from behind Peter—so that we see as if through his eyes—Peter notices a thief stealing Ellie's suitcase. Then, in a shot taken from Ellie's vantage point, Peter is shown rushing toward her and she concludes that Peter is making some weird sort of pass at her. Returning winded and disheveled from his pursuit of the thief, Peter assumes that Ellie understands his actions. She does not, however, and responds dismissively to his attempted explanation, "I don't know what you're raving about, young man. And, furthermore, I'm not interested" (*One Night*, p. 138).[5] When she finally understands what has transpired, she nonetheless tries to keep him at a distance—to accept his repeated offers of help might reveal her identity, something she must conceal to elude recapture. But Peter thinks Ellie is being needlessly distant and winds up expostulating, "Why, you ungrateful brat!" uttering the epithet with which he will continue to address her throughout the film.

Ellie and Peter are unable to communicate because of assumptions each harbors about class and gender, which blind them to the individuality of the other. But at the same time, *It Happened One Night* accords these assumptions a measure of validity. Thus, the film does not treat the assumptions simply as obstacles the two will have to surmount on the way to romantic intimacy. Each regards the other as a beneficiary of illegitimate social privilege, a position the film endorses. Thus, Peter's perception of Ellie as a spoiled brat becomes the film's verdict on the pridefulness of wealth—money authorizes the rich to treat others as mere instruments of their will. And Ellie's perception of Peter as an opinionated lout becomes the film's critique of masculinist pridefulness—specialized knowledge authorizes men to denigrate women. Ellie the brat and Peter the know-it-all thus figure forms of pride that inhibit true democratic reciprocity.

Ellie's Brattiness

In the Christian tradition, pride is the first of the seven deadly sins. It consists in an "overweening opinion of one's own qualities, attainments, or estate, which gives rise to a feeling and attitude of superiority over and contempt for others."[6] *It Happened One Night* exhibits Ellie's pridefulness in her wealth as an unreflective sense of entitlement vis-à-vis the ordinary Americans she encounters. On her journey with Peter, she will acquire greater respect for others and a correspondingly humbler estimate of her own worth.

Although Ellie is the main object of the film's critique of wealth, that indictment extends to her father as well. Alexander Andrews's use of force to keep Ellie from her husband dramatizes the film's critique of wealth as a form of pride. Those who possess it simply assume that they have the right to use other people as they see fit.

Andrews, it is true, wishes to spare his daughter the pain he assumes will be hers once she realizes her mistake in marrying King Westley. To convince Ellie that he has acted in her best interests, Andrews calls the aviator "no good" and "a fake," as if his contempt for Westley entitles him to kidnap his daughter from her own wedding. This Wall Street tycoon is accustomed to getting his way, through brute assertions of his wealth and power if necessary. In fact, when Ellie objects that his "idea of strategy is to use a lead pipe," Andrews boasts, "I've won a lot of arguments with a lead pipe" (*One Night*, p. 128). In the present context, however, it is pretty clear that this type of "strategy" will not work: The measures that Andrews has taken, even though motivated by well-intentioned concern for Ellie's welfare, will not secure her acceptance of his point of view. In fact, Ellie's marriage to King Westley continues her pattern of reacting to her father's wishes by doing just the opposite. When Andrews tells her, "You married him only because I told you not to" (*One Night*, p. 129), she acknowledges this. Her father's ruthlessness demonstrates the validity of Ellie's desire to escape his domination, but at the same time his insight into her motivation announces the narrative's goal for Ellie: to learn the positive content of her own desire.

Although Andrews claims to be employing strategy to get Ellie to change her mind, wielding a lead pipe is not her idea of a strategic way to get what one wants. The proposition that one can achieve one's ends by using one's wits is important to this story, for Ellie will herself accept creative improvisation as an approach to life. Her father's wealth has made it unnecessary for him to use real strategy to achieve his ends.

But if Andrews's tactics are wrong, his assessment of Ellie's marriage seems accurate. This raises the issue of how one can be made to see that one's understanding of a situation is mistaken, that there is another, better way of looking at it. We can call this the problem of education, and we find *It Happened One Night* continuing to address it during Ellie's travels with Peter. So far, the film has shown that Andrews's attempt to coerce a change of mind has only increased Ellie's stubborn determination not to do so. Exactly how using strategy is an alternative to force becomes clear as the narrative progresses.

That Ellie is very much her father's daughter, equally prideful in her wealth, is established when the bus passengers are given a thirty-minute breakfast stop after their night of travel. Ellie has awakened to find herself sleeping on Peter's shoulder—a first intimation of the possibility of romance—and tells Peter that she is going to the Hotel Windsor, presumably her sort of place. When Peter warns that she will miss the bus, she assures him, "Oh, no. No, they'll wait for me." To be on the safe side, she admonishes the bus driver as she leaves, "Driver, I'm going to be a few minutes late. Be sure you wait for me" (*One Night*, p. 141). Of course, the bus pulls off without her, much to Ellie's outrage: "Why, that's ridiculous! I was on that bus—I told them to wait" (*One Night*, p. 142). For all her rejection of her father, she shares his confidence that the world revolves around the needs of the rich.

In *Pygmalion*, Higgins's bachelorhood is both cause and effect of his failure to acknowledge his finitude, his need for others. Ellie is beset by an analogous problem: Because of her wealth, she does not see the need in her relations with others to, in Cavell's terms, acknowledge their otherness—they exist only to serve her ends.

It Happened One Night takes its criticism of wealth as a source of pride even further in Ellie's subsequent interaction with Peter. When she gets over her shock at the departure of the bus, she notices that Peter has waited for her. He explains that he is there because he has read a newspaper and found out who she is and what she is doing on the bus. When Ellie worries that he is going to expose her—"Listen, if you'll promise not to do it [i.e., turn her in to her father], I'll pay you. I'll pay you as much as he will" (*One Night*, p. 143)—Peter retorts,

> You know, I had you pegged right from the start. You're the spoiled brat of a
> rich father. The only way you can get anything is to buy it. Now you're in a
> jam and all you can think of is your money. It never fails, does it? Ever hear
> of the word "humility"? No, you wouldn't. I guess it never occurred to you
> just to say, "Please, Mister, I'm in trouble. Will you help me?" No. That'd
> bring you down off your high horse for a minute. (*One Night*, p. 144)

In this angry speech, Peter tells Ellie that she will have to learn the meaning of the word "humility", the paradigmatic Christian virtue. To relate to
others on the basis of a shared common humanity rather than on the pre-
rogatives of her wealth is the lesson in democratic citizenship that her trip
with Peter offers her, although not in the way Peter expects.

Peter the Know-It-All

It Happened One Night makes the irony of Peter's reproach to Ellie, that
she lacks humility, abundantly clear, although this aspect of the film is absent from Cavell's account of it. Peter's masculinist pretensions are subject
to as serious and sustained a critique as Ellie's moneyed hauteur.[7]

When we first see Peter in the bus station, he is slightly drunk and talking on a pay phone to his New York editor, Joe Gordon (Charles Wilson).
To the delight of a crowd of drunken but admiring fellow reporters, Peter
asserts his independence by refusing to accept the terms of his employment.
But when Gordon actually fires him for sending in an article written in free
verse—"Why didn't you tell me you were going to write it in Greek?" he
complains—Peter is briefly taken aback. He quickly recovers his poise,
however, and continues talking into the now-dead phone. He pretends to
tell Gordon off, announces that he is quitting the paper, and then expresses
his hope that "this [his quitting] will be a lesson to you!" Because he behaves
as if he does not care what his boss thinks, his act earns the admiration of
his credulous colleagues, all of whom resent their own bosses but lack
Peter's reckless self-assurance. When he hangs up the phone, his retinue accompanies him to the New York bus—his "chariot"—in a mock ceremony,
chanting, "Make way for the King!" (*One Night*, p. 133).[8]

Despite our own undeniable pleasure in Peter's performance, we know
that he needs the job from which he has been fired, so that his bravado,
which plays so well to the gallery, actually puts him in a precarious position. Because he cannot bear to be humiliated in front of his admiring audience, his pride causes him to jeopardize his future.

During his subsequent travels with Ellie, Peter's machismo is subjected
to extended and explicitly critical scrutiny. For example, when Peter at-

tempts to use donut dunking and hitchhiking as opportunities to impress Ellie with his savvy, she instead ridicules his inflated estimate of his own accomplishments. In two wonderfully comic episodes, the film shows how male epistemic display defeats democratic reciprocity.

The donut-dunking episode takes place at breakfast on the morning after Peter and Ellie have spent their first night on opposite sides of the hung blanket they call "the Wall of Jericho." (This blanket, subject to extensive interpretation by Cavell, functions to keep Ellie's virtue intact despite her sleeping in the same room with Peter.) As Ellie confesses that she has never before been alone with a man, Peter interrupts, apparently to fault her for dunking her donut in her coffee:

PETER: Say, where did you learn to dunk—in finishing school?
ELLIE: Aw now, don't you start telling me I shouldn't dunk.
PETER: Of course you shouldn't. You don't know how to do it. Dunking's an art. Don't let it soak so long. A dip, and plop, into your mouth. If you let it soak so long, it'll get soft and fall off. It's all a matter of timing. I ought to write a book about it.
ELLIE: Thanks, Professor.
PETER: Just goes to show you. Twenty million dollars and you don't know how to dunk. (*One Night,* p. 162)

At first, Ellie is surprised that Peter is concerned with how she dunks her donut rather than with the propriety of the practice itself. Then, more to the point, she ridicules Peter's evident pride in his donut-dunking expertise. She mocks the suggestion that dunking is the sort of activity about which one needs instruction. Indeed, Peter's idea of writing a book about it betrays the extent of his false pride. But, oblivious to her sarcasm, Peter concludes his failed lesson by pointing up the difference between Ellie's vast resources and her scant knowledge of the things that really count in life.

This is Peter's first attempt at instructing Ellie, but she certainly does not learn the intended lesson. The reasons for this failure, however, require some unpacking, for what we know and how we learn from others are subjects that this film repeatedly calls to our attention. Peter's conceit is that his possession of special knowledges that others lack makes him superior to them. In the present scene, it is this presumption that leads him to think of writing a book about donut dunking. But to Ellie, this idea is preposterous. Dunking a donut is just not an activity that requires what we think of as book learning. Peter is right that her donut will fall apart if she lets it soak, but the way in which he instructs Ellie shows us more about him than it does about donuts: We learn that Peter needs to compensate for this young woman's class advantage by trumpeting his own epistemic superiority.

Peter's inappropriate attempt to teach Ellie how to dunk a donut does not mean there is nothing that she needs to learn. Indeed, I argue in the next section that she acquires something vastly more important and subtle—an education in democratic values. The lessons that Ellie learns she learns from experience, however, not from a set of instructions such as one might find in a how-to book.

A second comic episode, the famous hitchhiking scene, deals Peter's pridefulness a more severe blow. This sequence occurs early one morning, after Peter and Ellie are forced to spend a night together under the stars to elude her pursuers. Ellie sits on a fence watching as Peter gives her a lesson in how to thumb a ride. Once again, Peter boasts that his expertise qualifies him to write a book. And once again, the film undercuts his boast, only this time Peter himself is forced to acknowledge that maybe he does not "know it all." As Peter moves to the road's edge, Ellie asks him,

ELLIE: But suppose nobody stops for us?
PETER: Oh, they'll stop all right. It's a matter of knowing how to hail them.
ELLIE: You're an expert, I suppose.
PETER: Expert! Going to write a book on it, called the "Hitchhiker's Hail"—
ELLIE: There's no end to your accomplishments.
PETER: You think it's simple, huh?
ELLIE (*exaggeratedly*): Oh, no! No!
PETER: Well, it *is* simple. It's all in the old thumb. A lot of people do it—(*waves*)—like this. (*Shakes his head sadly*) All wrong. Never get anywhere.
ELLIE: Ah! The poor things.
PETER: Yeah boy, that old thumb never fails. (*One Night,* pp. 183–184)

Peter goes on to demonstrate the three effective motions. But when he actually tries them, it is to no avail. After being passed by a flurry of cars, Peter retracts his boast:

PETER: I don't think I'll write a book after all.

ELLIE: Yeah. Think of all the fun you had though. (*He glares at her.*) Do you mind if I try?

PETER (*contemptuously*): You! Don't make me laugh.

ELLIE: You're such a smart Aleck! Nobody knows anything but you. I'll stop a car—and I won't use my thumb. (*One Night*, p. 185)

Of course, when Ellie proceeds to the curb, "lifts her skirt above her knees and pretends to be fixing her garter" (*One Night*, p. 185), a passing car immediately screeches to a halt (see Photo 3.1). In the next shot, we see Ellie comfortably ensconced in the back seat next to a humiliated Peter, to whom she has, she explains, "proved once and for all that the limb is mightier than the thumb" (*One Night*, p. 185).

In this delightful scene, Ellie not only ridicules Peter for his boasting, she shows him she is a good deal more resourceful than he thinks. The audience identifies with Ellie throughout as she teases Peter and then one-ups him. After all, it turns out that Ellie knows how to stop a car in a way that Peter cannot. Ellie's debunking once again shows up Peter's masculinist compulsion to appear more knowledgeable than any mere woman.

The sort of instruction that Peter thinks he has to offer Ellie consists of a fixed set of techniques, in this case for hitchhiking. And these stratagems are what he imagines including in his book. But Ellie's success comes not from following a recipe but from acting strategically, improvising. Recall her father's claim that in kidnapping Ellie from her wedding he was employing strategy. The hitchhiking sequence provides a competing interpretation of using strategy, namely, applying one's wits to adapt action to circumstance. *This* is the lesson Ellie has learned from observing Peter's handling of the various difficulties they have faced together on the road. *It Happened One Night* thus counterposes two concepts of learning: the acquisition of the kind of specialized know-how Peter takes such pride in versus the development of one's capacities for creatively responding to one's experience—the alternative opened to Ellie by her adventures with Peter.

Ellie's Education for Democracy

It Happened One Night is a romantic comedy of mutual transformation. The obstacles in the way of its unlikely couple are removed as Ellie finds she enjoys being with Peter and he comes to care about her. These dis-

Photo 3.1 Ellie shows she can use strategy, too

coveries lead the partners to reject that part of themselves that the other rightly views as representative of an oppressive social type. The flowering of romance between Peter and Ellie is thus a story about their education for democracy.

In contemporary terms, the personal has become the political in the specific sense that the triumph of their love symbolizes the possibility of a democratic culture. For Ellie, this means learning to encounter as her equals the Americans with whom she comes into contact during her travels with Peter. Whether it is waiting in line to shower in an auto camp or happily singing along with "common folk" on a bus, her road trip is one extended lesson in humility. In addition to discovering that she has suffered from the vice of pride, Ellie finds out that being a commoner can be a great deal more fun than being cocooned in her father's wealth.[9]

This lesson in democratic values represents the film's positive alternative to pride as a way of being-in-the-world. My analysis of the hitchhiking scene has already pointed the way to understanding the significance of creative improvisation in Ellie's education. She has come to prefer using strategy, living by her wits, to the life of stultifying privilege she has known. Although this is conveyed in a number of scenes, only one can be discussed here.

The scene in question takes place immediately after Peter's failed lesson in donut dunking. The couple's breakfast conversation is interrupted by the intrusion of Mr. Dyke, the owner of the auto camp, who is accompanied by two detectives sent by Ellie's father. Aware of their approach, Peter has seated Ellie on the bed, and as he combs her hair down over her face, he loudly recounts his conversation with Aunt Bellah from Wilkes-Barre. At first, Ellie has no idea what he is doing, but she quickly catches on and plays along with him (see Photo 3.2). When Peter feigns anger at one of the detectives to distract him from his quarry, Ellie jumps in to "calm" Peter. She even introduces her own variations on the story he has been fabricating. After Peter protests to Dyke, "They [the detectives] can't come in here and start shooting questions at my wife!" Ellie turns on him—"Don't get excited, Peter. They just asked a civil question"—capturing the bickering tone of old marrieds so well that it throws Dyke and the detectives off the scent. Ellie is so convincing as the aggrieved housewife that Dyke even comes to her aid, reproaching the detectives for causing an argument between this long-suffering "little woman" and her bullying husband (*One Night*, pp. 165–166).

Ellie clearly gets a kick out of pretending to be Peter's wife. Her pleasure stems not just from their success in putting one over on her pursuers, but from her delight in how they played off one another. In improvising the role of the abused housewife, Ellie is forced to use her wits. Indeed, she embroiders on Peter's script. Ellie's enjoyment derives from her discovery and exercise of capacities that her sheltered existence had kept hidden and unused.[10]

This incident is important to the evolution of the couple, for it causes Peter to realize that there is more to Ellie than the spoiled brat he has so far disdained—she has reserves of character undeveloped by her privileged way of life. As a result, both he and Ellie come to see other possibilities for their relationship:

PETER: Say, you weren't bad. Jumping in like that. Got a brain, haven't you.
ELLIE: You weren't so bad yourself.
PETER: We could start a two-person stock company. (*One Night*, p. 166)

Photo 3.2 *The Great Deception*

Impressed by Ellie's skill at improvisation, Peter playfully suggests a very different type of relationship, imagining Ellie and himself as a two-person troupe as a way of acknowledging that, with her quick wit, there is a fit between them after all. Although the stock company metaphor does not imply romance, it does symbolize a joint undertaking that transcends short-term mutual convenience.

Although this fantasy is Peter's, there are still limits to what he is willing to imagine. After he has given their performance a title, *The Great Deception*, Ellie adds that they could also do "Cinderella," invoking the fairy-tale romance of class ascent. Peter's curt rebuff, "No mushy stuff," indicates that he is not yet ready to entertain the idea of a romance with Ellie. On the other hand, Ellie's suggestion reveals that her imagination is already headed that way.

Peter and Ellie's masquerade exemplifies the film's understanding of how one changes the way one lives one's life. Ellie learns how to improvise by first observing Peter and then becoming a partner to his stratagem. And in doing so, she experiences the pleasures of a new kind of freedom. Neither Peter's attempts to instruct her nor her father's efforts at coercion have this power. Experience of a life lived among ordinary Americans is Ellie's best teacher, because it calls on her to cultivate her capacities for judgment and choice. This is the important lesson in democratic culture that Ellie learns on the road with Peter.

Men's Ways of Knowing It All

Although the trip to New York has transformed Ellie and her relationship with Peter, it has not yet, on the eve of their arrival, altered their explicit understanding of what ties them to one another. He is still intent on getting the story of her journey and she is still headed back to King Westley. Although each of them harbors feelings that could change the nature of their relationship, they are not able to acknowledge those feelings to one another. But if in the final scenes of the film the romance we have all eagerly anticipated blossoms, their relationship does not reach this stage without a serious breach, one that threatens to keep them apart for good. Only after weathering this crisis are they finally united.

Ellie has jettisoned her prideful behavior, but before she and Peter can become a couple, he will have to acknowledge his own pridefulness and see that he too needs a lesson in democracy. So long as he maintains his masculinist belief in a hierarchy based on knowledge, he cannot be an appropriate partner for Ellie. A rupture in their relationship challenges Peter to accord her equal authority, and only when this has been accomplished can these two come together as a couple.

The crisis that paves the way for Peter's transformation comes about as a result of Ellie's attempt to turn the relationship in a romantic direction. That Ellie has learned to use strategy is attested to in the sequence in which the two of them spend a last night together on the road. This is the first time in the film that she is depicted as having enough knowledge of her own desires and enough confidence in her own abilities to actually control the situation. Because Peter sees no reason for them to spend another night on the road when they are so near New York, Ellie creates a subterfuge to force the issue of their future:

PETER: If you ask me, I think it's foolish. I told you there's no use our staying here tonight. We could make New York in less than three hours.

ELLIE: Well, who ever heard of getting in at three o'clock in the morning. Everybody'd be asleep. (*One Night*, p. 190)

Relying on Peter's sense of her as spoiled and subject to whims, Ellie gets him to do something he thinks is unnecessary. Of course, the real reason for this dilatory tactic is to give Peter a final chance to express romantic interest in her. Unbeknownst to him, she has found out that her father has become reconciled to her marriage to King Westley, and this is her last chance to see if Peter loves her.

As the Wall of Jericho goes up in a now-familiar ritual, the two of them begin a conversation. Although clearly unhappy about parting from Ellie, Peter tells her that he does not plan to see her in New York because "I don't make it a policy to run around with married women" (*One Night*, p. 191). Peter is angry, feeling that Ellie has used him to deliver her to Westley, even though it was his idea to help Ellie in return for the story that would get him his job back. When Ellie goes on to ask him whether he has ever been in love, Peter responds with a rather lengthy soliloquy in which he tells her both of his fantasy of finding the woman of his dreams and his doubts about whether such a woman exists. Peter's reverie ended, he—and we, for the camera moves back from a close-up to a medium shot—find that Ellie has breached the wall and come to Peter's bedside. She now declares her love for him:

> ELLIE: Take me with you, Peter. Take me to your island. I want to do all those things you talked about.
> PETER: You'd better get back to your bed.
> ELLIE: I love you. Nothing else matters. We can run away. Everything'll take care of itself. Please, Peter. I can't let you out of my life now. I couldn't live without you.
> PETER: You'd better go back to your bed. (*One Night*, p. 193)

Several factors might explain why Peter rejects Ellie's overture. To accept would morally taint their eventual union, for in crossing the barrier between them, Ellie shows a willingness to transgress the prohibition on adultery. There may be some validity to this suggestion—when Peter and Ellie are finally reunited, it is neither as adulterers nor as bigamists—but there is another, more immediate, reason for his hesitancy. Recall that Peter has been counting on the exclusive story of Ellie's return to her husband to get him back his job at the paper. Accepting Ellie's declaration of love would jeopardize this plan, leaving him without the story he needs. As the subsequent scenes show, however, Peter does find a way to square the circle—it will be *their* story that he writes and sells.

Finally, Ellie's entreaty that he accept her as a lover threatens his control over his fantasies and his life. That this now-ardent, flesh-and-blood woman might actually be the woman of his dreams is as difficult for Peter to accept as it was for Higgins to see Eliza as something more than his creation. The two men share the masculine compulsion to flee from dependency on women. Peter cannot yet acknowledge to himself the fact of his love for Ellie.

After Ellie's passionate declaration, Peter lies awake, apparently working out a plan of action. But when he finally turns to Ellie to ask, "Hey, Brat—! Did you mean that? Would you really go? Hey, Brat—" (*One Night*, p. 194), the question comes too late, for she has cried herself to sleep. Peter then rashly decides that he has time to go to New York, sell their story, and then return to her with the proceeds to announce his love.

Things do not go as Peter has planned, however. The wife of the auto camp owner, who has noticed that their car is gone, gets her husband to awaken Ellie and throw her out. Ellie is shocked to discover that Peter has left without a word, concluding that her declaration of love has driven him away. Seeing no other solution to her predicament, she contacts her father and returns to Westley. Now it is Peter's turn to misunderstand the situation: He thinks that Ellie has played him for a fool. Instead of realizing that they do genuinely care for one another, each suspects that the other's motivation has been selfish all along.

This crisis marks a regression in their relationship. When Peter and Ellie first met, their attribution of class- and gender-specific faults to one another caused them to systematically misinterpret each other's intentions. With their adventures together had come mutual trust and understanding, but when Peter acts on his own, he violates that mutuality. As a result, suspicion returns and the couple is driven apart.

Before this final narrative problem can be solved, Peter's masculinism must be addressed. He has not yet undergone *his* transformation. As Peter's late night flight from Ellie demonstrates, he remains convinced that despite her jibes, he has all the answers. Before they can form the couple whose mutuality prefigures the democratic culture the film endorses, Peter, too, will have to learn humility.

The final scenes of *It Happened One Night* manage to reunite Peter and Ellie in a way that clears the path to marriage, but not before erecting a last obstacle. On the morning of her remarriage to Westley, Andrews shows Ellie a letter from Peter asking that he be paid the money he is owed. The letter further disheartens Ellie, for it suggests that Peter was, after all, only interested in her for the price on her head. Her resolve to go through with her repeat marriage to Westley is further strengthened.

This doubt about Peter's character—that he is mercenary—is not one the audience has previously entertained. Although at this point in the film a viewer may succumb to Ellie's skepticism about him, Peter has never before shown an interest in the reward. On the contrary, when Ellie had earlier offered him money in return for his silence, Peter contemptuously dismissed her attempt to buy him off.

As it turns out, Ellie's—and our—faith in Peter is restored. When he comes to Andrews's house to collect his money, he presents a bill for $39.60, a figure that represents only the expense he has incurred during his travels with Ellie, excluding even his own bus fare. Not only does this renew our confidence in Peter's integrity, it also shows that Peter is not after Ellie's money. On this evidence, Andrews judges Peter to be an appropriate partner for his daughter, his occupation and class status notwithstanding.[11]

Finally, when Ellie learns that Peter has no interest in the reward money, she bolts from her wedding ceremony and joins Peter in an auto camp. The news of the annulment of her marriage arrives and we hear a trumpet sound—the Wall of Jericho will, at last, come tumbling down.

But has Peter's masculinist pride really been humbled? Although here the film is not entirely clear, two pieces of evidence imply that it has. The first is Peter's dejection over his separation from Ellie. The buoyant, prideful Peter of old has not survived the breakup. He wants to be with her yet seems unable to find a way to make this happen. In *Pygmalion*, Higgins's inability to acknowledge his dependence on Eliza signaled his limitations, and in the end, Eliza is left without a man who could be her equal. Happily for Ellie, in *It Happened One Night*, Peter—Higgins's counterpart—is forced by his own feelings to admit his love.

The more explicit indication of Peter's transformation occurs in a final exchange with Ellie's father after Peter has received his check for $39.60. Andrews, convinced that Peter is not an adventurer, presses him to admit that he loves Ellie. Recall that in an earlier, less charged, context, Peter had rebuffed Ellie with a curt, "No mushy stuff." Now, Andrews forces the issue:

ANDREWS: Do you love my daughter?
PETER: Any guy that'd fall in love with your daughter should have
    his head examined.
ANDREWS: That's an evasion.
PETER: She picked herself a perfect running-mate. King Westley!
    The pill of the century! What *she* needs is a guy that'd take a sock

at her once a day—whether it was coming to her or not. . . . If you had half the brains you're supposed to have, you'd have done it yourself—long ago.

ANDREWS: Do you love her?

PETER: A normal human being couldn't live under the same roof with her, without going nutty. She's my idea of nothing.

ANDREWS: I asked you a question. Do you love her?

PETER: Yes!! But don't hold that against me. I'm a little screwy myself. (*One Night*, pp. 209–210)

Pushed into a corner, Peter acknowledges his love for Ellie, his incompleteness without her. More significant still is his recognition that Ellie is a woman he cannot really control. Ellie's initiative in "limbing" them a ride had caused Peter to resent her success, for it challenged his need to be in charge. As he attempts to dodge Andrews's pointed questions, Peter admits that Ellie is a woman he cannot dominate: Anyone who would fall in love with her, he says, is crazy. His assertion—which perhaps sounds less innocent to our ears than it did to a 1930s audience—that she needs to be "socked" once a day evidences his exasperation over her independence, and he adds that any normal man, ruefully excluding himself from that category, would be driven nuts living with her.

Ellie has changed Peter's idea of his own manhood. He can now admit that he loves her, although she is not exactly (or at all) the sort of woman he expected himself to fall in love with. Possessing desires and powers of her own, unlike Galatea, Ellie is not defined by her partner's imagination. The old, know-it-all Peter cannot smoothly incorporate this woman into the life he has imagined for himself—she will insist on an equal role in shaping their future together. Although we do not witness the details of Peter's transformation, his final exchange with Andrews is sufficient to register the fact of its having taken place. This is a real change from the position of masculine superiority that he had previously occupied. Now that he admits his need for Ellie, his dependence on her for his fulfillment, Peter's own education has been completed. Peter has now become a suitable partner for Ellie.

Conclusion

It Happened One Night is the story of Ellie's release from the confinement of great privilege and her initiation into the fluid world of American democracy. But it is also the story of how Peter grows to accept Ellie as his equal. The formation of this unlikely couple thus challenges both traditional masculinist postures as well as the pridefulness of wealth. Forms of social hierarchy defined by either class or gender position are antithetical to the film's democratic values.

Unlike *Pygmalion*, *It Happened One Night* was able to satisfy its New Deal era audience's desire to see this unlikely couple come together without compromising its critical ambitions. It thus marks a unique synthesis of social criticism and popular filmmaking, one that future instances of the genre will not have an easy time living up to.

Notes

1. Steve Neale and Frank Krutnik, *Popular Film and Television Comedy* (New York and London: Routledge, 1990). In the text, all future references to this book will be given parenthetically.

2. Stanley Cavell, *Pursuits of Happiness: The Hollywood Comedy of Remarriage* (Cambridge, MA: Harvard University Press, 1981), p. 102.

3. Cavell, *Pursuits of Happiness*, p. 5.

4. Pauline Kael, "Raising Kane," in *The Citizen Kane Book*, shooting script by Herman J. Mankiewicz and Orson Welles, notes on the script by Gary Carey (Boston: Little, Brown and Co., 1971), p. 19.

5. The published screenplays of *It Happened One Night* are not always accurate, so I have mentioned them in accordance with the actual dialogue of the film. Parenthetical references to *One Night* are to the script published in *Four-Star Scripts*, Lorraine Noble, ed.(New York: Doubleday, Doran and Co., 1936). References to a xerox of the screenplay by Robert Riskin (*It Happened One Night* [Hollywood: Script City, 1934]) are indicated parenthetically as *Script*.

6. *The Compact Edition of the Oxford English Dictionary* (Oxford, UK: Oxford University Press, 1971), p. 2297.

7. Cavell's interpretation of the film completely neglects this strand in the film's narrative. For him, the film is about the education of a woman by a man; thus, his reading does not question Peter's qualifications to be Ellie's teacher. As was true with class privilege, Cavell is blind to male privilege in his reading of the film.

8. By presenting us with two "kings" who will vie for Ellie's affections, the film also nods in the direction of Clark Gable's Hollywood nickname, "the King."

9. In *The Unruly Woman: Gender and the Genres of Laughter* (Austin: University of Texas Press, 1995), Kathleen Rowe offers an account of the film in which class issues are displaced onto gender and generational ones. The present section emphasizes the film's class theme—Ellie's education for democracy, as I term it—an element that is missing from Rowe's analysis.

10. In a self-reflexive moment, the film here calls attention to the limits of the power of the director. Peter can cast Ellie in a role, but only she can bring it to life and give it credibility.

11. Andrews has himself been transformed by the ordeal of Ellie's flight. Still wanting the best for his daughter, he will no longer jeopardize their relationship by trying to force her to do what he thinks she should.

4

Pretty Woman

A Fairy Tale of
Oedipalized Capitalism

Both *Pygmalion* and *It Happened One Night,* films from the 1930s, indict class and gender hierarchies as illegitimate forms of privilege. And although, as we have seen, the specifics of their indictments reflect differences in their respective social settings, both advance the same plot device—the romance of an unlikely couple—as the narrative pretext of their critiques.

On the face of it, the same seems true of *Pretty Woman,* Gary Marshall's 1990 updating of the *Pygmalion* story to post-Reagan America. Whereas Anthony Asquith's film skewered the pretensions of the British aristocracy, *Pretty Woman* takes aim at the newly ascendant finance capitalists who came to prominence during the Reagan era's rash of corporate takeovers and mergers. Thus, the film's male lead, its counterpart to the master linguist Henry Higgins, is Edward Lewis (Richard Gere), a highly successful takeover specialist modeled on the likes of Michael Milliken. Eliza Doolittle, Cockney flower girl, has been translated into Vivian Ward (Julia Roberts), a prostitute. And Higgins's bet that Eliza can be made to pass as a duchess has become Edward's gamble that his business associates can be made to accept Vivian as his girlfriend. Instead of the glitter of aristocratic London, we get the glitz of superwealthy American capitalists and their milieu.

Pretty Woman tells the story of Vivian's rise from streetwalker to high-bourgeois consort. Edward, who is in Los Angeles for a week engineering the takeover of a manufacturing firm owned by James Morse (Ralph

Bellamy) and his son, needs someone to pass as his girlfriend at the round of social gatherings he is expected to attend.[1] By the end of that week, Vivian's success at playing Edward's girlfriend results in her actually becoming his girlfriend (and, it is intimated, although never made explicit, his soon-to-be wife.) Like *Pygmalion*'s Eliza, then, Vivian ascends into the upper class through her ability to simulate already belonging to it. But unlike Henry Higgins, Edward will not be allowed to persist in his arrogant masculinism.

Given the similarities between their narrative structures, we might anticipate *Pretty Woman* would offer as biting a critique of contemporary American society as *Pygmalion* had of British society between the two great European wars. And indeed, various accounts of the film's genesis suggest that its original screenplay was a scathing indictment of contemporary American capitalism.[2] Once Disney acquired the screenplay, however, it demanded that the script be revised, transforming it from a tragic story "about a prostitute who ruined her life because she fell in love" into a "comedy, a fairy tale" that glorifies wealth and endorses male privilege.[3]

The question these accounts raise is whether the film itself bears traces of its process of creation. In articulating this issue, I find the Cold War metaphor of containment particularly apt. That is, I shall treat the film as aware of the potential for a serious critique of power and privilege in its ascent narrative, yet actively struggling to contain that potential, finally affirming the alchemical powers of wealth.

The crucial maneuver in this bait-and-switch strategy is to depict Vivian's ascent as the rectification of an earlier injustice. In celebrating her reversal of fortune, *Pretty Woman* conjures away its own awareness—and ours—of the inherent unfairness of hierarchical social structures. Here, the model is clearly the Cinderella story. And it will not be difficult to trace certain of *Pretty Woman*'s representational and narrative strategies back to that source, a debt the film acknowledges in a number of crucial, self-reflexive moments. So as well as updating *Pygmalion*, *Pretty Woman* gives us a Cinderella for the 1990s—the deserving L.A. hooker whose transfiguration by a go-go capitalist makes up for the abusive relationship that had thrust her onto the streets.[4]

A second element in *Pretty Woman*'s strategy of containment is a nostalgic recuperation of the family firm as a virtuous alternative to the morally problematic activities of corporate raiding and asset stripping. Through an Oedipalization of economic relationships, the film limits the scope of its critique of capitalism to the supposed excesses characteristic of the Reagan years. This narrative tactic betrays *Pretty Woman*'s agenda: to join in the suddenly fashionable denunciation of capitalist "greed," but only in a way that morally validates the possession of great wealth. Thus is the subversive potential of its ascent narrative safely contained.

Two Characters in Search of Salvation

Pretty Woman begins with a parallel montage sequence that introduces its two principals and establishes that despite the very apparent difference in their economic circumstances, Edward and Vivian each stand in need of rescue. That the film presents the lives of both corporate raider and street prostitute as damaged suggests that we are in for a wide-ranging social critique.

When we first see Edward, at a party given by his lawyer and business associate, Phillip Stuckey (Jason Alexander), he is on the phone with his live-in girlfriend, who is fed up with commands relayed through his secretary. To her threat to move out, Edward's response is swift and brutal: There is nothing to discuss—obey or get out, now! Later, as Edward leaves Phillip's house, he warns the young acolyte at his elbow to stay on top of business. Edward's social schedule—he has tickets for the Met back in New York the following Sunday—is not to be disrupted by delays in the Morse takeover. His abrupt departure from the party Phillip has thrown in his honor underscores his contempt for the flunkies with whom he has surrounded himself.

These initial displays of Edward's masculinist pride suggest that he is a character in the tradition of Henry Higgins and Peter Warne. But it is really Ellie Andrews that he more closely resembles, for, like her, his wealth has taught him that others are there to be used.[5]

Edward's surprise at the revelation by an ex-girlfriend encountered at the party that she, too, was closer to his secretary than to him confirms our feeling that Edward, despite his dawning recognition that something is amiss in his life, is in masculinist denial of his finitude. Indeed, when Edward first encounters Vivian, we realize that prostitution perfectly models his understanding of intimate relationship: In return for cash, she is at the beck and call of her client.

Recent feminist literature has argued that a masculinist approach to the world, although perhaps necessary in the public sphere, disables men from meeting the demands of intimacy.[6] By depicting its highly successful male lead as an emotional failure, *Pretty Woman* associates itself with this position.

This initial sequence, then, adumbrates the critique of capitalism implied in the film's opening line, "You know what they say, it's all about money," which *Pretty Woman* will spell out later.[7]

Intercut with shots of Edward's descent from Phillip's Beverly Hills home to his hotel in the valley below, we are shown Vivian awakening, then descending from her apartment to the streets where she plies her trade. Although the point of this parallel montage is, finally, to bring Edward and Vivian together on Hollywood Boulevard, we are convinced along the way that Vivian is in even greater need of salvation than Edward.

As the camera pans along the recumbent figure of the sleeping Vivian, we notice a number of snapshots hanging on the wall next to her bed. Each photo shows her with a man—but his face has been scissored out of the print. Only later do we learn that Vivian became a prostitute because she was seduced and then abandoned, penniless. These mutilated snapshots already indicate that there are other elements of her life that Vivian would like to cut out. We learn more about her problems when she starts out the door of her apartment, only to overhear the landlord asking her neighbor for the rent. Discovering that her roommate and fellow prostitute, Kit (Laura San Giacommo), has dipped into their rent-money stash, she is forced to descend the fire escape to avoid embarrassment.

Both unlikely partners inhabit worlds from which they need to escape. The opulence of one as well as the poverty of the other will be held up to critical scrutiny. From the outset, the film also establishes each as the likely agent of the other's salvation. In Vivian's case, her agency amounts to this: As the film's one acknowledged whore, she will not compromise herself as Edward's associates do but will treat him as an equal. Her very lack of guile, perhaps due, the film intimates, to her working-class background, contrasts sharply with the sycophancy of Edward's associates.

From their first meeting, Edward and Vivian do not behave as one would expect in a typical prostitute-client transaction. Shortly after Vivian hits the streets, Edward, thoroughly lost, spies her and stops his car. She approaches his Lotus Esprit, hoping to score at least a hundred dollars toward the rent; disappointingly, Edward is interested only in directions. Making the best of it, she demands five dollars for her information, raising the price to ten when he protests. Edward agrees to pay, but when he asks for change for a twenty that he offers her, Vivian promptly jumps into the car, grabs the bill, and puts it in her purse. For twenty dollars, she will personally conduct him to the Beverly Wilshire. Vivian's spontaneity and boldness upset Edward's assumption that other human beings can be compliantly ordered about. His obvious wealth leads most people to fall all over themselves to please him. But hoping for no more from him than some rent money, Vivian has no reason to defer, flatter, or cajole. Still innocent despite her social situation, Vivian treats Edward as an equal.

In this initial encounter, *Pretty Woman* depicts their class difference as enhancing, rather than detracting from, their interaction. Indeed, it is her very lack of deference that first allows Edward to see in Vivian more than the young prostitute and to move toward an understanding of who she could be for him that is not limited by her professional identity. From *Pretty Woman*'s perspective, the straightforward manner of this street-walker gives Vivian a moral authority lacking in Edward's manipulative associates who scramble for his favor.

Similarly, Edward's treatment of Vivian distinguishes him from the "bums" Vivian views herself as destined to attract. Even when he has only engaged her for one night, he treats her kindly—a scene that calls to mind Colonel Pickering's gallant treatment of Eliza Doolittle. For example, Edward's deferral of sex and attempts at conversation distinguish him from the average john. Indeed, his deferential treatment of her leads Vivian to quip that she wants to let him in on a secret: She is a "sure thing," so he need not bother with the elaborate seduction routine.

In its initial sequence, then, *Pretty Woman* gives us reason to anticipate an interesting critical trajectory. Issues of inequities of wealth that foster assumptions of superiority have been placed on the table. As we shall see, however, *Pretty Woman* is less committed to developing the critical potential of these beginnings than to showing that there are ways to mitigate their critical bite.

From Flower Girl to Prostitute

Before turning to an analysis of *Pretty Woman*'s strategies of containment, I want to explore prostitution's significance for the film's narrative. Because the profession of flower girl was commonly used as a front for solicitation, *Pygmalion*'s Eliza is constantly on the defensive. This is why, when she notices Higgins taking down her words as she attempts to sell Colonel Pickering a flower, she immediately suspects him of being a cop out to arrest her. Her repeated insistence—"I am a good girl, I am"[8]—is meant to convey how desperate she is to dissociate herself from prostitution.

The conventions of romantic comedy in general and of ascent narratives in particular generally require virtuous heroines. This both allows socially superior men to be in love with them and licenses condemnation of the injustice that consigned them to their inferior social status. *Pretty Woman*'s choice to make its female lead a prostitute—a profession in which the practitioners seem richly to deserve their misfortune—may therefore occasion surprise.

To understand this choice, we need to recognize important differences between the narrative and representational structures of 1930s romantic comedies and those of the post-Reagan era. As Steve Neale has argued, in the 1930s, industry censorship—the so-called Hollywood Code—and social attitudes generally, permitted sex between unlikely partners only upon marriage, as consummation and reward.[9] With the sexual revolution and the concurrent loosening of the code, films of the 1980s and 1990s present sex as a means of forging relationships rather than simply certifying them. Only after the unlikely partners have had sex does the question of committed romance arise. This change in the function of movie sex allows *Pretty Woman* to feature a prostitute as its female lead, and because extramarital sex is no longer proscribed, it becomes possible to depict her as virtuous, even deserving. Hence, the film retains the basic representational structure of *Pygmalion* despite Galatea's career change.

Vivian's response to Kit's theft of their rent money is but one of several incidents the film uses to establish Vivian's virtue. When Vivian finally confronts her roommate about having taken the rent money, Kit confesses that the money has gone for drugs. Vivian's evident disapproval is meant to distinguish her from the usual, morally depraved prostitute—she does not use drugs and she pays her bills.

In an interesting interpretation of *Pretty Woman*, Hilary Radner stresses the complex significance of Vivian's prostitution.[10] According to Radner, the film does not rely on a simple disjunction between Vivian's profession and her moral character but instead presents prostitution as a feminist form of venture capitalism: If Edward is in business, so too is Vivian.[11] Kit's boast, "We say who, we say when, we say how much," summarizes neatly her sense that the savvy sex worker can control men's desire to her own advantage. On Radner's unsentimental reading, the film tells the story of how one prostitute leverages her "assets" into a grand "corporate takeover," that is, marriage to her superrich john.

Despite her insight into the narrative's feminist possibilities, Radner condemns *Pretty Woman*'s unrealistic assessment of the situation of women: In its fantastic story of Vivian's relationship with Edward, the film offers the consoling illusion that such oppositions as domesticity/sexual desire, ambition/erotic desire, and agency/object of desire have been reconciled.[12] Indeed, even its makers cannot resist an ironic aside, slipping in two sequences—one early, one late in the film—in which a Rastafarian crossing Hollywood Boulevard reminds us that we are in "the land of dreams." This, says Radner, amounts to an admission that popular narrative cinema succeeds only when it presents a literally fantastic reconciliation of the irreconcilable.[13] In holding out the virtuous prostitute as a real possibility, *Pretty Woman* is essentially duplicitous.

Radner is undoubtedly on to something when she stresses the significance of Vivian's prostitution, but there are a number of serious problems in her explication. For example, she overlooks the deep ambivalence of *Pretty Woman*'s view of prostitution—for whatever the extent to which it is depicted as an empowering option, the film also makes clear how perilous a career choice it is. Having included a reference to the violent death of a sister prostitute, Skinny Marie, in its initial presentation of Vivian, the film unambiguously acknowledges prostitution's dangers.[14] And when Vivian angrily confronts Kit about the stupidity of squandering their rent money on drugs, her reproach—"Don't you want to get out of here?"—implies her own desire to escape the streets. But the options available to a woman in Vivian's situation seem severely limited. Eliza Doolittle's linguistic facility offered her a way out; we have yet to see how Vivian's rescue will be effected.

A second problem for Radner's interpretation is that it ignores an important plot element. When her relationship with Edward has progressed to the point of real intimacy, Vivian reveals how she was driven to prostitution. At the time, turning tricks had seemed a rational choice, the only available alternative to flipping burgers. Thus, Vivian's naïveté had led her first into a disastrous relationship and then onto the mean streets from which she now wants and needs to escape. Through this disclosure we learn—and we shall soon see just how central this is to the film's narrative—that Vivian's predicament is the result of having been wronged.

But the main problem with Radner's interpretation is that she sees Vivian in terms very different from those in which the film presents her: Rather than making Vivian out to be a woman cynically using her sexuality to leverage her social position, the film depicts her as an innocent in need of rescue from dire circumstances. In the end, then, and despite her acknowledgment of the importance of the Cinderella subtext, Radner fails to give sufficient weight to how that classic fairy tale determines the film's narrative and representational strategies.

"Cinderella" as a Tale of Moral Rectification

"Cinderella" is the story of a young woman's sudden rise from drudge to princess.[15] More to the point, Cinderella's heady social ascent rectifies a grievous moral wrong inflicted on an innocent. Although she is the biological daughter of their stepfather, her stepsisters, in collusion with their mother, cruelly reduce her to servitude. But when the Prince chooses Cinderella to be his bride, she is at once elevated above all the other women in the kingdom. We enjoy her elevation because she had been the victim of an injustice, and in redressing the wrongs Cinderella has suffered, the tale reassures us that the universe is just and that, in the end, one gets what one deserves.

Although Cinderella's fantastic rise may be read as a condemnation of class domination, it is actually less a criticism of hierarchy per se than of those who enjoy positions of social privilege undeservedly—for example, Cinderella's malicious steprelatives. In other words, hierarchy is justified so long as those at the top, like Princess Cinderella, really deserve to be there.

"Cinderella"'s legitimation of hierarchy depends on its validation of the idea of society as a meritocracy, in this case a moral meritocracy in which class position is a reflection of character, with the virtuous entitled to rule their moral inferiors. The division of society into two (or more) classes is claimed to follow from parallel moral distinctions among individuals.[16]

Initially, however, the world of "Cinderella" seems, if anything, to stand the ideal of a morally just universe on its head. True, the female characters in this story divide neatly into the good—Cinderella and her mother— and the wicked—her stepmother and stepsisters—but their relationship is an inversion of the meritocratic ideal, for here the wicked rule the good. Thus, Cinderella's household resembles that topsy-turvy world famously described by Hegel rather than the satisfyingly meritocratic one proposed as an ideal: "That what in the law of the first world is sweet, in this inverted in-itself is sour, what in the former is black is, in the other, white ... What is there south pole is here north pole."[17] Hegel's metaphor is of a world in which the natural order of things has been violated, and by analogy, Cinderella's household is the inverted world in relation to the ideal of moral meritocracy. Instead of being rewarded for her virtue, Cinderella has been indentured to her cruel and malicious steprelatives.

To align Cinderella's class position with her moral standing, thereby repairing society's moral fabric, an inversion of this first inversion will be necessary: Cinderella's suffering must be compensated, and her evil stepfamily appropriately punished. For this reason, the story's criticisms of hierarchy attack only those who enjoy the privileges of rank undeservedly, not the injustice of social ranking itself.

Two agents effect the necessary rectification of the inverted world of this fairy tale. First, there is Cinderella's dead mother, who has the ability to act through a charmed nature. It is her intervention that brings about Cinderella's transformation from charwoman to the elegant beauty her parentage has destined her to be. Then, of course, there is the Prince himself, for it is his love for Cinderella that gives sanction and permanence to that transformation.

Through the intervention of her dead mother, Cinderella's appearance has been made to correspond with her virtue. When Kant claimed that the beautiful was the symbol of the moral, he surely did not have in mind this folktale.[18] Nonetheless, it is precisely this relation that both explains the Prince's choice of Cinderella to be his bride and the meaning of his choice. But if it is Cinderella's beauty that attracts the Prince and fits her to be his wife, that beauty is not simply surface, it is also—and more importantly—a signifier of moral worth.

Nor does Cinderella's beauty indicate her social class to the Prince. Despite Cinderella's glamour, the fairy tale is quite clear on this. And because the Prince's choice of Cinderella to be his bride is not shaken by the fact that when he does find her, she is, to all appearances, a simple servant girl, the story has seemed to many to be democratic in spirit.

But does the lost-slipper stratagem really establish this? True, once Cinderella has fled the ball, having left the famous glass slipper behind, the only clue to her identity is her dainty shoe size. The Prince announces that he will marry the woman whose foot fits that slipper, and nothing else about Cinderella will count for him, not even her lowly station. The significance of this egalitarian moment needs to be contextualized within the larger scheme of moral rectification, however.

Feminist readers have bristled at the fairy tale's equation of physical appearance with moral character. This imputation is as true of Cinderella, whose virtue is affirmed right down to her tiny toes, as it is of her stepsisters, who, out of greed, mutilate their big feet to force them into the glass slipper. Aside from the obvious empirical inadequacy of this equation, it presupposes that a woman's beauty is a natural and not a social fact about her. The size of a person's foot is not—with certain exceptions—a social fact at all; rather, it is a physical attribute, the outcome of the genetic lottery. By allegorizing character as physical characteristic and then treating it as a rationale for social hierarchy, the fairy tale makes the well-known conflation of the social with the natural. Standards of beauty are clearly socially determined, as any film viewer ought to know.

With the rise and fall of its characters in accordance with their moral deserts, "Cinderella"'s narrative of rectification reestablishes society's disturbed moral equilibrium. The love of a prince for a serving girl turns the inverted world of this fairy tale right-side up. Cinderella will come at last to occupy that social position to which her virtue entitles her, as her wicked stepsisters will forever hobble about, punished for their wicked ways.

In a world in which hierarchy is unquestioned or at least is felt to be insurmountable, moral meritocracy appears as the only antidote to injustice. Because social power can be used to reward the good and punish the evil, rule by the best seems required to satisfy our hunger for justice. We are reconciled to the existence of social hierarchy because it promises reparation for the wrongs inflicted on us. After all, from where else in "Cinderella"'s moral universe but the castle can the wrongs she suffers be redressed? The infantile pleasure we take in this fable of moral rectification stems from this reassurance. At the same time, our enjoyment suffuses hierarchy with a positive glow: Dazzled, we acquiesce to a representational scheme in which privilege is self-evidently virtue's reward.

Shopping Esprit

Now that we are ready to look more closely at *Pretty Woman*, we will find, not surprisingly, that the trope of moral rectification dulls the critical sting of this film's ascent narrative. In this section, I propose an interpretation of three shopping episodes that, taken together, at once prepare the way for Vivian's final triumph and rehearse in miniature, as it were, the drama of moral rectification that animates the film as a whole. A close reading of these sequences establishes the complex mechanics that permit *Pretty Woman* to damn Edward's wealthy milieu yet celebrate the munificent powers of his own male, moneyed privilege. Specifically, *Pretty Woman*'s vindication of wealth turns on its use of women's beauty as revealed through/constituted by fashion operating as a perceptual marker of naturalized class difference. It is this chain of significations that justifies

Vivian's ascendancy over the shallow "suck-ups" Edward—and the film—despises.

The first of these shopping sequences takes place on the morning after Vivian and Edward spend their inaugural night together in his penthouse suite at the Beverly Wilshire Hotel. Vivian has just received a large sum of money from Edward to buy the clothes she will need as his companion. Still wearing her work uniform—hot pants and high boots—and to the sound of the song "Wild Women," Vivian enters a chic Rodeo Drive dress shop (see Photo 4.1). But a disdainful saleswoman virtually throws her out the door, telling the astounded Vivian, "I don't think we have anything for you. You're obviously in the wrong place. Please leave." Streetwalkers are clearly unwelcome in this smart boutique, never mind the fistful of dollars Vivian brandishes. Her appearance—the very outfit she wishes to replace—flags her as an unacceptable customer, her money notwithstanding.[19]

This scene demonstrates that more may be at stake in shopping in a capitalist society than simple satisfaction of basic human needs. Indeed, we might say that as a potent determinant of class identity, shopping has ontological significance. And this is especially true of fashion, since the clothes we buy not only cover our nakedness, they supply others with the signs they need to read that identity from our appearance. So as Vivian enters the Rodeo Drive boutique, class boundaries are being breached. And it behooves the sales staff, acting as a sort of social border patrol, to resolve the contradiction between Vivian's sluttish appearance and her presence in their exclusive store by refusing to serve her.

This scene disrupts any straightforward identification of class with money. In America, money is supposed to be the great equalizer—if you have it, you can buy whatever you want, and your money is as good as anyone else's. It is this deeply held faith in the democracy of the dollar that Vivian's ejection violates. For the saleswoman who ejects her, it is not enough to have the money, one must deserve to have it, or more accurately, one must be seen to deserve it. This attitude is strangely analogous to the hereditarianism of the British aristocracy: Some people are by nature better than others and so deserve their privilege. For an American woman, it is her physical appearance rather than her pedigree that counts.

It is at just this point that the film begins to deflect our expectations of a critique of class condescension, indeed, of class itself: Vivian will be shown to be so beautiful that she *deserves* to shop on Rodeo Drive. In "Cinderella"'s moral universe, a woman's appearance is a register of her

Photo 4.1 Vivian attempts to shop on Rodeo Drive

character, hence a measure of her entitlement. According to *Pretty Woman*, the problem with American society is not its class divisions, but the basis on which they rest.[20]

The film continues its presentation of the social and moral significance of shopping in a sequence that occurs after Bernard Thompson (Hector Elizondo), the manager of the Beverly Wilshire intercedes on Vivian's behalf when she has returned, distraught, from her first venture on Rodeo Drive. Thompson, playing the role of Vivian's fairy godfather, calls a friend at a second boutique and explains Vivian's situation to her. As a result, when Vivian arrives, she is treated courteously and purchases the dress she needs.

The payoff occurs in the following scene, when Edward returns to the hotel to pick up Vivian, who is to accompany him to an important dinner with the Morses. He enters the bar where she is supposed to be waiting and looks around but does not see her. There next follows a long shot of Edward walking up to the bar, then a cut to a medium shot taken from behind as he vainly searches the room. Now the camera retreats once again to a long shot in which we see Edward turning to leave, and behind Edward's back, that the woman sitting at the bar in an elegant black cocktail dress is Vivian. As Edward completes his turn, the camera records his recognition of Vivian by abruptly bringing her into focus (see Photo 4.2). The effect of this recognition is then emphasized in a series of shot/

reverse shot closeups of them simultaneously noticing one another and noticing their noticing. She walks up to him, says, "You're late," to which he responds, "You're stunning." Her reply—"You're forgiven"—ends their interaction as they leave the bar arm and arm, the perfect couple.

In narrative terms, this scene begins to assuage the humiliation Vivian suffered on Rodeo Drive. Edward's appreciation of her beauty confirms the transfigurative power of shopping: The little black dress reveals Vivian to be the woman adequate to this man's desire. The third and final shopping sequence will complete the process of reparation.

Before we succumb to the pleasures the film has planned for us, however, the antidemocratic irony in Vivian's success needs to be remarked: She is entitled to shop in Rodeo Drive's exclusive boutiques because she looks so good in the clothes they sell. Why, they look as if they had been designed for her—as, of course, they had. Indeed, the film suggests that Vivian/Cinderella has *more* right to shop there than many of the rich women who do so as a matter of course. The implication and central claim of this sequence, then, is that, by nature, Vivian deserves to be wealthy.

A series of equivalences establishes Vivian's right to class elevation, its visual crux being that Vivian's beauty evidently fits her to wear the kind of clothing sold in exclusive and trendy shops. Rodeo Drive chic is not for every woman, and those whom it suits are only those whom it makes beautiful.[21] But female beauty is not a simple matter of appearance, according to the film, for those who, like Vivian, are truly beautiful *deserve* to acquire and wear the clothes that display their beauty.

Pretty Woman thus attempts to convince us of Vivian's just deserts by means of a subtle visual strategy. First, her beauty is presented as a sign of individual merit; then, since clothes encode class, the fact that expensive fashions suit her beauty establishes her right to wear them; this means, finally, that Vivian deserves to be wealthy, for beauty is the "natural" basis for female social privilege. This analysis makes it clear why it is misleading to speak of a transformation of Vivian's character. More accurately, the film depicts the process through which Vivian's true but implicit upper-class identity is revealed, or brought forth.[22]

By using Vivian's beauty as a marker of her worthiness for a class upgrade, the film takes a very different view of hierarchy from that of *Pygmalion*. Where the earlier film saw Eliza's ability to pass as a duchess as evidence that there was no natural basis to class distinctions, Vivian's success identifies her as a member of an authentic upper class, from which

Photo 4.2 Edward finally recognizes Vivian

impostors deserve to be excluded. Thus, rather than pursue the democratic implications of its unmasking of the pretension of the capitalist
elite, *Pretty Woman* suggests an alternative foundation for class privilege,
one that rests on character and its visual correlate in women of beauty and
that facilitates reparation of the wrongs Vivian has suffered.[23]

That this really is *Pretty Woman*'s view of class becomes fully evident in
Vivian's third and final shopping expedition, which takes place on the day
following her humiliation. Edward expresses surprise that Vivian has
bought so few clothes with the money given her. She complains that she
did not find shopping much fun because the salespeople treated her badly:
"They were mean to me." Edward responds cynically, "Stores are never
nice to people. They're nice to credit cards."

Edward now takes Vivian to still a third Rodeo Drive boutique.
Although his ostensible goal is to finish outfitting her for the part she is to
play as his companion, he has a deeper purpose in mind as well: Edward
wants her to gain a greater sense of self-worth from being catered to, hand
and foot, by the salespeople in this store. To this end, Edward calls over
Mr. Hollister, the store manager, and tells him point-blank that they "are
going to be spending an obscene amount of money" and that they will require a lot of people "sucking up" to them because that is what they enjoy.

What a difference a day makes! With at least four people attending her,
Vivian greatly enjoys trying on different outfits. Her pleasure is empha-

sized by the strains of Roy Orbison's hit song—and the film's anthem—
"Pretty Woman," which accompanies her throughout the rest of this sequence. *She* has now become the pretty woman of the song's title. (The
song tells of a man's fantasy that an attractive woman he sees on the street
does not simply pass him by but actually turns around and walks back to
him. Vivian now qualifies as the sort of woman about whom a man can
have this fantasy.)[24]

Vivian leaves the store wearing a new white dress, high heels, and long
white gloves, her appearance so completely transformed that it actually
registers in her bodily comportment. Although the film does not thema-
tize this, she now carries herself with greater composure and restraint
than she did when dressed as a hooker. Men turn to look at her, but when
they do, they are no longer allowed the leering gaze of unmediated sexual
desire permitted them when she first entered the hotel with Edward.
Instead, Vivian, ex–"wild woman," has now become "pretty woman," that
is, her expensive and tasteful attire sublimates her sexuality in conformity
with high-bourgeois standards (see Photo 4.3).

One last bit of business remains in this minidrama of moral rectification. Vivian now returns to the store in which she was demeaned, finds
the offending saleswoman, and reminds her of their earlier encounter.
After assuring herself that the woman works on commission, Vivian
flaunts the packages she is carrying, and jeers, "Big mistake. Big. Huge. I
have to go shopping now." The scene ends with Vivian collapsed in a
stuffed chair in her hotel room, a self-satisfied smile on her face.

Vivian's slight has been redressed and the film expects us to participate
in her triumph by accepting it as simple justice—her day and ours has
been made.[25] But to see Vivian's new wardrobe as quite the victory for her
the film claims, we need to endorse its "Cinderella" premise that class distinctions have moral significance.

Pygmalion's narrative of class ascent condemned England's class structure. *Pretty Woman*'s only complains that American society privileges the
wrong people. This fable of transfiguration by shopping spree pretends
that there are those who by nature are entitled: Vivian's beauty, revealed by
her flair for high fashion, justifies her membership in this authentic elite;
other women—usurpers—lack her natural beauty and only wear expensive clothes because they can afford them.[26]

Vivian now possesses a wardrobe that permits her beauty to emerge, but
she is still a prostitute. The greater injustice that propelled her onto the
streets will only truly be rectified once she has been anointed, Cinderella-

Photo 4.3 "Pretty Woman" on Rodeo Drive

like, the partner of her wealthy prince. There still are some important obstacles to be overcome if her inverted world is to be righted, not the least of which is Edward's masculinist arrogance. He requires a transformation more fundamental than Vivian's before this fairy tale reaches its inevitable happy conclusion.

Oedipus in the Boardroom

Whereas Vivian's transformation happens on Rodeo Drive, Edward's takes place in his suite at the Beverly Wilshire. Edward comes to recognize that his workaholism stems from unresolved Oedipal issues. And once having acknowledged the sources of his compulsions, he embraces a "kinder, gentler" path to capitalist accumulation, one that allows the film to deflect its critique of wealth per se onto a critique of "destructive" forms of its pursuit.

As Vivian's relationship with Edward develops from a one-night stand into a weeklong relationship, the two of them become more intimate. Nestled between her long legs in his suite's Jacuzzi, Edward reveals that the satisfactions corporate raiding bring him have their roots in childhood trauma. His father deserted his mother for another woman and left them destitute. Ever since, Edward has been engaged in his own project of moral rectification, symbolically punishing his deadbeat dad by besting father surrogates in corporate combat. Edward is now locked into an endless cycle of repetition—his satisfaction short-lived—acquiring new companies against the wishes of owner/father figures like James Morse. Indeed, the third victim of Edward's professional spite was his own father!

Early on, Vivian is confused about what Edward actually does, taking him for a lawyer. When he explains his work to her, she compares him to her high school friends who stole cars, "chopped" them, and sold the parts for cash, exactly the process to which Edward subjects the companies he acquires. Implicit in this comparison is a negative judgment—stripping corporate assets is as destructive, hence as immoral, as stripping stolen cars.

Initially annoyed at the naïveté of Vivian's comparison, Edward finally comes to share her assessment. This shift is registered after the Morses have angrily walked away from the dinner meeting with Edward for which Vivian had bought her outfit. Shaken by their disgust at his tactics, Edward realizes, as he puts it to Vivian, "We both screw people for money."[27]

The narrative significance of this scene lies in its embrace of Vivian's apparently naïve distinction between productive and unproductive activities: Dismantling corporations for profit is now viewed as destructive. Where the film had earlier endorsed Edward's dismissal of this evaluative dichotomy, it is here rehabilitated through his act of self-recognition.

Edward expresses his acceptance of this valuation in a conversation with Phillip. Now poised to achieve his goal—he can sink the loan the Morses need to fight his takeover—Edward hesitates to do so. While idly constructing a tower of drinking glasses, he explains to the disbelieving Phillip that as a child, he loved building things. The implication is that he ought to be satisfying this mature desire, literally creating something, as do the Morses, who build destroyers for the Navy.

Edward decides to back away from the deal, then, because he realizes that the Morses' determination to fight for control of their company has a worthier source than his desire to acquire it. Whereas he is driven by an Oedipal will-to-power, they are engaged in running a socially useful, productive enterprise. Although the film's choice of arms manufacture as its example of productive activity seems a disingenuous hint by its makers that the distinction between productive and destructive activity cannot withstand critical scrutiny, we need to understand exactly why a morally principled distinction between corporate raiding and running a family firm is unsustainable.

To begin with, the film's portrayal of the Morses as major players in the defense industry is implausible. Any firm with major Department of Defense contracts, as Morse Industries is alleged to have, cannot be family owned, for, as Tom Riddell already pointed out in 1985, "Defense contracting for the last twenty-five years has been concentrated in the largest firms."[28] The sorts of players he had in mind were Lockheed, Boeing, United Technologies, McDonnell Douglas, and Grumman, the five largest defense contractors in 1975.[29] Although a mom-and-pop or, in this case, pop-and-son operation might have a role as a minor subcontractor in the defense industry, no such firm could possibly go toe to toe with the multinationals and win. The film resorts to such an unrealistic option because it wants to do two things: on the one hand, endorse the growing critique of the Reagan era's vast increase in inequities in wealth; and on the other, contain the scope of that critique, applying it only to the excesses of that era rather than to the existence of wealth and social hierarchy per se. To succeed at this balancing act, the film has to exhume an acceptable alternative to the corporate raider to stand as the sign of the kinder, gentler nation America seemed to hope it could become.

James Morse may be the longed-for good father, but he can hardly figure as the model capitalist for the 1990s; instead, he represents nostalgia for an economic era that is long since past and—to those of us who have read Dickens, never mind Marx—was always morally problematic, anyway. But because *Pretty Woman* refracts its economic options through vulgar Freudianism—rebellious son is reconciled to the rule of benign father—we ignore the bogus economics, rejoicing at Edward's successful resolution of his Oedipal travails and accepting, along the way, the terms of the film's portrayal.

A Happy Ending

Taken together, *Pretty Woman*'s shopping sequences—from Vivian's humiliation to her final act of vengeance—enact, on a reduced scale, the trope of moral rectification that structures the film's overall narrative development. Edward's choice of Vivian to be his bride completes the reparation of the wrongs that had led her to a life on the streets. To the extent that we thrill at the rightness of this fairy-tale ending, we accept the film's brief for hierarchy as the necessary price for the fulfillment of our desires.

Edward's decision is precipitated by the final crisis that occurs once he has agreed to work with, rather than against, the Morses. Having concluded his business in California, Edward makes Vivian an offer he considers very generous: to set her up as his mistress in Beverly Hills. Vivian responds that she might have accepted such an offer a week earlier, but no longer.[30] She explains her reaction by recalling that as a child, whenever her mother would lock her in a closet—a form of punishment worthy of Cinderella's stepmother and bringing with it its own demand for reparation—she would dream she had been transformed into a princess awaiting rescue from her confinement by a dashing knight on horseback. When she demands the fulfillment of this dream, Edward balks, unable to bring himself to acknowledge her as his equal. Not to worry, though, for, echoing the opening scenes of the film, a closing parallel montage sequence brings the two together, this time for keeps.

But first, her knight having momentarily failed her, Vivian leaves the hotel, determined not to return to the street. With the money she has earned during her week as Edward's escort, she now has the wherewithal to transform her life. Packing to leave for San Francisco, Vivian tells Kit that she intends to pursue her education.

Meanwhile, Edward is brought to acknowledge his need for Vivian through the agency of Bernard Thompson, who once again functions as her fairy godfather. As Edward pays his hotel bill, he asks Thompson to return the necklace that he had borrowed for Vivian to wear to *La Traviata*.[31] Admiring the necklace, Thompson remarks, "It must be difficult to let go of something so beautiful." And in case the audience has missed his double entendre, he adds that the same driver who will be taking Edward to the airport had driven Vivian home the day before.

Thompson's intervention prepares the way for the film's fairy-tale ending, which enacts Vivian's dream: Edward races to her rescue in his trusty sunroofed limousine, determined to scale the tenement/tower in which his princess is held captive. But to reach her, Edward must overcome a fear of heights and climb the fire escape ladder she had earlier descended to avoid her landlord. When finally he has met the challenge—knees trembling and roses gripped between his teeth—Edward finds himself uncertain of his next move. Turning to Vivian—the expert on her own dreams—he asks for guidance: "So what happened after he climbed the tower and rescued her?" Her response—"She rescued him right back"—registers the film's contemporaneity. Knights and princesses are now codependent. As she and Edward embrace high atop the fire escape, Vivian's social elevation is accomplished. With the fulfillment of her dream, we are assured of the possibility that the damaged child within each of us may someday receive redress for our suffering.

But to experience these pleasures, we need to accept the terms in which they are presented, ignoring the deeper issue, put on the table by *Pretty Woman* itself, of whether inequalities in wealth are merited. If the film succeeds in moving us, it is only by deflecting our attention from that very question. In confining its narrative of class ascent within a drama of moral rectification, *Pretty Woman* succeeds in containing the critical potential of its own premise.

Notes

1. Bellamy's presence—he played the inappropriate male partner in such films as *The Awful Truth* (1937) and *His Girl Friday* (1940)—also serves to evoke the world of 1930s comedies.

2. See, for example, Ron Grover, *The Disney Touch: Disney, ABC, and the Quest for the World's Greatest Media Empire* (Chicago: Irwin, 1997), pp. 221–224.

3. Terry Gross's interview with Barry Primus, *Fresh Air,* August 27, 1992.

4. Evidence of the impact of *Pretty Woman's* ascent narrative can be seen in a story about Slavic women becoming prostitutes (*New York Times,* January 11, 1998, pp. 1, 6). The film is cited as a factor in women's willingness to become prostitutes.

5. Although the film's early scenes represent Edward in much the same terms as *It Happened One Night* represents Ellie, the later Oedipal narrative of his father's desertion suggests that he cannot be as inexperienced and sheltered as these scenes suggest. Here, the momentary demands of the narrative seem to overwhelm the makers' desire for consistency.

6. See, for example, Nancy Chodorow, *The Reproduction of Mothering: Psychoanalysis and the Sociology of Gender* (Berkeley: University of California Press, 1978).

7. All quotations from *Pretty Woman* are from my transcription of the sound track.

8. See, for example, *The Collected Screenplays of Bernard Shaw,* Bernard F. Dukore, ed. (Athens: University of Georgia Press, 1980), p. 229.

9. See Steve Neale's interesting discussion of the development of film comedy, "The Big Romance or Something Wild?: Romantic Comedy Today," *Screen,* 33:3 (Autumn 1992): pp. 284–299.

10. Hilary Radner, "Pretty Is as Pretty Does: Free Enterprise and the Marriage Plot," in *Film Theory Goes to the Movies,* Jim Collins, Hilary Radner, and Ava Preacher Collins, eds. (New York: Routledge, 1993), pp. 56–76.

11. Radner ("Pretty Is as Pretty Does") treats this equation literally rather than metaphorically.

12. The illusion is that it is possible to simultaneously satisfy two criteria that are articulated as mutually exclusive. So, for example, a woman cannot fulfill the roles of homemaker and sexual partner at the same time.

13. Thus, despite her attention to the economic aspects of the narrative, Radner's critique of the film involves the Lacanian-inspired claim that narrative film dwells in infantile fantasy.

14. Radner admits that Skinny Marie's murder shows the dangers of prostitution. She sees this aspect of the narrative only as a cautionary tale, however, one that shows "what happens when a young woman invests her capital unwisely," not as a criticism of prostitution itself ("Pretty Is as Pretty Does," p. 66).

15. Jacob and Wilhelm Grimm, *The Complete Grimm's* [sic.] *Fairy Tales* (New York: Pantheon Books, 1944), pp. 121–128.

16. It is not at all obvious that moral meritocracy implies rigid class distinctions. There might be many differences in individual moral merit that a class structure would not reflect.

17. G. W. F. Hegel, *Phenomenology of Spirit*, A. V. Miller, tr. (Oxford, UK: Oxford University Press, 1977), p. 97.

18. Kant makes this claim in the *Critique of Judgment*, Werner S. Pluhar, tr. (Indianapolis, IN, and Cambridge, MA: Hackett Publishers, 1987), §59.

19. It is worth noting that clothes are not the only means used to encode social location. Vivian's bodily comportment functions as another signifier of class. In early scenes, she gestures wildly, throwing her limbs about in a way that indicates lack of refinement. Her chic wardrobe brings with it greater restraint in the way she carries herself.

20. If women's class privilege is based on beauty, what justifies male privilege? An obvious option is that wealth functions as beauty's male analogue. We shall see how the film resolves the conflict between this view and its critique of Edward's amoral pursuit of wealth.

21. Among other options, women's clothes can be stylish or trashy, as Vivian's two outfits make clear. Radner's equation of these two styles with voyeurism and fetishism, respectively, misses the film's use of beauty as a marker of character ("Pretty Is as Pretty Does"). Interestingly, more recent fashions—especially those designed by the late Gianni Versace—deconstruct the opposition between high style and whorish.

22. A similar point is made by Robert Lapsley and Michael Westlake, "From *Casablanca* to *Pretty Woman:* The Politics of Romance," *Screen*, 33:1 (Spring 1992): pp. 27–49.

23. *Pretty Woman*, like Henry Higgins in *Pygmalion*, thus supports hierarchy, although on a different basis from the one prevalent in their respective societies: Higgins endorses a hierarchy based on knowledge rather than blood, and *Pretty Woman*, one based on character rather than wealth alone. The difference between the films is that the earlier film criticizes Higgins for his acceptance of hierarchy, a narrative element missing from the later one.

24. Grover reports that the film's association with the Orbison song was coincidental. See *The Disney Touch*, p. 224.

25. When Vivian lords it over the saleswoman who slighted her, we may not endorse the moment as fully as the film wishes, for Vivian is here being cruel, sadistic. We may wonder why it is not enough for her to be appreciated by others, why she has to stick her success in her tormentor's face.

26. It is too simple to say that the film represents beauty as a class marker for women and wealth as a class marker for men. Edward's good looks are also important to the film's representational strategy. It is also worth repeating that beauty, although based in biological characteristics, is a socially constructed norm that varies from society to society and even within social groups.

27. Both Radner ("Pretty Is as Pretty Does") and Kathleen Rowe (*The Unruly Woman: Gender and the Genres of Laughter* [Austin: University of Texas Press, 1995], p. 198) simply accept Edward's cynical equation of his and Vivian's professions without criticism, a fact that betrays the limitations in their understanding of the film. Although his pun is meant to register both his growing identification of himself and Vivian as well as his increasing dissatisfaction with his work, it succeeds only through a confusion of the literal and the symbolic. Although Edward's ironic identification of himself as a prostitute allows him to condemn his own profession symbolically, he simultaneously degrades Vivian's through his conflation of the literal and the symbolic meanings of screwing. There are several issues about prostitution and the film's portrayal of it that I am sidestepping here and that would have to be raised in a complete discussion of this film. In particular, the question of whether prostitution is a form of sexual exploitation is left unexamined.

28. Tom Riddell, "Concentration and Inefficiency in the Defense Sector: Policy Options," *Journal of Economic Issues,* 19:2 (June 1985): p. 452.

29. Tom Gervasi, *America's War Machine: The Pursuit of Global Dominance* (New York: Grove Press, 1984), p. 332. The recent merger of Boeing and McDonnell Douglas has reduced this number to four.

30. There is a further reason for Vivian's demand—to reassure the audience that her interest in Edward is not motivated by his wealth. Vivian's unwillingness to accept Edward's money on his terms establishes the purity of her desire for him.

31. *Pretty Woman* uses a number of techniques to equate Vivian with Violetta, including having Vivian cry as she watches *La Traviata*. But Violetta's self-sacrifice for the love of another has no parallel in Vivian's story and may be a trace of the original, tragic screenplay.

5
White Palace
Dustbuster Epiphanies

Although *White Palace,* too, is concerned with issues of class and gender, Luis Mandoki's 1990 film focuses as well on differences of religion and age. This mix of obstacles confronting its unlikely couple complicates the film's socially critical labors beyond what we have already seen.

These self-imposed burdens aside, *White Palace*'s real uniqueness as an instance of the genre lies in the way its critique is conveyed—less through personal transformation, as in the other films so far considered, than through the vicissitudes of the unlikely relationship itself. Because the male partner has internalized the values of his reference group of young urban professionals—infamously acronymed "yuppies" in the 1980s—he cannot unambivalently accept a romantic attachment that conflicts with the group's partnering norms. As a result, to keep his un-likely relationship totally hidden from his peers, he is shown repeatedly dissembling. The film censures him—and by extension, his social mi-lieu—for affirming values that would proscribe so vital a relationship. Dazzled by surfaces, they are blind to the deeper and more significant realities concealed beneath.

In *Pygmalion, It Happened One Night,* and *Pretty Woman,* the romantic couple is achieved through the elimination of the social difference(s) be-tween the partners. *White Palace* suggests, to the contrary and interest-ingly, that these differences are precisely what make their connection so significant for its lovers. The very unlikeliness of their attraction liberates the partners from social norms that stultify passion and so defeat the pos-sibility of a life lived more authentically. Although by no means a great film, *White Palace*'s innovative presentation of the positive role that difference can play in the lives of individuals and, by implication, societies heightens its claim on our interest.

An Overdetermined Unlikeliness

The tense drama between the partners' attraction to one another and the conventions that stigmatize it as unlikely exists primarily in the consciousness of *White Palace*'s male protagonist, Max Baron (James Spader). Max is torn between the conformist pressure to accept his social group's verdict on Nora Baker (Susan Sarandon) and his awareness that Nora's gift of intimacy has reawakened his deadened spirit. When Max's nouveau riche Jewish friends dismiss Nora—an older, working-class, non-Jewish "shiksa"—as unfit to partner the handsome, young executive, it threatens to overwhelm his hitherto throttled desire to live his life more fully and more deeply.

Max, a yuppie adman, earns lots of money, a fact made obvious during the title sequence, as we see him driving his new Volvo to his home in a swanky apartment complex, having picked up on the way a number of identical, freshly dry-cleaned and pressed suits. Nora is a waitress at the White Palace, the fast-food joint from which the film takes its title. Her ramshackle house, in which she later seduces Max, starkly conveys the economic gulf between them.

A second gulf separating Max from Nora is age. Although a widower, Max is only twenty-seven, thus a "young" man. At forty-one, Nora is past the age when women are normally judged desirable, a fact registered, for example, by Max's mother when she remarks on first meeting Nora, "She's no spring chicken." Of course, this age difference is an obstacle to their romance only because of certain gender stereotypes, stereotypes that the film mobilizes. Were their ages reversed—he, forty-one, say; and she, twenty-seven—few eyebrows would be raised.[1]

Finally, Max is Jewish; and Nora, a lapsed Catholic, a difference actually more complex than is conveyed by this simple statement. For if religious faith is important to neither, the fact of Max's Jewishness *is* significant because it defines his social milieu. Their religious difference, then, is really a synecdoche for a more general difference in the role other people play in their lives. Nora is portrayed as virtually asocial. The only relationships we are shown are with the bartender in the bar where she encounters Max, a black coworker with whom she rides the bus, and a sister from

Photo 5.1 The yuppie meets the waitress

whom she has been estranged for years. This means, among other things, that Nora has no reference group the views of which could affect the couple's formation. Because only Max's circle is allowed to judge the relationship, the film can hedge on how much narrative weight Nora's class identity is allowed. Thus, the question of what it is to be a working-class woman is raised—or rather, elided—in terms that already compromise the film's ability to answer it.

Max, on the other hand, is virtually submerged in a clique, the nucleus of which is composed of young men, all of whom are Jewish and professionals. This clanlike social group rejects people of inferior socioeconomic status as outsiders; people like Nora can never be received into its familiarity (in the literal sense).[2] To these nouveau riche Jewish yuppies, who know how to interpret her social-structural characteristics—her class, religion, and (gendered) age—Nora is a hopelessly inappropriate partner for Max. Middle-aged, working-class shiksas, available and sexually canny, are fine for affairs, for dalliances; but to "bring one home," to take such a liaison seriously, is grotesque.[3]

This attitude exemplifies the familiar dichotomous schema that assigns women to one of two mutually exclusive categories: bad girl/good girl; whore/virgin; girlfriend/wife; blonde (dumb)/brunette. Whatever the specifics, women exemplifying the first term are seen as sexually exciting but not fit to be wived, whereas women instancing the second lack sexual allure but are what men must settle for when they settle down. Max's association with Nora is understandable, indeed enviable, so long as it is kept within well-understood limits, but Max's emotional investment in his relationship with Nora challenges the clan's right to define what is appropriate to its members.[4]

This dichtomizing representational strategy displaces class differences among women onto differences in their sexuality. That is, *White Palace*'s use of the bad girl/good girl schema projects class differences among women onto differences in their sexual comportment—working-class women are bad; women of Max's class, good. Since class appears in the form of gender/sexual stereotype, the manner of its (displaced) presence functions to obscure its real existence.

But *White Palace* does not simply employ this regime of sexual stereotyping, it subjects it to critical scrutiny by showing that contrary to type, Nora *is* the appropriate mate for Max. Using sexuality as a means for interrogating social difference, the film problematizes the assumption that an individual's structural social characteristics—her class, race, gender, age, and so on—sufficiently determine the grounds of her connection to another human being. The film asserts that "disqualifying" social differences notwithstanding, indeed, in part precisely because of them, Nora is not merely an appropriate partner for Max, but Max is lucky to have found her.[5] *White Palace* thus raises the question of how two individuals so obviously unsuited to one another could come to form a couple.

The Source of Connection

Having conjured up all the stereotypes that tell against its unlikely couple, *White Palace* must now set to work to defeat them. This is made easier by the casting of James Spader and Susan Sarandon as its leads, for the audience's reception of the film's narrative, which determines the being of the characters as fictional, is inevitably "contaminated" by its awareness that Max and Nora are being played by two attractive stars. And it is not just that Spader and Sarandon are stars, but that they are precisely these stars—whose recent films had endowed them with sexually intriguing identities—that justifies the audience's anticipation of eventual sex. James Spader's breakthrough role as the sensitive but damaged videographer in *Sex, Lies, and Videotape* (1989) had just established him as a lead actor and Susan Sarandon had already rehearsed Nora's persona as the older sexual initiator of men in such films as *Bull Durham* (1988). Playing on these resonances, *White Palace* sets up our expectation of a similar relationship between the characters these stars will play in this film.[6]

This anticipation of a Max-Nora couple does not, however, explain how the audience can be persuaded that Nora really is a suitable partner for Max. Indeed, our expectation that a sexual relationship between the two will develop could just be a symptom of the same stereotypical understanding of women of Nora's type that Max's clan exhibits. We therefore need to dig deeper to understand how the audience becomes convinced that Max and Nora deserve be more to one another than just sexual partners.

In fact, it is another dichotomizing difference separating Max from Nora—neatness/messiness—that although not specifically social, lends plausibility to this couple. The film shows us that to judge what is fitting on the basis of apparent difference is a mistake, for contrary appearances may conceal deeper levels of affinity.

From the first scene in which he figures, Max is depicted as fanatically, even obsessively, neat. As he comes home from work and enters his apartment, he stops twice to rearrange the nap on his expensive and tasteful Persian rug. When he puts his freshly cleaned suits in the closet, we are invited to see his many identical suits, all hung neatly in rows. There is nothing in this apartment that is out of its place, no trace of an unruly item escaping Max's control.

By contrast, Nora's slovenliness seems almost a caricature. When Max first enters her home, a house in a "bad" part of town, it is strewn with refuse like an abandoned shack. In a subjective shot taken from Max's point of view, we experience for ourselves the disarray that confronts Nora's visitor. It really does look as if it had been hit by a cyclone, and we share Max's queasy reaction to what he sees. The problems that Nora's messiness portend are somewhat heavy-handedly prefigured as Max discovers and then discards a half-eaten sandwich during their first sexual encounter.

Taken at face value, this difference between Max and Nora could stand for a deep and final incompatibility. Reconciling his exaggerated need for order with her abandonment to chaos would seem like mixing oil with water. In an incident early in their courtship, Max arrives at Nora's house for dinner one evening carrying a present. She excitedly unwraps it only to find that Max has bought her a mini–vacuum cleaner, as if her lack of one were responsible for the messiness of her home. Nora's response is to throw Max out: Flowers or perfume make an appropriate gift, she angrily insists, not a dustbuster. But as a chastened Max leaves the house, he—and we—glimpse Nora's now sparkling kitchen and a dinner table with candles and flowers that presaged plans for a romantic evening together. Nora's messiness must be, in some sense, a choice she has made.

The significance of this sequence emerges in the course of the film, as Max's compulsive neatness and Nora's equally determined messiness are revealed as more than idiosyncratic tics. In fact, this issue becomes a pretext for exploring what makes two people suited to one another, and what we learn is instructive: Their exaggerated and opposite behaviors are actually different responses to similar personal tragedies, so this apparent incompatibility reveals a source of deep existential connection.

Max and Nora had each suffered a devastating loss—Max, his wife, Janey, killed in a car accident; Nora, her son, Jimmy, dead as the result of substance abuse. For both, losing a loved one initiated a catastrophic break. Nothing that has come after is the same as it had been before. Max has sought impossible levels of control over his experience, as if his obsessive neatness could ward off further suffering. And Nora, her life now bereft of purpose, has lost interest in her existence, and her slovenly housekeeping is just one symptom of this letting go.

A common experience of loss provides the ground of a sympathetic attentiveness to one another that breaks through the surface characteristics that keep Max and Nora apart. For Max's yuppie friends, you are your demographics—Nora is just an over-the-hill, lower-class shiksa—but *White Palace* condemns such superficiality, requiring its audience to acknowledge that similar experiences can undercut the social categories that divide people. This might tempt one to see the film as relying on the idea of an essential commonality of human experience more basic than social distinctions, but such an interpretation is not necessary. It is enough to see the film as positing a source of connection in the individual biographies of these two human beings that is not reducible to a common social category. Precisely because they share the experience of loss, Max and Nora are more similar than their obvious differences would lead one to expect.

But at the same time, it is these differences that allow them to attain the intense connection elsewhere unavailable to them. Their peers cannot see them for what they are: The working-class men in the bar Nora frequents size her up as just a sexually available older woman, a lonely waitress looking for some company; to the avid women whose voices we hear on Max's answering machine, he is the demographic jackpot, with all the qualifications they deem necessary in a partner. But both Max and Nora have chosen nothing rather than settle for so little. Hence, the film suggests, only by going outside their respective groups will either find someone with whom to share his or her deepest hurts and hopes.

Nora as Marilyn

In the most notorious scene in *White Palace*, Nora seduces the sleeping Max. Earlier in the evening, he repeatedly deflects Nora's sexual overtures. But when he falls asleep on her couch, she ignores his rebuffs and begins to fellate him. As in other post–Reagan-era films—*Pretty Woman*, for example—sex opens up the possibility of a committed relationship. But *White Palace* goes further, asserting that in itself, Nora's seduction of Max establishes her suitability to be his partner. To see why this makes sense, we need to appreciate how the film connects Nora with Marilyn Monroe, for it is through this narrative strategy that *White Palace* makes its point.

From the moment we learn more about Nora than that she works in a hamburger joint, her obsession with Monroe is emphasized. When Nora first runs into Max in a bar, she suggests that he looks like Tony Curtis. Although this may seem a rather bizarre association—James Spader does not look anything like Tony Curtis—the key to its meaning becomes clear when Nora proceeds to quote a line Monroe utters in *Some Like It Hot* (1959): "I had a wonderful dream. I was sorting your shells and mixing your cocktails and when I woke up, I wanted to swim right back to you."[7] Nora is thinking of Curtis as he appeared in that film and casts herself as Monroe, an identification emphasized further by the posters of Marilyn that adorn Nora's walls (see Photo 5.2). On entering her home, Max notices these and asks, "What exactly is there between you and Marilyn Monroe?" to which she replies, "Oh, she's just so fucked up and glamorous, and losing and fighting all the time, losing and fighting." Nora clearly identifies with Marilyn, and to understand Nora's view of her relationship to Max, as well as the meaning of her identification with Monroe, we need to turn to *Some Like It Hot*.

The relevant aspect of that film is the development of the romance between Sugar Cane (Marilyn Monroe) and Joe (Tony Curtis). Joe, a

Photo 5.2 Max inspecting Nora's collection of Marilyn Monroe Posters

womanizing saxophone player, hides out from pursuing gangsters by disguising himself as Josephine, a female saxophonist in an all-woman band. There, he meets Sugar Cane, a character in the "dumb-blonde" tradition, who is vulnerable to seduction by men like himself.[8]

The stock figure of the dumb blonde promises sexual availability without too much bother about a "relationship." Kathleen Rowe calls attention to the use of this cliché in films of the 1950s, including *Some Like It Hot*.[9] For her, the supersession of the unruly woman of 1930s comedies by the dumb blonde marks a retreat from the progressive sexual politics of those Depression-era films, a view that misses *Some Like It Hot's* critical thrust.

Some Like It Hot interrogates the dumb blonde cliché, implying that there is more to Sugar than a projection of male desire: Beneath the stereotype, there is the deeper reality of persistence in the face of pain and loss. Sugar has remained a caring and vulnerable human being despite repeated desertions by the callow musicians to whom she is fatally attracted. In a film in which male characters are constantly disguising themselves, appearing to be other than they are, the tension between what appears and what lies beneath the surface is repeatedly invoked. *Some Like It Hot* proposes to show us that there is more to its dumb blonde than her alluring curves.

To seduce Sugar, Joe invents for himself a character rich enough to attract her, but wounded so as to enlist her sympathy. He poses as the multimillionaire heir to the Shell Oil fortune, who, incidentally, sounds a lot like Cary Grant. "Shell Jr.," as Sugar calls him, confesses to impotence, grief at the accidental death of his fiancée having unmanned him. Courting her on a yacht that is not his own, Joe sets up Sugar to try to cure him of his tragic disability.

Like *White Palace, Some Like It Hot* features a morally questionable seduction. If Billy Wilder's film expects us to take pleasure in Joe's conquest and to suspend our moral qualms, Sugar must be both alluring and laughable. That she swallows Joe's outlandish seduction story licenses us to enjoy watching her participate in her own victimization. (At the same time, of course, we anticipate her ultimate victory over him.) And our pleasure is doubled in that it is Monroe who plays Sugar, for this is part of her image as well. Thus, *Some Like It Hot* becomes a metaspoof of the dumb blonde tradition that its narrative critiques.

Audiences tend to pass over the content of Joe's fantastic story, but from the vantage point of *White Palace*, it is worth some attention. In earlier chapters, I have argued that what I have called "masculinism" is an evasion of human finitude. The seduction sequence from *Some Like It Hot* plays on another aspect of our dependence on others: The fact that the death of those we love can destroy our happiness. Shell Jr.'s feigned impotence suggests that an alternative source of the masculinist refusal to connect is that caring for another makes one vulnerable to the pain of loss.[10]

The result of Sugar's attentions is, not surprisingly, Joe's (Shell Jr.'s?) arousal, but contrary to his intentions, he falls in love with her. Her innocence and vulnerability, the very qualities that make her such an easy mark, finally endear her to him, and so Joe is caught in the web of his own seduction. Moved by Sugar's generosity, Joe realizes—as do we—that the stereotype is not adequate to the reality of Sugar/Monroe. His successful seduction is thus a Pyrrhic victory, for the dumb blonde winds up winning the heart of her would-be seducer, offering him the possibility of true intimacy. Joe's masculinism, ruled by a logic of conquest, as well as the invented and inverted masculinity of Shell Jr., ruled by a logic of frozen withdrawal, are both defeated by Sugar's ministrations. The serious critical point made by the film's comic antics is that these male postures are impoverished ways of being a man. No mere projection of masculinist desire, *Some Like It Hot*'s dumb blonde frees her partner for a richer experience of his manhood.

Because Nora frames her self-understanding through the narrative of *Some Like It Hot*, *White Palace* asks us to identify her seduction of the sleeping Max with Sugar's gesture toward Shell Jr. Unlike the socially ambitious women of his social class, Nora understands that in response to Janey's death, Max has retreated from his own sexual desire. She will be his Sugar, releasing him from his icy withdrawal to reexperience his manhood sexually.

White Palace explores the phenomenology of grief more fully than its comic exemplar, however: Max's sexual disengagement is both emblem and symptom of his desireless being-in-the-world. In seducing Max, Nora is acting out of an understanding of what he really needs, which requires her to override his rejection of her sexual come-on. In reawakening his manhood, she expects that analogously to Joe/Josephine/Shell Jr., Max will come to see her as a fit partner.

Common to both *Some Like It Hot* and *White Palace* is the suggestion that a full sexual experience can shatter the social stereotypes that otherwise confine our possibilities. It is the force of his renewed desire that binds Max to Nora; that eases his fear of losing control of his life; and that, finally, allows him to experience his manhood more expansively than his peer group's stultifying norms allow.[11]

With all its clever intertextual play, *White Palace* is making a serious claim for Hollywood film, so often dismissed as superficial. Nora's insightful use of *Some Like It Hot* models the way in which these films have been, and can be, a source of moral instruction for their audiences—at their best, questioning the routinized, often cruel, categories of common sense. *White Palace* thus challenges the usual oppositions: entertainment versus art, pleasure versus significance. The film's overt critique of the masculinist assumption that attractive working-class women—Sugar, Nora—are superficial and dumb is equally a defense of Hollywood against an elitism that equates production values with vacuity.[12]

Overcoming Ambivalence

Despite the impact of their sexual encounter, Max is unable to free himself from a sense of embarrassment at being seen with Nora. By now, we viewers have made the judgment about her fitness to be his partner that

Max has still to accept. In due time, he is brought to this realization for himself. But before this happens, Max's ambivalence, his inability to accept Nora completely and for whom she is, is explored in discomforting detail.

At first, the film shows us—but not Nora—that Max acts as if he were ashamed of her. For example, out walking with Nora, he spies a business associate and, to avoid being seen, subtly alters their path. Nora, who is engrossed in conversation, is oblivious to this stratagem, but a long shot that reveals what Max has done lets us anticipate the trouble to follow.

Max's failure to publicly acknowledge Nora soon becomes a serious issue for the couple. Obliged to attend his friend Neil Horowitz's (Jason Alexander) wedding to Rachel Fine (Eileen Brennan), he lies to Nora, telling her that he must spend that evening helping his mother with her taxes. When her electricity is cut off, Nora calls Max at his mother's, only to learn the truth. This discovery causes Nora to confess her insecurity, her worry that each time he leaves her, it will be the last. Nora understands that Max feels she is not the right sort of person for him, but she warns him that although she forgives him this time, she will not excuse a second lie, for it strikes too deeply at her own self-esteem.

As if in response to her threat, a crisis promptly ensues. The difficulty emerges when Nora realizes that Max has not been able to shed his sense of her as an embarrassment. Ironically, her realization comes at an occasion Max takes to demonstrate precisely the opposite: He invites Nora to Thanksgiving dinner at the Horowitzes', where all the members of his clan are to gather. Nora does not see this as a free act of acknowledgment, however, but as an attempt to balance her demands with those of his clan. Although the couple will eventually transcend this crisis and be reunited, for the moment this incident creates too wide an abyss for their relationship to bridge.

Nora understands Max's gesture as duplicitous because of an earlier incident at a local supermarket, to which she and Max had gone to shop. Max abandoned her at the checkout line while he searched for an item that he had forgotten: freshly ground parmesan, not the déclassé canned stuff she had chosen. On his quest, he encountered Rachel and, acting as if he were alone, hedged about bringing "his mystery woman" with him to her Thanksgiving dinner. Returning to the checkout counter, Max lies to Nora, describing Rachel as an acquaintance whose name he could not remember.

Meanwhile Nora, who accepts Max's explanation, believes that her invitation to the Horowitzes' means he no longer needs to conceal her. She is very nervous about the impression she will make, but Max seems surprisingly untroubled by his lie, as if sure that Nora will not remember Rachel. Or perhaps, Nora's anxieties about being compared to his dead wife, Janey, have simply distracted him.

In any case, from the moment the couple nervously enters the Horowitzes' home, things begin to unravel. First, Nora does recognize her hostess as the woman in the supermarket whose name Max had supposedly forgotten. She now interprets Max's failure of nerve to mean that he had been trapped by circumstances into bringing her. Recalling that she had heard Rachel's invitation on his answering machine, she concludes that Max simply had to ask her to come with him to avoid another scene. Not to have done so—by either lying once again or by not going himself—would have let slip that he still was ashamed of her. But it now seems clear to her that Max's gesture did not signify the commitment to their relationship that she had assumed.[13]

At last seeing Max with his friends, Nora comes to believe that he and she are not merely an improbable couple but an impossible one. The members of Max's nouveau riche Jewish social set treat him as if he were family, talking of "our boy, Max," and such. Although Max's friends behave cordially, Nora knows that she stands out; that she does not belong there; indeed, that there is nothing that she can ever do to win real acceptance.

One of the most interesting and intelligent things about *White Palace* is its depiction of Nora's response to her awkward situation. At first, she tries to maintain an ironic distance, as Larry Klugman (Corey Parker), one of Max's close friends, asks her what she thinks of "our boy." His possessiveness—matched by that of Max's other friends—seems intended to exclude Nora, to make her feel as if she had lured Max away from this circle of intimates. Larry's opening has a prurient edge, for he acts as if he knows that this older, working-class woman had used her sexual cunning to ensnare Max. This is bad enough, but as if to keep Nora from establishing intimacy with anyone at the party, Larry's wife, Sherri (Barbara Howard), interrupts the conversation to call her husband's attention to the Horowitzes' kitchen chairs: "Just what we've have been looking for." Nora's, "Hey, you better get a peek at those chairs, Larry," overheard by Sherri, is indicative of both her growing unease and of her derisive attitude toward Larry's domestication at the hands of his wife.

Further contributing to Nora's unease is the company's failure to get her name right and their seeming disapproval of her dress. Although she has taken pains with her appearance, her judgment as to what is appropriate underscores rather than undermines the stereotype of the sexually experienced shiksa. Her dress keeps slipping off of her shoulder to reveal more skin than is consistent with her hosts' decorous standards. To Max's clan, Nora's predicament is interpreted as a blatant display of the sexual wares that have fuddled poor, naïve Max.

Seeking relief for her battered self-esteem, Nora retires to the bathroom to cool out with a friendly cigarette. But Sherri walks in on her by accident. To make conversation, she asks Nora what she does and, on learning that Nora is a waitress in a fast-food restaurant, observes that Max is "quite a catch" and wonders how Nora "did it." Offended by the implication she hears in Sherri's question, Nora responds with a coarse, "Give a good blow-job, I guess." To Sherri's quip, "I bet you do," "I bet you don't" is Nora's comeback. But echoing one of the central themes of this film— "What you see is not always what you get"—Sherri has the last word, suggesting Nora is too quick to dismiss other people's blow jobs.

There is irony in Nora's exchanges with Larry and Sherri, for they convey truths unrecognizable to those not equipped to hear them. Although it *is* Nora's sexual prowess that has "captured" Max, neither the leering husband nor his cynical wife understands what this means. On the other hand, Nora is herself not innocent of stereotyping, for she treats Sherri as if she were nothing but her own inverse—virgin to Nora's whore.

Once seated at dinner, Nora can hardly contain herself as Neil's father, Sol (Steven Hill), holds forth on the contemporary political scene, excoriating the Republicans for having created a deficit that will dominate the agenda of the country and burden its working people for generations to come. Feeling ever more the outsider to this well-off Jewish clan, Nora explodes at what she perceives to be their liberal hypocrisy. What goes on in Washington makes no difference to her, she rails, for she will be "flipping burgers" no matter who is in the White House. She storms out of the apartment, with Max and his mother in close pursuit.[14]

Denouncing Max for having once again deceived her, Nora makes good her earlier threat: This time, his lie will not be forgiven. Despite all Nora has meant to him, Max cannot free himself from the prejudices of his clan. And so Nora is forced to choose between their relationship and her self-esteem—and here it is important to recall that, unlike Max, she has no context to call on for support. She has no choice but to reject him and leave St. Louis.

Only with Nora's departure is Max's ambivalence resolved. Her significance descends on him in an epiphany at a party given by Heidi Solomon

(Kim Meyers), an attractive Jewish yuppie, the embodiment of all that the clan values: sophistication, beauty, artistic taste, wealth. But as Max looks around at his friends, he sees them with eyes from which the scales of conformity have fallen. "How do you know who's right for each other?" he asks them, as he points out the grim realities of their relationships—the divorces, the bad-mouthing. Agitated, he rises from the couch on which he has been sitting and, to the consternation of the other guests, inspects Heidi's dustbuster, exclaiming, "There's no dust in it!"

The climax to these fevered ruminations recalls the earlier dustbuster debacle at Nora's. Then, the mini-vacuum was a symbol of what Max would not accept in her; now, it represents the emptiness of the lives of Max's friends. At last, he realizes that Nora is the appropriate partner for him and all that remains is for the film to engineer their reconciliation.

A Problematic Ending

Unfortunately, the upbeat narrative closure *White Palace* provides the saga of Max and Nora backs away from its premise that the very unlikeliness of their attraction has freed them to love one another. In fact, the film's ending is ambiguous, but on either of its two most plausible readings this harsh judgment must stand.

The more natural of the two interpretations would have the couple's re-union privilege working-class values. According to this view, Max's reconciliation with Nora is secured by his rejection of his old social nexus—his yuppie friends and even his mother. Max is set down in a world totally determined by Nora's values: in New York, where he is alone, living in a run-down apartment with a view of garbage, thus embracing disorder and ugliness, and hoping to work as a teacher, resuming a career he had given up for reasons never clarified, but at least no longer in advertising, that profession most concerned with appearance rather than reality. Through a mechanical inversion of everything he had been, he breaks down Nora's reluctance to resume their relationship. This Prince Charming gets to have his Cinderella not by bringing her to his castle but by relocating to her hovel.

Instead of exploring how Max might build a life responsive to his own needs rather than one acceptable to his friends, the film chooses a familiar Hollywood option—the faux populist route of turning Max's life into a replica of Nora's. In effect, the ending valorizes one term of each of the divisions (except age) that separate Max and Nora. Every aspect of Nora's gritty working-class existence is now represented as superior to the glittery artifice of Max's former world.

Rather than maintain its subversion of the hold of hierarchic rankings on our thought and conduct, the film now embraces the superficial view of social difference it had criticized earlier. Max's inversion of values results in as inauthentic a form of life as one dominated by his friends' judgments of appropriateness. In rejecting their values, Max rejects not only their superficial snobbery but aspects of his own life that had previously mattered a great deal.

This point is brought home by the film's use of musical taste as a class marker. Early in the film, in a scene in which Max drives Nora home from the bar, she asks about the music on the car stereo. When he responds that the opera to which he is listening is the most beautiful music in the world, this is the first evidence we see in him of passion. Only in relation to this music does Max betray deep feeling; otherwise he struggles to keep emotion at bay. Nora reacts by asking him if he has anything by the Oak Ridge Boys. Max, the upper-class sophisticate is an aficionado of opera, whereas the working-class waitress predictably likes country music. At that point, however, although we recognize Nora's lack of sophistication as an obstacle to their relationship, we also enjoy her refusal to be intimidated by elite cultural values. No hushed respect from her.

But in the final scene in the deli where Nora now works, having given up his home, his job, and his family to be with her, Max goes still further and, in response to her request that he order, himself asks for some Oak Ridge Boys. The message here is that he is now truly fit for her because he has cast aside the "highfalutin" art of opera in favor of the "low" art of country music. This final act of renunciation initiates the vulgar sequence in which Max symbolically screws Nora on one of the deli's tables.

Max's gesture shows that despite its sensitive exploration of the complex and often hidden bases of relationship early in the film, *White Palace* has retreated from its brave attempt to see both high and low as legitimate sources of moral and aesthetic experience, or, put another way, has backed away from its brave attempt to reject a hierarchically structured system of social valuation.[15]

The second, alternative reading of Max's reunion with Nora would begin by emphasizing the narrative significance of Max's mother, Edith (Renée Taylor), who plays an ongoing but relatively minor role in the film. We are introduced to her when she and Max visit the grave of Max's late wife, the day after his first sexual encounter with Nora. Upset that Janey's grave has not received the care for which they had paid, she falls to her knees and starts pulling up weeds. Max's discomfort is evident as he attempts to reassure her that he will see to the care of the grave site. Edith's extravagant behavior suggests that Max's attraction to the more refined world of his circle of St. Louis yuppies may have a psychologically complex origin: Instead of simply being his taken-for-granted context, that milieu may represent a haven from his embarrassing social origins.

This sense is reinforced by Edith's behavior during the ill-fated Thanksgiving dinner that sparks Nora's decision to break off with Max and leave St. Louis. When Max picks up his mother, her house seems more like Nora's dump than his own fancy digs. Edith has prepared a noodle dish, as if she had been invited to a potluck, not an elaborately prepared holiday table. Later she spills a drink and, losing her composure, falls to her knees yet again, this time to clean up the mess she has made. As the camera moves to Nora, we hear Edith apologize to Max for embarrassing him in front of his friends, as if this were no isolated occurrence.

On this evidence, then, Edith can be seen as the source of Max's hunger for social acceptance. His loud, unpolished mother is clearly not of the same social class as the parents of his yuppie friends, the Horowitzes. (Although it is tempting to read Max's reaction as a case of Jewish self-hatred, it is class and not Jewishness that is the focus here.) If Max's persistent embarrassment over Nora, his inability to fully honor her, is rooted in his relationship to his mother, then to accept Nora is also to accept his mother, a working-class Jewish woman, and—finally and most important—to accept his own class origins.

Interpreted in this manner, the couple's reunion once again diminishes the power of their unlikeliness. If, in the old fairy tale, Cinderella ascends to her rightful class position through the mediation of Prince Charming, in the film Max is declassed through his relationship with Nora. Thus, in a surprising twist, *White Palace* sends its upstart young male back to the class from which he has come.

At the film's start, there is a disparity between the wealth Max has acquired as an advertising executive and his inherited class status. On to this interpretation, rather than being socially inappropriate, Max's union with Nora attaches him to a partner from the class into which he was born. On this reading, then, the ending of *White Palace* demonstrates the futility of attempting to rise above one's social origins, for one's "real" class status will always out.

White Palace's ending thus marks a retreat from its earlier subversion of hierarchic rankings and affirmation of the value of social difference. By reverting to stereotypical portrayals of class—through either Max's embrace of Nora's working-class values or an assertion of the untenability of his social ascent—*White Palace* betrays its ambition to make a statement that transcends the familiar narrative permutations of the unlikely couple film by destabilizing the categories that structure them.

This sense that, in the end, the film loses its nerve is not just an artifact of its reception; it is present in the text of the film itself. The final sequence shows Max symbolically screwing Nora on a table that he has cleared with a sweeping, macho gesture. The cheers and applause of the deli's patrons, who now watch this scene much as do we, disrupt the film's hitherto naturalistic assumptions. By interposing this second audience between us and the film's two main characters, our absorption is overtaken by self-consciousness.

But *White Palace*'s winking invocation of the specular nature of film is not a simple gesture of self-awareness on its part. Instead, by calling attention to the process of viewing, *White Palace* also calls attention to the contrivance of its own ending. The parodic character of the final sequence is its guilty acknowledgment that it has proceeded in bad faith.

So, by adopting an ending of this type, *White Palace* ultimately aligns itself with Hollywood's reluctance to affirm the fruitfulness of social differences. It is particularly ironic that this film, which shows so brilliantly the impoverishing effects of social conformity, winds up caving in to the Hollywood system's demand for narrative closure. *White Palace* fails to achieve what it held out as a possibility for its male lead, namely, the ability to liberate oneself from the constraints of a deadening conformity.

Notes

1. A number of unlikely couple films, including *Sunset Boulevard* (1950), *All That Heaven Allows* (1955), and *Harold and Maude* (1971), focus on age difference. Although the latter two are critical of society for seeing "older" women as inappropriate for "younger" men, *Sunset Boulevard* brilliantly explores the difficulties a once-glamorous sex symbol has with the aging process.

2. Although his friends' parents are part of the group, Max's mother is not, as we learn when Rachel Fine (Rachel Levin), the wife of one of the clan's alpha males, apologizes to Max for inviting her to Thanksgiving dinner. I discuss the relevance of this later in the chapter.

3. Sexual stereotypes thus function as the embodiment of class, religious, and age differences among women. This demonstrates the need to think of identity in nonadditive terms. For an explicit argument concerning this point, see Elizabeth Spelman, *Inessential Other* (Boston: Beacon Press, 1991).

4. In many unlikely couple films, men are also used to represent types. This is quite obvious, for example, in *It Happened One Night*, where Ellie Andrews's potential husbands, Peter Warne and King Westley, are contrasted. Their relationship to sexuality is not, however, the marker of the differences between them.

5. It is easy to see this film, as some feminist critics no doubt do, as reinforcing the stereotype that women are, in essence, nurturers of males. Although this interpretation is true to the film, it should not keep us from seeing that there is more at issue here than gender stereotyping.

6. The nontransparency of the film actor marks an important way in which Hollywood cinema differs from other art forms, for the audience's awareness of the identity of the actors never becomes fully transparent or, to be more precise, is always something that can lose its transparency and emerge into the audience's awareness, thus allowing for a tension between character and actor that is not possible in, say, a novel or even a play. Virginia Wright Wexman argues, in *Creating the Couple: Love, Marriage, and Hollywood Performance* (Princeton: Princeton University Press, 1993), that the audience's awareness of their stars is central to understanding the appeal of Hollywood films.

7. This and future quotations from *Some Like It Hot* are from my transcription of the film's sound track. The same holds for quotations from *White Palace*.

8. For an interesting discussion of Monroe in light of this tradition, see Richard Dyer, "Monroe and Sexuality," in *Women and Film*, Janet Todd, ed. (New York: Holmes and Meier, 1988), pp. 69 ff.

9. Chapter 6 of her book, *The Unruly Woman: Gender and the Genres of Laughter* (Austin: University of Texas Press, 1995), is titled "Dumb Blondes."

10. For my purposes here, I ignore the film's implicit view of Shell Jr. as gay. In her interpretation in *The Unruly Woman* (pp. 183–190), Rowe misses this aspect of the film.

11. Sex is therefore a symbol in these films, standing for an aspect of reality that is absent in lives governed by social stereotype.

12. In this sense, we can see the entire narrative as an allegory of the nature of film itself.

13. The film does not problematize Nora's understanding of Max's motivation. Instead, it simply accepts her interpretation. The problem this causes for the film's conclusion might have been avoided if the film had taken the timing of the characters' interpretations to be more significant. That is, Nora does not allow for the possibility that Max's attitude may have changed since his supermarket deception. The film could then have portrayed how ignoring temporality leads to significant misunderstandings in relationships.

14. One problem, as we shall see, is the film's failure to maintain its distance from Nora's perspective. Once she confronts Sol, it is as if the film adopts her perspective, neglecting the element of hypocrisy in her total dismissal of Max's nouveau riche clan.

15. The film's portrayal of the working class is not as positive as the ending suggests. Indeed, there are a number of respects in which it portrays working-class life in negative terms. There is Nora's asocial nature, as if working-class people had no social nexus. This contrasts especially starkly with Max's highly social definition of self. Second, there is the film's portrayal of working-class men, for example, in the scene in which Nora and Max meet in the bar. At least part of the answer to why Nora is interested in Max, aside from his physical beauty, is that he is not like the crude working-class males, one of whom the film foregrounds as Nora circumnavigates the bar to talk with Max. The idea is that his androgyny is preferable to the machismo of these men for whom Nora is simply a one-night stand. Thus, despite its ending's valorization of the working class, *White Palace* exhibits a highly ambivalent estimation of working-class life.

Part Two

Race

6
Guess Who's Coming to Dinner
Does Father Really Know Best?

Guess Who's Coming to Dinner (1967) is the first of the four films I discuss in which the unlikely couple is an interracial one.[1] All four films straightforwardly assume the injustice of antiblack racism. Reflecting the different historical conjunctures in which they were made, and, in one case, a non-American context, and although necessarily staking out different positions on this intractable phenomenon, all advance the same narrative premise—transgressive romance—to explore the possibility of eliminating racism.

Guess Who's Coming to Dinner tells the story of an upper-class, white husband and wife, who at first disapprove of their daughter's intention to marry a black man but later come to embrace the idea. Because the political turmoil of the 1960s—from the civil rights movement to its more radical offspring such as the black power movement—had resulted in a heightened awareness of the injustices of America's racialized society, the film can use this story to address the viability of liberalism, with its commitment to integration as a means of undermining racial hierarchy and, thus, achieving equality for blacks. Since the Draytons are "lifelong liberals," their initial hostility to the prospect of a black son-in-law calls liberal integrationism into question. The charge that the film investigates is that when the chickens come home to roost, liberals cannot be counted on to honor their ideals.

But the liberals in this film—and this is its point—do not desert the cause of racial justice, despite their initial difficulty in living up to its consequences. By the film's end, both Christina (Katharine Hepburn), the mother, and, more importantly, Matt (Spencer Tracy), the father of the young bride-to-be, endorse their daughter's impending marriage. Indeed, the focus of the film is on Matt's arduous struggle to come to accept it. In the end, not only is this father of the bride saved from the charge of hypocrisy, but his embrace of his prospective son-in-law vindicates liberalism as a political philosophy and, with it, integration as the solution to the racism of American society.

Guess Who's Coming to Dinner was a popular success when it was released, grossing between seventy and eighty million dollars and winning two of the ten Academy Awards for which it was nominated (for Best Actress [Katharine Hepburn] and Best Screenplay [William Rose]). From the time of its release, however, critics have been nearly unanimous that the terms in which this film tells its story undermine its ability to make a serious political statement—foremost among their complaints, that the black male lead is so extraordinary and contrived a human being as to be simply unbelievable. A particularly barbed example is Joseph Morgenstern's sarcastic characterization of John Prentice as "a composite Schweitzer, Salk, and Christ colored black for significance."[2] Film scholars have also generally dismissed this film for its lack of realism. Representative of these is Donald Bogle, who labels the film "the last of the explicitly integrationist message pictures" and dismisses it as "pure 1949 claptrap done up in 1940s high-gloss MGM style."[3] Similarly, Thomas Cripps cites *Guess Who's Coming to Dinner* as merely one in a line of films that signaled the decline of Sidney Poitier's career and that demonstrated "the exhaustion by 1968 of the genre [of the message movie] and the ennui of its audience."[4]

These harsh assessments did not go unanswered. Pointing out that he repeatedly encountered difficulty in funding the film—more than once, Columbia threatened to retract its financial support—Stanley Kramer, the film's producer and director, defended the film's subject as "the touchiest of all issues between blacks and whites: interracial sex and marriage."[5] He also offered an interesting explanation of how John Wade Prentice, the character played by Sidney Poitier, had been developed: "We took special pains to make Poitier a very special character. . . . We did this so that if the young couple didn't marry because of their parents disapproval, the *only* reason would be that he was black and she was white."[6] Kramer's strategy was thus calculatedly political. By making John a man of great personal integrity and world renown, the film excludes factors other than race that might justify parental opposition to the marriage. From Kramer's point of view, this artifice frees the film to concentrate on the question of white liberal racism.

Sidney Poitier also defended the film's representational strategy, but with a somewhat different emphasis. He contended that the critics failed to recognize Hollywood's complicity in American racism:

> In 1967 it was utterly impossible to do an in-depth interracial love story, to treat the issue in dead earnestness, head on. . . . But Kramer . . . treated the theme with humor, but so delicately, so humanly, so lovingly that he made everyone look at the question for the very first time in film history. *Guess Who's Coming to Dinner* is a totally revolutionary movie. . . . What the critics didn't know and what blinded them to the great merit of the film, was that Hollywood was incapable of anything more drastic in 1967.[7]

According to Poitier, in 1967 the compromised state of the film industry—and by implication, American society generally—required the film to proceed by indirection. Without Kramer's reassuringly tactful handling, this drama of interracial love could not have been produced.

Poitier's characterization of the film as revolutionary reminds us that *Guess Who's Coming to Dinner* did break some long-standing taboos. For example, coming shortly after the repeal of the Hollywood Production Code, it was Hollywood's first film to show a black man romantically kissing a white woman, even if that explosive image was confined to the rearview mirror of a taxicab (see Photo 6.1).[8]

Also, Poitier is right to insist that *Guess Who's Coming to Dinner* be seen as a compromise between the desire to make a politically significant statement about interracial romance—and through it, about liberalism and integration—and a realistic assessment of the obstacles posed to such a project by a racist film industry and society. But his defense of the result ignores the cost to principle of having effected that compromise. As I shall demonstrate in this chapter, *Guess Who's Coming to Dinner* fails to vindicate liberal integrationism in large part because the representational and narrative strategies it adopts to forestall racist responses undercut its antiracist intentions.

Defending Liberalism and Integration

Guess Who's Coming to Dinner was an intervention in the highly charged debate about the civil rights movement's successes and failures. By 1967,

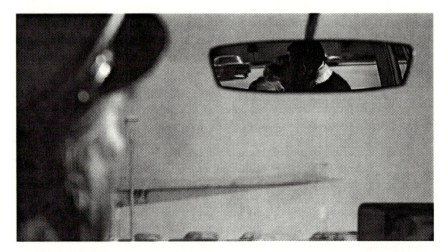

Photo 6.1 Hollywood's first interracial kiss

the assassination of black leaders like Martin Luther King Jr., the emergence of the black power movement, and uprisings in cities all across America had challenged the viability of integration as a political solution to segregation and racism. The film frames its response to these challenges by asking whether the residues of racism in white liberal consciousness invalidate liberal political commitments. If, as the film hopes, people like the Draytons can overcome their atavistic prejudices when faced with the climactic challenge of their daughter's proposing to marry "one," then the answer will be affirmative.

Ironically, *Guess Who's Coming to Dinner* fastidiously avoids contextualizing its own politics, placing the only two references to the tumultuous racial struggles of the 1960s in the mouth of the white couple's maid, Tillie (Isabelle Sanford). Both comments are sarcastic references to that context. Watching John climb the stairs of the house, she comments, "Civil rights are one thing. This here is something else." Later, warning John not to take advantage of his fiancée, she threatens that if he does, "You'll find out what Black Power really means."[9] This marginalization of the film's raison d'être both coyly acknowledges its political agenda and betrays its anxiety about how the audience will react.

The interracial couple whose romance is at the center of this film comprises Johanna Drayton (Katharine Houghton)—the twenty-three-year-old daughter of Matt, a white, liberal newspaper publisher, and his wife,

Christina, the owner of an avant-garde art gallery—and John Wade Prentice—a thirty-seven-year-old African American doctor whom she met while on vacation in Hawaii. He is the son of a retired mail carrier, John Sr. (Roy Glenn Jr.), and his wife, Mary (Beah Richards). The film's action takes place during one afternoon in which the two lovers stop over in San Francisco, the Draytons' home. Johanna thinks that they are there simply to introduce John to her parents, but he has a different purpose in mind.

Johanna has assured her fiancé that his race will not be an issue for her parents, but the older and less naïve John is hardly sanguine about how they will react to the news that their daughter intends to marry a black man, even one as accomplished as he is. Because Johanna is so young and so close to her parents, he has decided to place the couple's future in the hands of the elder Draytons: Unbeknownst to Johanna, he will propose that should either of them express any reservations about the marriage, he will break off the engagement. But John has business to attend to in Geneva—he is on his way to a new, important position at the World Health Organization—so the Draytons will have only a few hours to decide whether they will give the couple their blessing.[10]

Initially, the prospects for liberalism are poor, for both of Johanna's parents recoil with shock and disapproval from her announced intention to marry John. We witness Christina's reaction first. She has rushed home because Hillary St. George (Virginia Christine), the manager of her art gallery, has told her that her daughter has unexpectedly arrived in town. John is in Matt's study, phoning his parents, when Christina enters the living room. Johanna gushes excitedly about having fallen head over heels in love, to Christina's evident pleasure. The film then toys with its audience, having Johanna tell her mother that there is one thing about her fiancé that she must tell her. Of course, we expect Johanna to disclose that he is black, but instead we learn of a previous marriage. As Johanna pronounces her fiancé's name, she is stopped dead in midphrase by the look of shock that she—and we—see on Christina's face. The reason—revealed in a midrange shot that places the two women in the foreground as John, in the background, enters the living room from the study—is that Christina has seen that her daughter's fiancé is black. Her distress is so extreme that John advises her to sit down lest she faint, and this normally self-possessed professional woman is reduced to stuttering, "Doc . . . Doc . . . Doctor Prentice, I'm so pleased to meet you."

Matt Drayton's reaction, although not quite as dramatic, is no less troubling. Returning home from work on his way to a golf game, Matt finds

Christina, Johanna, and John sitting on the terrace having lunch—but not before Tillie has warned him that "All hell's done broke loose now." Matt handles things well until he realizes—stopping in midstride as he walks through the living room—what Tillie's warning means. Once he understands the significance of John's presence, Matt decides that here is a problem serious enough to justify abandoning his golf game.

Matt's initial opposition to the marriage takes the form of his worry about whether John is a suitable partner for his daughter. As soon as he and Christina are alone in his study, Matt telephones his secretary and asks her to check into John's background. When his secretary calls back with the news that John is an outstanding doctor and scholar, Matt's hopes for an easy solution to his dilemma are dashed. Since opposing the marriage simply because of John's race would force Matt to admit his hypocrisy, he takes refuge in a different concern: that the racism of American society will cause the couple unacceptable suffering. As a father, he blusters, he must be the "rational" one, the one who will not be swayed by "emotion," the one who can therefore "realistically" assess the couple's clouded prognosis.

Privileging Romantic Love

Faced with the prospect of a black son-in-law, both Christina and Matt squirm with discomfort over where the teaching of their liberal ideals has led their daughter. But Christina has the easier time overcoming her anguish, moved by evidence of how deeply in love her daughter is. She expresses her change of heart to Matt in a sequence filmed from inside Matt's study. The scene begins with a close-up of a brief conversation between John and Johanna, who are outside on an adjoining terrace. Johanna admits to John that she had been worried that her parents might let her down and John teases her for covering up her nervousness with assurances that everything would be okay. This brief exchange is itself significant, for we are meant to see how comfortable they are with one another.[11] The camera then makes a reverse zoom that ends with a long shot of the two taken from slightly behind and to the right of Christina, whose shoulders and head frame one side of the shot (see Photo 6.2). A reverse shot to a close-up of a teary-eyed Christina is followed by a cut to Matt, who has been watching the scene from behind his wife; as he approaches her, she confesses that she can no longer oppose this marriage, because she can see the joy that John has brought her daughter.[12] "Joey has always been a happy person," Christina says:

But I don't think I've ever seen her so happy as she is now. And I have to be happy for her, Matt, and I am. And proud of the fact that we helped to make her. And whatever happens now, I feel glad that Joey's Joey.

Christina's speech cites two reasons for her change of heart. The first—a conventional one—is the obvious happiness that Joey's love for John has brought her daughter. The second is much more interesting and to the point: She is proud of the fact that she has raised a daughter who does not attribute significance to the color of her fiancé's skin. Christina is able to give their marriage her blessing because she has changed her way of perceiving the couple; rejecting dominant social norms that would stigmatize the couple as problematic, she comes to see its interracial makeup as exemplary. Her daughter has become the embodiment of the color-blind ideal with which the Draytons had raised her.

Although Matt eventually succumbs, he has a great deal more difficulty doing so. His initial reaction to his wife's about-face—"And I'm thinking only of her own welfare," he insists—is to reproach Christina for not "having her [Joey's] best interest" in mind. At this critical juncture in her life, he cannot concede his twenty-three-year-old daughter the right to make choices for herself and live with their consequences. In his zeal to "protect" Johanna, he is oblivious to the effect that his prohibition of the marriage would have on their relationship. As Christina tries to make him see, rather than sparing Johanna pain, Matt's opposition will not only prove futile, but will likely also cause her to doubt his integrity.

Spencer Tracy had once before played the role of a father who had great difficulty accepting his daughter's marriage. In *The Father of the Bride*, made in 1950, the problem facing its eponymous hero is his fear that his daughter's love for her groom will mean an end to her love for him. In *Guess Who's Coming to Dinner*, Matt's paternalism surfaces in his concern that the young couple does not understand the depth of the racism that they will have to face in 1960s America. Although everyone else attributes Matt's opposition to his daughter's marriage to an African American to the hypocrisy of a white liberal patriarch, he thinks of himself as a realist, someone who is not simply smitten, as his wife is, by the sight of the two young lovers, but who can think rationally about the pros and cons of their situation.[13]

Interestingly enough, it is Mary Prentice, John's mother, who gets Matt to relent and support the marriage. Instead of assaulting him with arguments about the irrationality of his position, she addresses him in psychological terms, asking that he think about his position as an aging male:

Photo 6.2 Christina observes the "passionate" couple

> What happens to men when they grow old? Why do they forget everything?
> I believe those two young people need each other like they need the air to
> breathe. Anybody can see that by just looking at them. But you and my hus-
> band, you might as well be blind.

Mary here, and Christina earlier, have spoken up for the film's idea of
color-blindness, the ideal realized by Johanna and John. The problem
with the older generation, or at least with its male members, is precisely
that they see something—race—where they should not. But now, the man
who claims to see clearly is told that he is blind. Mary challenges him to
see something else in the young lovers, something other than an affront to
the social norms that, ironically, he has himself dedicated his life to chal-
lenging. What Mary sees is the passion the two have for one other, and
for her this trumps all of Matt's objections. His problem, she continues, is
"that men grow old and when sexual things no longer matter to them,
they forget it all, forget what passion is." Matt and John Sr. have forgotten
the power of sexual passion:

> Now the two of you don't know. And the strange thing for your wife and me
> is that you don't even remember. If you did, how could you do what you are
> doing [i.e., stand in the way of the marriage]?

Mary's hope is that Matt will be able to recall his own youthful passion.

And he does: "I admit that I hadn't considered it [i.e., love], hadn't even thought about it," he tells her as he addresses the assembled cast in the film's climactic scene.

> But I know exactly how he feels about her. And there is nothing, absolutely nothing, that your son feels about my daughter that I don't feel for Christina. Old? Yes. Burned out? Certainly. But I can tell you the memories are still there: clear, intact, indestructible. . . . The only thing that matters is what they feel and how much they feel for each other. And if it's half of what we felt, that's everything.

Matt has risen to Mary's challenge, his recollected passion for Christina awakening his sympathy for the young lovers.[14] Endorsing a version of the cliché that love conquers all, he argues:

> And I think that now, no matter what kind of case some bastard could make against your getting married, there would be only one thing worse, and that would be, knowing what you two are, knowing what you two have, and knowing what you two feel, if you didn't get married.

Matt's speech affirms the power of love to transcend whatever obstacles John and Joey will encounter. Indeed, to insist on these obstacles—as Matt had so recently done—one would have to be a bastard.

This speech is the one moment in the film that contemporaneous critics singled out for praise, although this had more to do with the fact that it is Spencer Tracy making this speech, and doing so under the eyes of his on-screen wife and off-screen lover, Katharine Hepburn.[15] When Matt/Spencer talks about what he and Christina/Katharine had, viewers could not help but recall the many classic romantic comedies in which they had starred together. Moreover, this was the last speech that Tracy was ever to make on film, for he was very ill at the time and died just days after the filming was completed.

Guess Who's Coming to Dinner thus privileges the romantically constituted couple in order to defeat the racist attitudes of nearly all its characters. Either acquiesce to the marriage, demonstrate one's understanding that the love the two young people have for each other is more significant than their racial difference, or else be seen as racist. What tension we feel as viewers is relieved once Matt redeems himself in our eyes and proves that he is not the hypocrite he appeared to be.[16]

Matt's change of heart registers an important acknowledgment by the father of this film's bride, although the sexist nature of the narrative makes it difficult to see this. For Matt to give the marriage his blessing, he needs to reconcile himself to John's assumption of power over Johanna as a replacement for his own. This is a difficult transition for fathers to make in any case. Recalling his own youth and the love he felt as a young man for his then-young wife, Matt accepts John as an appropriate husband for his daughter.

Looked at in this way, the film instructs us on patriarchy's strategy for accommodating racial integration. Rather than compromise men's power over women, patriarchy will admit black men to the ranks of the privileged. And like Matt, individual white men will be able to overcome their reluctance to do so by identifying in their young black successors the passionate youths they themselves once were.

Matt's transformation not only restores our faith in him, it seals, in its makers' eyes, *Guess Who's Coming to Dinner's* vindication of liberalism. His opposition to his daughter's marriage to a black man raised doubts about whether liberals could be trusted to act on their principles. Those doubts have been laid to rest. But although the film offers us the satisfactions of narrative closure, this does not mean that the film's vindication of liberalism is successful or even coherent. In fact, there are a number of serious problems with *Guess Who's Coming to Dinner's* politics—some internal to liberalism, others the product of its makers' narrative and representational strategies—and I now turn to a consideration of some of these.

Representing Racism

A first problem with *Guess Who's Coming to Dinner,* internal to the liberal political orientation it champions, is that it understands racism as an effect of the prejudices of individual social actors. For this reason, the film is unable to acknowledge racism's systematic, structural aspects. Thus, to say that *Guess Who's Coming to Dinner* represents antiblack racism as essentially an effect of individual prejudice is to point out how the film locates racism's source in feelings, beliefs, and actions that unfairly discriminate against others because of such inherent characteristics as their skin color, physiognomy, and so on.

There are two scenes at the very beginning of the film in which our unlikely couple provokes racist reactions.[17] In the first, we see the taxi driver (John Hudkins) who takes the lovers from the airport to the Draytons' home react with distaste when he glimpses their kiss in his rearview mirror and then almost refuse the cab fare that John hands him. In the second of these racist vignettes, Hillary, Christina's employee at her gallery, cannot help showing her surprise and disapproval when she realizes that John and Johanna are involved with one another. The narrative function of these scenes is to build toward the Draytons' encounter with their future son-in-law, but along the way they also exemplify the film's understanding of racism. These minor characters betray their own race prejudice, for they see this relationship as offensive because of the difference in its partners' skin colors.

The same analysis of racism as prejudice underlies the film's representation of Johanna, who embodies its conception of the solution to the problems it addresses. Johanna's color-blindness is, at the level of individual character, the necessary corrective to the moral flaw of prejudice. Because Johanna is color-blind, that is, fails to perceive the (social significance of the) difference between white and black, her actions are untainted by prejudice. She cannot treat blacks as different from whites because she does not see them as different. Johanna's color-blindness can be presented as the solution to American racism precisely because the film views racism as prejudice based on skin color.

It is this understanding of racism and its antidote that accords with the liberalism that the film sets out to vindicate. Seeing racism as prejudice makes it a problem in the moral character of individual white Americans, a problem that can be solved by pointing out that such attitudes contradict a belief in the essential dignity and equality of all human beings.

In the mid-1940s, the Swedish sociologist Gunnar Myrdal had articulated an analysis of American racism in just these terms, claiming in *An American Dilemma* that the "Negro problem" was really a problem in the consciousness of white Americans, a conflict between their moral ideals and their attitudes toward black Americans:

> The American Negro problem is a problem in the heart of the American. It is there that the interracial tension has its focus. It is there that the decisive struggle goes on. . . . At bottom our problem is the moral dilemma of the American—the conflict between his moral valuations on various levels of consciousness and generality. The "American Dilemma," referred to in the title of this book, is the ever-raging conflict between, on the one hand, the valuations . . . where the American thinks, talks, and acts under the influence of high national and Christian precepts, and, on the other hand, the valuations on specific planes of individual and group living, where personal and local interests; economic, social, and sexual jealousies; considerations of community prestige and conformity; group prejudice against particular

persons or types of people; and all sorts of miscellaneous wants, impulses, and habits dominate his outlook.[18]

The conflict between the Draytons' belief in equality and their racist reaction to their daughter's match is a paradigmatic example of the predicament Myrdal's famously influential study anatomized. And by the 1960s, *An American Dilemma* had become American liberalism's common sense on the race issue.[19]

As self-evident, then, as *Guess Who's Coming to Dinner*'s understanding of racism as the effect of individual prejudice appeared, it is nonetheless inadequate. For even if Americans were suddenly to decide that skin color has no moral significance, there are structural aspects of racism that would not thereby be eradicated.

For example, consider the Draytons' relationship with their maid, Tillie. The film presents her role in the Drayton family as that of a "mammy," that is, a black woman who has come to identify strongly with the family she selflessly nurtures.[20] Tillie's identification with the Draytons is so strong that she attacks John for attempting to marry Johanna. To the question, "Is there racism in the Draytons' relationship with Tillie?" we might be inclined to respond, "No, for the Draytons treat her as a family member, and without a hint of prejudice." On the other hand, one could argue that the Draytons' attitude—and even the filmmakers'—toward her is, at times, patronizing. But putting this objection aside, it would not at all follow that the situation that links Tillie to the Draytons is free of racism. Black women like Tillie were employed as live-in maids by people in the Draytons' social class as a result of historically conditioned economic factors that limited their life chances. Without access to wider educational and employment opportunities, they were forced in large numbers into low-paying, low-status jobs as domestics, service workers, and so on. So even if none of the Draytons discriminate against Tillie on the basis of her skin color, her role in the household is an invidious, racially determined effect of the structure of American society.

But consistent with the ontological individualism of liberal social theory, *Guess Who's Coming to Dinner* treats Tillie's situation as unproblematic. If the film seeks to vindicate liberal integrationism by contriving a black male paragon, its success implies nothing about the racialized division of labor of which the Drayton household is a microcosm. A conception of racism as a structural phenomenon privileging white Americans just because they are white is simply beyond the film's representational possibilities.

Naturalizing Integration

As the civil rights movement made clear, the racial integration of American society could only be achieved by means of a political struggle. But *Guess Who's Coming to Dinner* naturalizes the process of integration by treating it as the inevitable result of generational succession. In this way, despite its condemnation of American society for its racism, the film adopts narrative and representational strategies that encourage its audience to passively await the arrival of integration rather than actively work for its realization.

This prospect of an immanent generational eclipse of racism partakes of a general sense that *Guess Who's Coming to Dinner* conveys—and that marks the film as a product of the late 1960s—that its present is a time of ferment that is leaving the older generation behind. The film registers its sense of rapid social development by depicting Matt Drayton as bedeviled by the ubiquity of dizzying change.

One example of the way in which time has speeded up is the prominence of air travel, from the title sequence in which we see a large jet land at the San Francisco airport, to John's brief stopover before hurrying on to Geneva. The mere forty minutes that it takes for the Prentices to arrive from Los Angeles is mentioned a number of times.

Other scenes stress instead changes in Matt's social environment—for example, in a discussion between him and John of the racial dilemma in which they find themselves, John assures Matt that things are changing for the better. Matt's response, that nowhere are they changing quite as fast as in his own backyard, indicates his discomfort with the pace of these changes. In a later scene, Matt and his friend Monsignor Mike Ryan (Cecil Kellaway) argue about Matt's opposition to the marriage, Matt protesting that he knows what the couple is up against: "I happen to know they wouldn't have a dog's chance. Not in this country. Not in the whole stinking world." But Mike persists: "They are this country, Matt. They'll change this stinking world."

The change that counts most to the film's narrative, however, is the emergence of a postracist white youth. Whereas, with the exception of Mike Ryan, all the members of the parental generation are infected by bigotry, Johanna's generation is presented as color-blind, free of their elders' prejudices.[21] This is the meaning of the sequence in which a white delivery boy (D'Urville Martin) arrives at the Draytons' bringing steaks for the ever-expanding list of dinner guests. When he agrees to provide a

lift for Tillie's assistant, Dorothy (Barbara Randolph), the two exit, bo-
ogying to the rock-and-roll blasting from his truck radio. These members
of the "new" generation of Americans seem oblivious to racial difference;
they simply enjoy dancing together to *their* music. This idea of an emer-
gent, color-blind youth culture is central to the film's representation of
racism as a generational phenomenon, doomed to pass away as naturally
as one generation succeeds another.

In a rather more extended scene, in which Matt and Christina go out
for ice cream, this naturalization of racism's eclipse is reiterated, albeit
with a slightly different emphasis. This time, Matt's belief that American
racism justifies his opposition to Johanna's marriage is expressly shown to
be old-fashioned, out of step with the times and, in particular, the youth
culture of the 1960s.[22] The drive-in to which they go is a hangout for
teenagers, who sit around in their hot rods and sports cars listening to
loud rock music on their car radios. When the young, gum-chewing
carhop (Alexandra Hay) asks for Matt's order, he tells her he cannot remember what he had last time. After she lists a number of flavors, he decides he must have eaten Fresh Oregon Boysenberry, but when she brings
him his cone, he takes a first taste and grimaces—this is the wrong flavor.
After calling the carhop back, intending to return the ice cream, he takes a
second taste and decides that it is not so bad after all. When she finally
appears, he lamely informs her that although it was not the flavor he had
in mind, he likes it. As he and Christina exit the drive-in, he tells the
carhop to remind him of it the next time he comes in.

As the sequence progresses, the carhop's reaction to Matt changes.
Initially polite, by the time he leaves, she has come to see him as a trying
old man whom she has nevertheless to humor. Still the patriarch in his
own household, in the broader social setting Matt no longer seems powerful but instead seems to be slipping into his dotage.

The obvious differences in their tastes in music and cars serve to emphasize the generational gap separating Matt from the teenagers by
whom he is surrounded at the drive-in and with whom his daughter is
identified. More subtly, Matt is portrayed as unsettled by change—he
wants things to remain the same. On the other hand, his reaction to an
unfamiliar ice cream flavor suggests that he is not entirely inflexible: Since
he finds Fresh Oregon Boysenberry delicious, despite his initial aversion,
perhaps Johanna's chocolate boyfriend will be to his liking too once he
gets over his initial, and habitual, negative response to novelty.

Guess Who's Coming to Dinner uses this analogy to develop its understanding of racism as an effect of prejudice. Despite the seemingly trivi-

alizing nature of the parallel, it does dramatize an ontological assumption underlying the film's optimism. For whether someone finds a food pleasing is generally assumed to be simply a subjective fact about that person, and a fact that can be changed. In drawing the analogy, the film proposes that a person's response to the race (i.e., skin color) of another is also just a matter of taste—of individual, subjective preference for white skin over black or vice versa—and so as ephemeral as a preference for one or another ice cream flavor. This undergirds the film's optimism that racism can be eliminated. Matt will eventually get used to the color of his daughter's husband, just as he got used to an unfamiliar flavor of ice cream.[23]

Given the importance accorded the themes of change and generational succession, it is surprising that these do not figure as reasons for Matt's change of heart. Although he is repeatedly forced to confess that he is at sea in a world that no longer quite accords with his expectations, he never explicitly acknowledges what this implies about his own opposition to the marriage, namely, that it is based on empirical claims that do not reflect the realities of a rapidly changing society.

The reason for this is that this aspect of the film is addressed exclusively to its viewers. By depicting racism as sclerotic, the audience is pressured to support a more up-to-date politics of race. The only option the film allowed 1960s audiences who wanted to think of themselves as "with it," in touch with American reality, was to embrace the color-blindness the film associates with the hip younger generation. Although Matt is deeply troubled over his daughter's prospects, the film's confidence that racism is bound to disappear through generational succession sought to reassure that audience about the young couple's fate.

But if there is something to be said for the film's optimism, its strategy of representation gives the audience an easy out. For its white members are placed in the comfortable position of identifying themselves as supporters of integration while believing that nothing is required of them to bring it about. If racism will be eliminated through the natural process of generational succession, what need is there for social activism? So, despite their restored faith in Matt at the film's end, viewers can also feel superior to him, for they know that his anguish is unnecessary, much ado about nothing. The film's premature hopes for an inevitable eclipse of racism allow its white viewers to evade the critical self-scrutiny that would be entailed by a serious confrontation with racism; instead, they are permitted to remain as spectators while momentous struggles over the fate of America's Second Reconstruction rage about them.

Conflicting Strategies

The last problem with *Guess Who's Coming to Dinner* that I shall discuss, a conflict between its representational and narrative strategies, arises because of its makers' desire to preempt racist reactions to the on-screen portrayal of a passionate interracial romance. As a result, the film's narrative insistence on the passion rings hollow, for its representational strategy denies the audience convincing visual confirmation. The attempt to defeat racist outrage thus results in the sacrifice of the film's coherence.

We have seen that the makers of *Guess Who's Coming to Dinner* were acutely aware that their story of a love affair between a black man and a blonde woman skirted dangerously close to one of the central racist apparitions in America's psyche, an apparition the movie version of which the film scholar Donald Bogle has called "the brutal black buck" and which he traces back to D. W. Griffith's 1915 classic, *Birth of a Nation:*

> Bucks are always big, baaddd niggers, oversexed and savage, violent and frenzied as they lust for white flesh. . . . Griffith played on the myth of the Negro's high-powered sexuality, then articulated the great white fear that every black man longs for a white woman. Underlying the fear was the assumption that the white woman was the ultimate in female desirability, herself a symbol of white pride, power, and beauty. . . . Thus the black bucks of the film are psychopaths, one [Gus] always panting and salivating, the other [Silas Lynch] forever stiffening his body as if the mere presence of a white woman in the same room could bring him to a sexual climax. Griffith played hard on the bestiality of his black villainous bucks and used it to arouse hatred.[24]

The black male is in effect demonized, represented as in the grip of a sexuality both vicious and, in the presence of white women, uncontrollable. As Bogle points out, this involves the fantasy that white women possess a universal appeal, to which black males are particularly vulnerable.

Even though a half century separates *Birth of a Nation* from *Guess Who's Coming to Dinner*, it was no mistake to fear that many viewers would still, in 1967, identify John Prentice with the demonic sexuality of Griffith's blackface villains. If the film was to achieve its political objectives, it had to tell its story in a way that would not activate this most powerful of all racist tropes; otherwise the audience would not accept John and Johanna as romantic partners.

Earlier, we saw Sidney Poitier explain that the film could not address the issue of interracial romance squarely. We are now able to understand more precisely why. The continuing hold on the white imagination of the figure of the brutal black buck meant that the film had to develop a strategy for defusing viewer aversion and hostility to the representation of an attractive black male romantically involved with a beautiful, young white woman. To square this circle, *Guess Who's Coming to Dinner* must visually portray the passion between John and Johanna—about which we hear so much—with extraordinary discretion. Hence, the lengths to which it goes to exceptionalize John, to dissociate him from those ravenous black despoilers of white womanhood featured in *Birth of a Nation*. Only a lunatic racist could suspect this highly educated and refined man of an uncontrollable sexual desire for white women.

The film includes a number of specific narrative elements the sole purpose of which is to dissociate John from the stereotype of black male sexuality. For example, early in the film, her mother asks Johanna whether she and John have slept together. Johanna explains that they have not, but adds that it is John—and not she—who is responsible for this. This exchange serves no function other than that of acquitting John of lusting after white flesh. In a similar vein, to emphasize that John's sexual interest is not limited to white women, he is shown appreciatively eyeing Tillie's young assistant, Dorothy.

But by far the most important of these obliquities is *Guess Who's Coming to Dinner*'s determinedly desexualized representation of its central love affair. To prevent John from being seen as sexually voracious, we are offered no visual evidence of his passion for Johanna. For example, in the terrace scene discussed earlier that Christina, Matt, and we witness through a window, the two behave in such adolescent terms that the actors have trouble rendering their lines convincingly.

The importance of these representational choices, understandable though they are, is that what we see on-screen contradicts what we hear in the film's dialogue. Remember that central to its explanation of first Christina's and then Matt's change of heart is the evidence they are given for the unlikely couple's passionate attachment to one another. But it is difficult to credit these claims given the total lack of visible erotic energy between John and Johanna, even allowing for the greater sexual reticence one would expect in a film made in 1967. The film's attempt to make their passion a decisive reason for supporting the relationship finds no direct support in the viewers' experience.

To repeat, my goal in exposing these inconsistencies has not been to establish that *Guess Who's Coming to Dinner* is really a bad film. After all, there seems nearly unanimous agreement among both film scholars and the contemporaneous critics that the film is deeply flawed. But what neither these writers nor the film's makers have acknowledged is the extent to which this is due to the desire to achieve popular success with an audience whose racist attitudes made it difficult to believably portray a grand passion between a black man and a white woman. If *Guess Who's Coming to Dinner* is neutered by the contradiction between its narrative and representational strategies, that is less evidence of inferior filmmaking than of the highly problematic project underlying it. Indeed, in my view, the film warrants more sympathetic treatment than many of its dismissive critics allow, if only because the problematic social context in which and for which the film was made deserves to be factored into an assessment of its merit.

Guess Who's Coming to Dinner, then, is an appropriate film with which to begin our study of the interracial unlikely couple film for it bears witness to the complex political and aesthetic cross-currents such films must navigate. The legacy of racism is not simply a subject at issue in their narratives, it is inscribed in the very means by which such films tell their stories of unlikely love, stories in which they seek to assess the significance of racism and the prospects for its elimination.

Notes

1. Recently, there has been a growing recognition that "race" is a social construction in that there is no biological reality supporting the classification of human beings into different races. Theorists have reacted in different ways, some urging that the term be simply eschewed, others that the term always be placed in quotation marks. Although I continue to use the term "race" without any special markers, I acknowledge the constructed nature of race. For discussion of these issues, see, for example, Kwame Anthony Appiah, *In My Father's House: Africa in the Philosophy of Culture* (Oxford, UK: Oxford University Press, 1992), and David Theo Goldberg, *Racist Culture: Philosophy and the Politics of Meaning* (Oxford, UK, and Cambridge, MA: Blackwell, 1993).

2. "Spense and Supergirl," *Newsweek,* December 25, 1967, p. 70.

3. Donald Bogle, *Toms, Coons, Mulattos, Mammies, and Bucks: An Interpretive History of Blacks in American Films* (New York: Continuum, 1996), p. 217.

4. Thomas Cripps, *Making Movies Black: The Hollywood Message Movie from World War II to the Civil Rights Era* (New York and Oxford, UK: Oxford University Press, 1993), p. 289.

5. Stanley Kramer with Thomas M. Coffey, *A Mad, Mad, Mad, Mad World: A Life in Hollywood* (New York: Harcourt Brace & Company: 1997), p. 218. There is some question about the validity of Kramer's claim and, indeed, whether the

film does not compromise itself by using an interracial couple composed of a black man and a white woman to question the viability of liberal integrationism, since such a couple represents the racist fantasy of what is at stake in the politics of integration more generally, namely, giving black men access to white women, a view fatefully recorded, for example, in *Birth of a Nation* (1915).

6. Quoted in Donald Spoto, *Stanley Kramer: Film Maker* (New York: G. P. Putnam's Sons, 1978), pp. 275–276.

7. Spoto, *Stanley Kramer*, pp. 276–277.

8. This is recognized by Stanley Kauffmann ("Recent Wars," *The New Republic*, December 16, 1967, pp. 19 and 30) and Arthur Knight ("The New Look," *Saturday Review*, December 16, 1967, p. 47).

9. All quotations from *Guess Who's Coming to Dinner* are from my transcription of the film's sound track.

10. The time pressures the Draytons are under in deciding whether to approve the marriage increase during the course of the film when Johanna decides to accompany John to Geneva that same evening rather than join him in a couple of weeks.

11. This scene is a good example of the disparity between the actual presentation of the romantic relationship—one characterized more by their teasing affection than deep passion—and the paeans to that passion that other characters sing. I discuss this issue at length later in this chapter.

12. The long reverse zoom causes the audience to view the young couple's easy tenderness with one another as if seen through Christina's eyes. The intended result is that we should experience her sentiments as our own.

13. Even in 1991, there was still a strong aversion among whites to interracial marriage. According to the General Social Survey reported in the *New York Times*, December 2, 1992, 20 percent of whites thought that black-white marriages should be illegal, and 66 percent said they would "oppose a close relative's marrying a black person." These rather sobering figures should make us realize that there is still a strong sense among white Americans that interracial marriages are wrong, so that, *pace* the film, the attitudes Matt Drayton imputes to his fellow white Americans to justify his position have persisted.

14. The specific focus of Mary's claim—that male impotence is responsible for the two fathers' lack of sympathy for the couple—is transformed in Matt's speech into a claim about their inability to remember the significance of romantic love.

15. See, for example, Brendan Gill, "Good Causes," *The New Yorker*, December 16, 1967, pp. 108–110.

16. John Prentice Sr. has not changed his mind by the end of the film, but Matt patronizingly assures everyone that he will.

17. It might seem problematic to assume that a character's disapproval of this interracial couple is necessarily a sign of his or her racism, since there are other grounds on which to oppose exogamous (cross-group) marriage. But in the context of racist America in the 1960s, white opposition to an interracial couple

could be used as an index of racism. Generally, an individual's reservations about exogamous marriage can stem from other factors, such as a desire to preserve an imperiled group.

18. Gunnar Myrdal, *An American Dilemma: The Negro Problem and Modern Democracy* (New York: Harper and Row, 1944), p. lxxi.

19. An index of the influence of this study is its citation in footnote 11 of the Supreme Court's decision in *Brown versus Board of Education of Topeka*, 347 U.S. 483, 74 S.Ct. 686, in 1954.

20. The mammy is one of the central stereotypes discussed by Donald Bogle in *Toms, Coons, Mulattos, Mammies, and Bucks*. For a discussion of the reality behind this stereotype, see Deborah Gray White, *Ain't I a Woman? Female Slaves in the Plantation South* (New York and London: W. W. Norton & Co., 1985), pp. 46–61.

21. From this point of view, the most significant fact about John Prentice is that, at thirty-seven, he stands between the two generations of adults/parents and youths/children. The reason for this is that the generational structure of the Drayton family does not fit that of the broader society. Although Johanna is twenty-three, her naïveté makes her seem younger than that. The parental generation, however, is actually much older than is usual. That is, her parents are more of the age of standard grandparents. This nuclear family spans three generations, with the absent middle generation represented only by the intrusion of this black man. It is worth remembering that Martin Luther King Jr. was a member of this middle generation.

22. Released in 1967, the means the film uses to signify the 1960s are not those that we tend now to associate with that era.

23. It is worth noting explicitly that Matt's understanding of prejudice as resistant to generational eclipse has proved more prescient than the film's own view.

24. Bogle, *Toms, Coons, Mulattos, Mammies, and Bucks*, pp. 13–14.

7
Jungle Fever
Souring on
Forbidden Fruit

Angie, this love will overcome everything is in Walt Disney films. I've always hated Disney films. . . . You got with me despite your family because
you were curious about black . . . and I was curious about white.[1]

With these words, Flipper Purify (Wesley Snipes) announces to his lover,
Angela Tucci (Annabella Sciorra), that their affair, which forms the narrative center of Spike Lee's film *Jungle Fever* (1991), must end. Angie's hope
that their liaison might continue is a Disneyesque fantasy, he implies, alluding to the unrealism characteristic of Hollywood romances. And here,
although Flipper supplies no specific reference, he must have in mind
films—like *Guess Who's Coming to Dinner*—in which love triumphs over
adversity. According to Flipper, the reason they embarked on their affair
was their curiosity about what it would be like to have sex with a member
of another racial group.

The suspicion that, in this scene, Flipper serves as a mouthpiece for the
film's director is confirmed by an interview in which Spike Lee echoes
Flipper's disparaging remarks about standard Hollywood fare:

I am a romantic at heart. I do believe now, as Luther Vandross [a character
in Lee's film, *Do The Right Thing* (1989)] says, in the power of love. But at
the same time, we have to make a distinction between that which is real and
that fake Hollywood, Walt Disney walk into the sunset hand in hand. That
shit's never been real.[2]

Lee's explanation of why the affair had to end again echoes Flipper's lines:

> This film is about two people who are attracted to each other because of sexual mythology. She's attracted to him because she's been told that black men know how to fuck. He's attracted to her because all his life he's been bombarded with images of white women being the epitome of beauty and the standard that everything else must be measured against.[3]

Thus, according to Lee, sexual mythology creates the desire that his characters feel for one another. As a result, each is not really interested in the other as an individual but rather as merely the embodiment of a social stereotype. Once their curiosity has been sated, there is no reason for the affair to continue.

Lee's use of the expression "jungle fever" as the title of his film accords with this analysis. The term originated during the 1920s, the period of the Harlem Renaissance, and was used in connection with those whites who ventured Uptown for a taste of its club scene. The association is of blacks with the jungle, hence, with nature—and more to the point, with uninhibited sexuality. In other words, the black body—exotic, forbidden, alluring—is the object of the desire of those whites suffering from jungle fever. Lee's appropriation of the term is meant ironically, Flipper's attraction to Angie being a racially inverted version of the phenomenon.

By presenting Flipper's affair as the result of his desire to experience the Other socially denied to him, *Jungle Fever* invokes the trope of the forbidden fruit to tell the story of its unlikely couple. The lure of forbidden fruit is created by the interdiction against eating it. But the actual eating ever proves a disappointment, for the fruit does not have—cannot have—the sweetness anticipated. The moral is thus a conservative one: Those who have tasted sex with the Other return to socially sanctioned arrangements now convinced of their rightness. Given this narrative trajectory, the unlikely couple will help one or both of its partners to come to a clearer understanding of who they really are, but cannot in the end itself function as a source of support and affirmation for either. Rather, the paltriness of its satisfactions allows the partners to see how integral their socially appropriate relationships are to their authentic selves.

In what I call the "official interpretation," *Jungle Fever* employs the narrative figure of the forbidden fruit to focus attention on the way in which racial stereotypes produce the attraction that leads to the affair between Flipper and Angie. The film itself tells a deeper and more complex story, however, one only partially accounted for by the official interpretation.

There are two important elements to this unlikely romance that the official interpretation does not acknowledge: First, in telling Flipper's story, *Jungle Fever* is making a clear political statement about the need for separatism if blacks are to achieve racial equality with whites; second, the official interpretation fails to recognize that Angie's perspective on the affair is very different from Flipper's.

The film presents Flipper's interest in Angie as an extension of his overall attempt to integrate into white society, an attempt that proves a failure. From this point of view, the film is the story of Flipper's growing realization of the futility of the project of integration and his consequent embrace of black separatism. This aspect of *Jungle Fever* advances an implicit critique of the liberal politics of *Guess Who's Coming to Dinner* and of blacks like John Prentice who think that integration provides the solution to America's race problem.[4]

Jungle Fever argues that since white America cannot shed its racism, integrationism is a political strategy that will not bring blacks the equality they seek. Flipper's affair with Angie serves as one important element of the process of self-exploration that leads him both to acknowledge this and to identify with the entire black community as a whole. In addition, *Jungle Fever* ridicules *Guess Who's Coming to Dinner*'s view that "love is all there is," insisting that other social practices and institutions can make equally powerful claims on people's loyalties.

Although the formal structure of the film—which stresses the parallels between Flipper's and Angie's lives—suggests that their situations are fundamentally alike, Angie's class, gender, and ethnicity make her experience of the affair very different from his. Flipper claims that he was just curious about her as a white woman, but Angie actually falls in love. In making this plausible, *Jungle Fever* critiques the machismo of Italian American males. For Angie, Flipper's identity as a black is less important than his way of being a man, so different from what she sees in her Bensonhurst neighborhood of Brooklyn. Angie is attracted to Flipper's mode of masculinity because it is more adequate to her own sense of what she wants in a partner.

So although Flipper's entrance into the affair signifies further alienation from his blackness, Angie's acceptance of Flipper as a lover marks a positive step in her own self-development, despite the film's inability to find a narrative closure that can acknowledge this. Just as important as the film's critique of black males who pursue integration is its exploration of the racist and sexist masculinity of working-class, Italian American males.

Jungle Fever is thus a more complex and socially critical film than its formidably intelligent director allows. Desiring to tell a story that has a simple political moral, yet one that illuminates the realities that resulted in the brutal murder of Yusuf Hawkins, a young black who was looking for a used car in Bensonhurst, Lee has crafted a film that insistently belies his own perspective on it. The conflict between Lee's two intentions—to show that black men belong in the black community beside black women and to explain the race hatred that led to the bludgeoning of Hawkins—produces a film that, for all its shortcomings, presents interesting angles on both the black and white communities on which it focuses.

Being Black in White America

One way to think of *Jungle Fever*'s social analysis would be to treat the demise of the Flipper-Angie couple as an instance of a general truth that interracial romances are doomed by antiblack racism. The film's rough treatment of Angie lends emotional credence to the claim, for one does feel the plot of the film is being made to subserve an ideological intention. So broad a claim would be misleading, however, for the film is not concerned with the general question of whether interracial couples can survive in a racist society. Indeed, the film portrays a romance between white Paulie Carbone (John Turturro) and black Orin Goode (Tyra Ferrell) in sympathetic terms. In discussing the issue of the film's attitude toward interracial couples, Spike Lee has pointed to this subplot to rebut the charge that the film is a blanket indictment of interracial romance. Paulie and Orin's relationship is different from Flipper and Angie's because "their initial attraction is based on genuine feelings" rather than on sexual mythology.[5]

In distinguishing interracial couples on the basis of the grounds for their partners' attraction to one another, Lee thus distances himself from the universal opposition to interracial romance that some African American leaders have maintained. Malcolm X, for example, declared, "We do oppose intermarriage. We are as much against intermarriage as we are against all of the other injustices that our people have encountered."[6] Lee's inclusion of the Paulie-Orin couple in *Jungle Fever* emphasizes his rejection of such global condemnation of interracial love.

But how, then, are we to understand the broader significance of the film's portrayal of the failure of the Flipper-Angie couple? Although the complexities introduced by its maker's tangled intentions make it impossible to give a simple answer to this question, we can begin by attending to the way Flipper's experience of the relationship is represented. As we have seen, there is a virtual identity between Spike Lee's and Flipper's explanations of what the affair is about. By delving more deeply into their perspective on the affair, we will be able to unpack the moral/political message the film wishes to communicate.

Flipper is the archetypal "buppie"—black urban professional. Although married to a (light-skinned) African American woman, he has achieved professional success working as an architect in an all-white firm. Although he attempts to maintain a sense of himself as a black man—by requesting, for example, an African American secretary—Flipper wants to make it in the white world. Indeed, by most measures he has succeeded admirably, for his work allows him to ensure a high standard of living for his wife and daughter in the elite Sugar Hill section of Harlem. Flipper's situation at the outset of the film suggests that integration into American society is a possibility for those blacks who work hard.

The plot of the film shows that this premise is incorrect. Because whites are and will remain racist, the goal of integration cannot be realized. Flipper will not achieve the sort of acceptance by whites that he has struggled to get, for he will never be treated as an equal. Whites in the 1990s may allow blacks—or at least, certain blacks—a larger piece of the pie than in the days of legal segregation, but they will not accord them the equality that is the measure of a fully integrated society that has eliminated racial hierarchy.[7]

The film's attitude toward integration comes out very clearly in the subplot that revolves around Flipper's job at Mast and Covington. When the film opens, Flipper has been working at the firm since its founding and is responsible for much of its success. Nonetheless, the firm's two white partners do not give him the respect he thinks he deserves. This becomes clear when they hire a white secretary for him, disregarding his request to fill the position with a "sister." When they respond to his protests with specious arguments about always hiring the best person for the job, he sees condescension toward himself and cynicism toward the demands of African Americans to be treated fairly.

As a result of this slight, Flipper decides to ask to be made a partner. In a scene shot in a series of reversing 360-degree pans, Flipper reminds his bosses that he played an important role in the firm's rise and announces that the time has come for him to be rewarded. Playing good cop–bad cop, the two partners alternately dismiss his demand; assure him of their high regard; and urge that if he will just remain patient, they will someday give him the recognition he seeks. Infuriated by their attitude, Flipper quits.

In the following scene—in which Flipper tells his friend Cyrus (Spike Lee) about his affair with Angie—Flipper expands on his plans now that he has left the firm. Instead of worrying about being unemployed, he expresses his intention to start a firm of his own, one in which he will reap the benefits of his labor.

Even a schematic rendering of this subplot makes it clear that it is meant to establish the futility of African Americans' attempts to integrate into white society. The patronizing comments of Flipper's bosses substantiate the film's view that although white Americans benefit from the skills and efforts of African Americans, they are not capable of shedding their racist attitudes. Even though Flipper has made important contributions to the firm, its two white partners are intent on retaining control of the firm they see themselves as having built. The only way a black man can achieve equality in American society, the film suggests, is by forging his own destiny independent of whites—a strategy that Flipper opts for when he decides to start his own architectural firm.

This subplot, an allegory of the situation of African Americans in the United States, is meant to show that although some African Americans may be allowed a certain measure of success in white society, they will never be treated as equals. White Americans remain racist despite the efforts of intelligent and competent African American coworkers.

In making this argument, *Jungle Fever* repeats a view of the persistence of white-American racism that has many exponents in scholarly circles. For example, in responding to William Julius Wilson's influential *The Declining Significance of Race,* Kenneth B. Clark has written, "It is a fact that in the struggle for racial justice, American blacks are now confronted with more subtle and sophisticated manifestations of racism." Going on to discuss the ways in which such racism is manifested in relation to blacks in high-status jobs, he writes,

> Tokenism, rather than genuine compliance with Affirmative Action and Equal Employment Opportunity requirements, remains the rule in spite of the Civil Rights Act of 1964. In spite of some few exceptions, even these few blacks [in executive, managerial, and policymaking positions] are not yet fully accepted in terms of their qualities and characteristics as individuals. They tend to be perceived as symbols. . . . Not infrequently these blacks are not held to the same standard of on-the-job performance; they are either evaluated more severely or more leniently than others.[8]

The subplot concerning Flipper's job seems devised to illustrate Clark's point. The racism of his white bosses, although somewhat subtler than outright prejudice, reveals the hollow promise of integration.

This belief in the intractability of white racism clearly distinguishes *Jungle Fever's* social analysis from *Guess Who's Coming to Dinner's*. Relying on Gunnar Myrdal's view that the racism of white Americans would be defeated by the "high national and Christian precepts" they profess,[9] *Guess Who's Coming to Dinner* espouses a confident integrationism. *Jungle Fever's* less sanguine view of white America's willingness to change reflects bitter historical experience. Three decades after the civil rights movement's successful challenge to the legal framework of America's racial hierarchy, African Americans remain subject to racial prejudice and discrimination. *Jungle Fever* cannot share the optimism of *Guess Who's Coming to Dinner* that white Americans will finally accept African Americans as fully equal citizens of the Republic.

Flipper's response to his employers' racism exemplifies the self-help philosophy of black nationalism, the central tenet of which is that African Americans need to control the economies of their own communities. In different contexts and for various reasons, this separatist strategy has been advocated by black nationalists since at least the time of Booker T. Washington, who argued that the best means of "elevating" the black race was for blacks to "own and operate the most successful farms [and become] the largest tax-payers," for political rights and recognition will then follow.[10] In the 1910s and 1920s, Marcus Garvey promoted "economic cooperation through racial solidarity" as the means that would allow American blacks to spearhead the redemption of Africa.[11] More recent black nationalists have returned to Washington's original vision of economic separatism as the only viable strategy for ameliorating the situation of blacks in America. For example, in words that strikingly echo those of Washington, Malcolm X declared,

> When the black man in this country awakens, becomes intellectually mature and able to think for himself, you will then see that the only way he will become independent and recognized as a human being on the basis of equality with all other human beings, he has to have what they have and he has to be doing for himself what others are doing for themselves.[12]

In a similar vein, Elijah Muhammad, Malcolm's mentor, repeatedly emphasized the need for economic self-help:

> The white Man spends his money with his *own kind*, which is natural. You, too, must do this. Help to make jobs for your own kind. Take a lesson from

the Chinese and Japanese, the Puerto Rican and the Cubans, and go all out and support your own kind. . . . The so called American Negro . . . is today in the worst economic condition of any human being in the wilderness of North America. Unemployment is mounting and he feels it worst. . . . You, the black Man, are the only member of the human race that deliberately walks past the place of business of one of your own kind—a black man, and spend your dollars with your natural enemy.[13]

Taking for granted the racism of white Americans, Elijah Muhammad here urges his black followers to band together to ameliorate the condition of black America.

Jungle Fever's advocacy of a similar economic strategy allies its political perspective with that of black nationalism. The film does more than simply portray Flipper's eagerness to succeed in the white world, however; it positions his integrationist ambitions historically as a response to the ineffective and morally suspect attitudes of his parents' generation. The elder Purifys are meant to embody two no-longer relevant models of blackness, and it is against this background of historical irrelevance that Flipper's pursuit of integration is presented. The problem with this choice, according to the film, is that it is achieved at the expense of his identity as a black man. The film therefore requires him to find a way of being-in-the-world that allows him to embrace his blackness.

Flipper's father, the Good Reverend Doctor (Ossie Davis), provides a first model of blackness. When we initially encounter him, the Good Reverend Doctor is reading aloud the passage from 1 Corinthians in which Paul explains the origin of marriage: "Nevertheless, *to avoid* fornication, let every man have his own wife, and let every woman have her own husband."[14] The Good Reverend Doctor lives in a world he cannot fathom without the moral guidance provided by the Bible. Through its portrait of the Good Reverend Doctor, the film depicts a black religiosity of bombast, out of touch with the real problems of contemporary African American life: In a later scene, Flipper angrily asks his father, "Do you ever just talk?" For this obdurate patriarch, the Devil is responsible for all those who stray from the path of Biblical righteousness. Because Flipper believes that individuals are alone responsible for what they do, he sees his father's use of religion as an evasion.

Flipper's long-suffering mother, Lucinda (Ruby Dee), provides a second model of blackness. The butt of indignities from both her husband and her children, she simply accepts them for the sake of the illusion of domestic peace. This woman wants to do the right thing for her family, but she can offer them only an all-excusing, ineffectual love.

The futility of both models is established through the subplot involving Gator (Samuel L. Jackson), Flipper's older brother and a crack addict. When Gator arrives at his parents' apartment, his father orders him from the house because he sings and dances, ungodly behavior the Good Reverend Doctor cannot condone. But his mother slips him some money and then lies to her husband about what she has done.

Both ways of coping with Gator are inadequate. Banning him from his home thrusts him deeper into the world of drugs that is his undoing. (As if this were not clear, the Good Reverend Doctor winds up killing his own son without regret to keep him out of the house.) But providing him with money to feed his habit, although it sustains the familial connection, does nothing to confront the problem of drugs itself. In fact, Lucinda only succeeds in deceiving herself as well as her husband about what Gator really needs.

Since neither religious escapism nor uncritical familial protectiveness are adequate to the complex and difficult realities of being an ambitious young black in the 1990s, Flipper's need to forge a new mode of life for himself is understandable. Given these alternatives, the option of integrating into white society seems eminently preferable.

The Education of Flipper Purify

Even as *Jungle Fever* portrays Flipper's pursuit of integration into the world of white professionalism, it also demonstrates the futility of his striving. In depicting his affair with Angie, the film deepens its critique of Flipper's integrationism by expanding it beyond his work life: Flipper, it argues, has taken this path because of his black self-hatred. By the end of the film, *Jungle Fever* shows him identifying with the black community as a whole, achieving thereby a more adequate sense of self.

Angela Tucci is the white temp Flipper's bosses have hired against his wishes. Although upset that they have not honored his request for an African American, he decides not to push the issue. Their affair occurs as a result of an intimacy that develops between them as they eat take-out meals together while working late. Angie prefers long hours at the office to cooking dinner for her father and brothers. As they get to know one another, desire begins to stir. After a third late night, as Angie prepares to leave, Flipper volunteers, "You know, Angie, I've never cheated on my wife before." She turns to go, he calls her back, the two kiss, and they make love on his drafting table (see Photo 7.1).

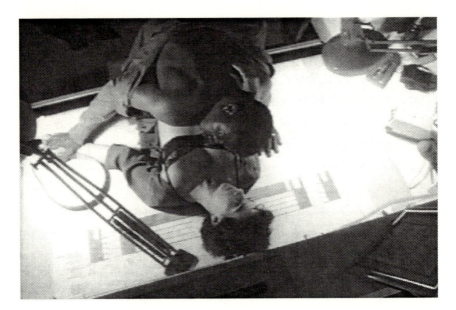

Photo 7.1 Tasting forbidden fruit

As we have seen in Chapter 6, the makers of *Guess Who's Coming to Dinner* were so concerned about white outrage over the on-screen presentation of a sexually potent black male that they went out of their way to desexualize John, the Sidney Poitier character; in this scene of heated interracial love making, Flipper's sexuality is frankly depicted.

There are a number of reasons why *Jungle Fever* could allow itself a more directly sexual representation of its unlikely relationship than could *Guess Who's Coming to Dinner*. First, the intervening years have seen a significant relaxation in the standards of what can be shown on-screen. *Jungle Fever* thus benefits from an overall atmosphere of greater freedom in the treatment of sexuality. Second, insofar as there has been a decline in prejudice among those segments of American society likely to see a Spike Lee film, there is less chance that an interracial sex scene will be negatively received. Furthermore, the fact that Lee is a self-consciously *black* filmmaker means that he is not exclusively concerned—not even primarily concerned—with the responses of his white audience.

The question of why Flipper actually starts this affair is one the film never answers directly. From the beginning, Flipper's relationship with his wife, Drew (Lonette McKee), is portrayed in idyllic terms. We first see them as the camera tracks into their bedroom to reveal the couple making love. Their early morning love making is passionate and, we later learn, a daily occurrence. Evidently, marital difficulties are not the motive for Flipper's dalliance.

Whenever the question of why he is involved with Angie is put to him, Flipper becomes inarticulate. With his friend Cyrus, Flipper says, "I have to admit, I've always been curious about Caucasian women." When his brother, Gator, finds Angie in Flipper's Greenwich Village apartment, Flipper mumbles in discomfort, "Gator, it's complex, man." And when Angie responds to Flipper's assurances that he has a great marriage and loves his wife by asking what he is doing with her, the best he can manage is, "I honestly don't know." The only real explanation he offers is "jungle fever"—he was drawn into their affair by a desire to see what it would be like to have sex with a white woman.

But even if Flipper's account of his own motivation is accurate, it still leaves too much unexplained. More light is shed on this question by Flipper's now-estranged wife, Drew, who throws him out of the house after learning of the affair. When Flipper approaches her in the department store in which she works, to seek a reconciliation, Drew is too deeply hurt to take him back, and repulsing his overture, she tells him why. Flipper's desire for a white lover calls into question the grounds of his love for her, Drew explains. Light-skinned, herself the product of an interracial marriage—her father was white—she recounts how she was made to suffer as a youth, enduring such epithets as "yellow bitch," "octoroon," "quadroon." This has sensitized her to how the black community has internalized white racism's obsession with skin color.[15] She accuses Flipper of having desired her for her light skin and now having gone a step further—into the arms of a real white woman—as a result of hatred for his own dark color.

Drew's analysis of Flipper's attraction to Angie provides the best explanation for the affair the film offers. By his involvement with a white woman, Flipper has advanced his project of integration. Drew charges that this desire is fed by black self-hatred: Her husband rejects the black world he sees both in his parents' home and on the streets of Harlem. To deny his own membership in this community, to rid himself of feelings of inferiority, Flipper repudiates those whose skin color resembles his own—as if such acts will make him less black.

Once Flipper's behavior is understood as rooted in self-hatred, the trajectory of the narrative becomes clear: The affair constitutes a step toward

Flipper's full embrace of his own identity as a black man, something he has resisted up to now. We have already seen him affirm his black identity in one important aspect of his life: quitting the white firm for which he has worked to start his own practice. His rejection of Angie will mark a second crucial step in this process.

Other narrative elements in *Jungle Fever* also mark Flipper's growth toward self-acceptance, his relationship to the black underclass being the most important of these. This issue is an immediate one for Flipper because Gator is a crackhead. At the outset of the film, Flipper wants nothing to do with his older brother, whom he simply wishes to avoid. At first, albeit reluctantly, he gives him some money with which to buy drugs, but he later refuses to do even this. It is as if Gator's mere existence belies the Flipper he has chosen to be, as if the shame of having a brother like that is all that Flipper can think about when confronted by Gator.

Although Gator's death robs Flipper of the chance to embrace him as a brother, Flipper is given the opportunity to make such a gesture, if only symbolically. He is twice accosted by a child prostitute, evidently an addict, who offers to "suck his dick" for first five dollars and then two, the first time as he takes his daughter, Ming (Veronica Timbers), to school. Horrified, he thrusts the young prostitute away and hurriedly drags Ming across the street, hurting and frightening her. When they reach the other side—and are thus safe from contamination—he yells at the frightened Ming that he will kill her if he ever catches her using drugs.

Flipper panics because he feels defiled by the approach of this pitiful and desperate young prostitute. His threat to kill his daughter if she ever uses drugs—foreshadowing his own brother's fate—indicates the extremity of his need to distance himself from the underclass. Since this scene occurs after he has separated from his wife and daughter, it may also stem from his awareness that his own absence may make Ming more vulnerable to the temptation of drugs.[16]

In the film's final scene, Flipper, who has now ended his affair with Angie and begun the process of reconciliation with Drew, again encounters this same child prostitute. But this time he hugs her to him and screams the anguished "No!" that ends the narrative. Flipper's embrace and cry seal his symbolic identification with the underclass and so measure the distance he has traveled toward self-acceptance, assuming responsibility for his community with all the anguish this implies.

By the end of *Jungle Fever*, then, Flipper has learned who he is; his story is one of growth and self-discovery. This seemingly successful African

American's pursuit of a politics—both public and personal—of integration is shown to stem from racial self-hatred. Thus, Flipper's growing awareness of his need to accept his own blackness requires him to turn toward separatism in both the public sphere—to found his own practice—and in his personal life—to reject his white lover and return to his family.

In presenting the story of Flipper's abortive affair with Angie as an example of the motif of the forbidden fruit, *Jungle Fever* adopts a narrative structure more usual in romances involving cross-class couples. One of the partners—customarily of the inferior class—has the idea that life in the upper reaches of society is more exciting; ascent is attained by means of a sexual liaison with a social superior; once the affair has been consummated, however, the ascending partner discovers that desire for the Other had only been a case of forbidden fruit—seemingly sweet because prohibited, but sour once tasted; the sobered climber returns home and the structure of society is reaffirmed. Instances of this plotline are legion, recent among them such films as *Someone to Watch Over Me* (1987), *Angie* (1994), and *Crossing Delancey* (1988).

Clearly, the figure of the forbidden fruit implies a very different narrative logic from the familiar schema of "love conquers all" embodied in a film like *Guess Who's Coming to Dinner* and ridiculed by *Jungle Fever*. Their choice of narrative line is surely due to underlying differences in the two films' understanding of race and racism. Where *Guess Who's Coming to Dinner* was predicated on the possibility of a color-blind society, *Jungle Fever's* use of the forbidden fruit narrative makes sense precisely because it sees racism as intractable, impossible to eliminate. In the climate of late-1960s racial activism, *Guess Who's Coming to Dinner* attempted to vindicate liberal integrationism by showing that white Americans could rise even to the challenge of intermarriage. At the beginning of the 1990s, *Jungle Fever* sees such faith as illusory: White America, it says, is and always will be racist. The only plausible solution for the black community is to turn its energies to building institutions it can control.

Necessarily, therefore, the two films also differ in their assessment of the possibilities of interracial romance, although *Jungle Fever's* insistence that Flipper does not love Angie obscures the contrast. For *Guess Who's Coming to Dinner*, nothing should or could stand in the way of romantic love; *Jungle Fever* argues that there are other, equally compelling, claims on our commitments. Because neither the black nor the white community is willing to accept Flipper and Angie into its midst—a point made by an interaction with a waitress in a Harlem restaurant and by a confrontation with white policemen—the couple becomes socially isolated. Flipper's rejection of Angie can be seen as an acknowledgment that he needs more than love, that playing a role in the black community is necessary to confirm his identity.

Jungle Fever's forbidden fruit narrative illustrates how an abortive affair can play as important a role in personal development as a successful romance. In this respect, the film inverts the usual claim of unlikely couple films. Flipper attains a more adequate sense of himself because the affair with Angie does *not* give him what he needs—namely, acceptance of his identity as a black man. It does, however, allow him to see what is necessary for him to achieve such self-acceptance: a more complete identification with his community. Thus, unsuccessful affairs can foster moral development by revealing that what is taken for granted is itself nourishing and important.

Because *Jungle Fever* treats Flipper's commitment to integration as an expression of self-hatred, it is able to present his rejection of Angie as a step in his growing acceptance of his own skin color. In so doing, *Jungle Fever* asserts that there is a specific way of being black for an upper-middle-class African American man, one that involves identification with the entire African American community and, especially, its most oppressed members.

Although Flipper's story may make sense as a psychological portrait, it cannot be made to serve the purpose the film assigns it, that is, a general analysis of the inadequacy of integration as a political strategy for African Americans, unless, implausibly, every African American committed to integration can be shown to suffer from racial self-hatred. But *Jungle Fever's* psychologizing of the politics of race is reductive in any case, for it assumes that the legitimacy of the political agenda it opposes can be undermined by providing a psychological account of why individuals are attracted to it. An adequate critique of integration needs to do more than develop a psychological analysis of its adherents. So, despite its interest as a story about one man's confrontation with his own internalized racism, *Jungle Fever* cannot bear the political weight its maker intends.

Angie's Story

One of the most pronounced narrative features of *Jungle Fever* is the formal parallelism it sets up between Flipper's and Angie's lives. A number of crucial scenes work to emphasize this similarity. For example, after Flipper tells Cyrus about the affair, Angie tells two of her girlfriends. Or, after Flipper is thrown out of his home by his wife, Angie is thrown out of hers by her father. And after their affair has ended, the film makes an effort at symmetric narrative closure, with both returning to the homes from which they had been expelled. The film even presents their stake in the relationship as similar: Both stand to lose ties to family and community.

This insistent narrative parallelism seems intended to give the impression—one that Lee makes explicit in his enunciation of the official interpretation—that Flipper and Angie engage in their affair for the same reason. Since Flipper says outright that he has been motivated by a curiosity about the other race, the assumption is that Angie too has acted out of similar motivation.

In assessing this interpretation, we first need to acknowledge that Angie, although not prejudiced, is not color-blind. She is right to fear that her family will be shocked to hear of the affair and skin color does play a role in her attraction to Flipper.[17] But despite her awareness of Flipper's race, this is not the primary reason for her attraction to him. Indeed, the film actually depicts Angie resisting Flipper's attempt to assimilate her experience of the affair to his. In the scene with which I opened this chapter, Flipper begins his speech: "Angie, I don't think there's anything left to talk about. I give up. I don't love you and I doubt if you ever loved me." To which Angie replies, "Don't tell me what I felt or didn't feel." Although this is hardly a full account of her own experience of the relationship, it is sufficient to establish that Angie's feelings differed from those acknowledged by Flipper. The suggestion is, in fact, that she loved Flipper, if only for a time.[18]

The film's depiction of Angie is one of its most serious flaws. On the one hand, she is presented as an interesting human being trapped in a suffocating environment, and because of this, the audience develops a great deal of sympathy for her. On the other hand, she is not really allowed to express her own perspective on her relationship with Flipper. She is treated as simply a foil for Flipper, the real star of the film. It is as if the audience's sympathy for Angie must not be allowed to extend too far.

One reason for this ambivalent attitude lies in the conflict between the director and the actress who played her about what was motivating Angie. Lee wanted Angie's story to mirror Flipper's, but Annabella Sciorra apparently believed that something else moved her character. After the filming, it was generally acknowledged that Sciorra had refused to play the role in the way that Lee had demanded, insisting that Angie be allowed to express her perspective more fully. Lee actually testified to this fact in an interview with Arsenio Hall in which he admitted that he had quarreled with the actress: "I couldn't put a gun to her head and it was too far along in the shoot to fire her."[19]

The ambivalence manifested toward Angie is deeper than this explanation allows, however, springing from the very conception of the film. In developing its plot, Lee wanted to do two things: First, as we have seen, he wanted to tell a cautionary tale about a black man who has chosen to define his life through integration. Thus, *Jungle Fever*'s "morality tale"[20] has to end with a clear message to the effect that blacks need to help themselves rather than look to white society. This is why the predominant difference in the couple must be a racial one.

But Lee also has said that his first inspiration for the film was the incident in which Yusuf Hawkins, a young black man from Harlem, was killed because a group of Italian American youths in Bensonhurst thought that he was dating a woman from their community. In fact, the film, which begins by projecting a photograph of Hawkins on the screen, is dedicated to him. Attention to this story about the prejudices of the Italian Americans in Bensonhurst and their fears of black sexuality is therefore important for understanding the film. As Lee put it,

> Harlem and Bensonhurst for me are more than just geographical locations; it's what they represent. Yusuf was killed because they thought he was the black boyfriend of one of the girls in the neighborhood. What it comes down to is that white males have problems with black men's sexuality.[21]

Hence, the film includes many scenes in Paulie's candy store that show the racist attitudes of Bensonhurst's Italian American men and link these attitudes to their sexual insecurities. The reactions of Angie's father to his discovery that she is dating a black man, as well as of Paulie's father when he finds out that his son is seeing a black woman, emphasize the violent racism of this community. The Italian Americans in this film still harbor the crude racist attitudes that many social theorists have claimed are no longer prevalent in American society.

But one of the awkward consequences of trying to shed light on the fate of Yusuf Hawkins is that class issues are raised that impact on the racial story that is supposed to be at the center of *Jungle Fever*. To make the film relevant to Hawkins's tragic fate, Lee chose to have Angie come from Bensonhurst. This meant that she would have to be a working-class woman. As a result, the unlikely couple she forms with Flipper is separated by class as well as racial difference. This means, in turn, that the two characters may accord different weights to either difference. Thus, even though Flipper sees Angie as primarily a white woman, thereby allowing her working-class status less weight in his relationship with her, Flipper's class identity may weigh more heavily with Angie than his race.[22] And in fact, from her point of view, the dominant difference in the couple is class. Although Lee's concern to tell a story with a particular moral does not allow him to validate this difference of perspective, his own aspirations for the film require its expression.

If Angie's primary significance for Flipper is her whiteness, this is ironic. As Gator notes when he meets her, Flipper's choice of a dark-haired, Italian American, working-class woman as the white woman with whom to have an affair is doing things "the hard way." Johanna Drayton is more the type one normally associates with black male desire for a white woman—wealthy, liberal, and blonde.

In any case, to see how Angie's view of Flipper privileges his class identity over his race, we only need ask why Angie is interested in having an affair with him in the first place. After all, given the prejudices of the men in her life, such an affair is likely to spell trouble. As with Flipper, there must be some strong motivation for pursuing this unlikely affair.

And indeed there is: Angie is willing to break with the norms of her community and enter into a sexual relationship with a black man because she is suffocating in Bensonhurst, her aspirations stifled by the limited horizon of the men of the community. With the exception of her boyfriend, Paulie, *Jungle Fever* portrays the men of that working-class Italian American neighborhood as menacing louts. In a number of scenes in Paulie's candy store, the repartee among the young men who hang out there reveals them to be ignorant and racist. These are the sorts of men, the film is saying, responsible for the murder of Yusuf Hawkins, and its blunt portrayal is intended to explain how they could come to see him as a threat to their community.

But even more important than these unattractive generalities is the film's depiction of Angie's home life. The signal scene in this regard takes place when Angie comes home from her first day of work at Mast and Covington. Her father and two brothers sit on a couch in their living room watching a baseball game as the grocery-laden Angie opens the door to be met by complaints about how late she is and how hungry they are for their dinner. Even so, Angie is left to prepare dinner alone, because her brothers refuse to help, apparently a routine occurrence. There follows a cut to her serving the food and her father telling her brothers to thank their sister for the meal. But her younger brother, Jimmy (Michael Imperioli), complains that he preferred his mother's cooking, whereupon the whole place erupts in a loud argument, totally disrupting the dinner. The scene closes with Angie's exasperated, "What a fucking life."

Angie's is a classic case of the "second-shift" problem, where working-class women who perform a full day's labor outside of the home must continue to assume all of the tasks within the home mandated by the traditional gendered division of labor.[23] The fact that Angie had an exhausting day, including a long commute to and from Manhattan, does not affect the expectations of the male members of her family that she, as the sole woman of the house, is still responsible for such chores as cooking dinner. The contrast between the attractive and vivacious young woman we encounter at Mast and Covington and the put-upon drudge she becomes when she returns home to Bensonhurst lets us see that Angie is in a trap from which she does not know how to escape.

This sense of Angie's life as a dead end is exacerbated when Paulie comes to pick her up for the evening. Angie's brothers goad him, warning that he better not be "fucking their sister" (see Photo 7.2). In the next scene, Angie tells him that she is upset he does not stand up to her brothers, but just takes their abuse.

Paulie's passivity, although it marks a way of surviving as a sensitive human being in this appallingly restrictive social environment, and is more appealing to Angie than the imbecilic machismo of her two brothers, ultimately disqualifies him as a romantic partner. Paulie is himself dominated by his father and seems unable to take control of his life by, for example, setting limits to the demands his father makes on him or even by asking Angie to marry him.

Jungle Fever attempts to portray the men of Bensonhurst in a way that makes it understandable how they could have killed a young African American simply because they suspected that he was the lover of one of their woman. In the process, the film necessarily depicts the harsh constraints such attitudes impose on the lives of the women of that community. As a result, Angie engages our sympathies because she emerges as a true victim of sexism and racism.

Against this backdrop, it is not surprising that Angie finds herself willing to have an affair with Flipper, for he represents a way of being assertively male that avoids both the violence-tinged working-class masculinity of Angie's brothers and also Paulie's passivity. Flipper's refine-

Photo 7.2 Angie's brothers hassle the passive Paulie

ment, superior to that of the men with whom Angie lives in Bensonhurst, is due in large measure to his class status. This means that Angie views him as a man more from another class than of a different race. In fact, Flipper's class location links him to a world that has been closed off to her. Although there may be some racial aspects to the world that he opens for her, its primary aspect is class. To put it epigrammatically, whereas Lee seems to think of Flipper as representing Harlem to Angie's Bensonhurst, to her he actually represents Manhattan and all that is contained there. He provides her with access not so much to black sexuality as to upper-class masculinity. And this seems to promise her a means of escape from the slow death she had been living in Bensonhurst. The sexual curiosity Flipper (and through him, Spike Lee) attributes to Angie plays some role in her attraction to him, but it is not its most important factor, and it does not, in any case, explain the extent of her interest in him. Instead, the overwhelming reason for Angie's interest is that he represents desired possibilities. Flipper's way of being a man and the life that he leads, rather than his race, are what attract her to him.

This is why the attempt to see Angie as simply a victim of jungle fever is so problematic. In Angie, the film has drawn a rich portrait of a young woman who wants more for herself than her education, gender, and class

allow her to have. Her affair with Flipper holds the promise of an enlarge-
ment of her life. Lee's allegiance to a racialized understanding of Angie,
however, causes him to treat her in a manner inconsistent with that rich
portrait. When, after her affair with Flipper has ended, Angie returns
home to Bensonhurst, with her tail between her legs and with not even
the prospect of resuming her relationship with Paulie, she is not acting as
the film has led us to believe she would. Ruled by his desire for a formal
parallelism consistent with his simple moral message, Lee will not allow
Angie to move in directions he has opened up for her. There seems no
reason for her to slink home, especially since it is clear that whatever
awaits her there will be unpleasant at best. In the terms it has set out for
her, the film could have allowed her to accept the end of the affair, but
given her the psychic resources to forge a life beyond the narrow constraints of Bensonhurst. As Angie returns home, we have no sense that
anything will come of her affair but the destruction of her life's possibilities. Although Flipper has endured pain, that pain has some meaning; in
Angie's case, not only has she suffered at Flipper's hands, but the film itself dismisses her suffering, for she is not allowed to have gained anything
as a result of her efforts.

Conclusion

Given the pathos of Angie's life, Spike Lee's refusal to acknowledge this
aspect of the film is a striking indication that the significance of her relationship with Flipper exceeds the understanding that the film's director
permits himself. For him, his film is a morality tale, a didactic exercise
aimed primarily at upper-middle-class African American males. The lesson they are supposed to take away from a viewing of this film is that their
desire for relationships with white women may be fed by racial self-
hatred.

   This aspect of the film represents Lee's attempt to counter *Guess Who's
Coming to Dinner*'s message that integration is a viable strategy for overcoming the racism of American society. The fate of *Jungle Fever*'s unlikely
couple is intended to show the futility of that strategy.

   To convey that message, Lee not only treats race as the dominant difference in the Flipper-Angie couple, he claims that it is the only difference that counts. As we have seen, however, this story has another dynamic, one fueled by class and gender differences rather than simply racial
ones. Although the film refuses to fully develop this story, enough of it is

present for us to see it as a separate narrative strand undermined only by the film's ending. If there is a real tragedy in/of this film, it is Angie's failure to realize a better life for herself.

In a way, the most interesting thing about *Jungle Fever* is the fact that it combines these two narratives in a single story. Unfortunately, Spike Lee's desire to convey a simple political line results in a failure to give both narratives their fullest development. Nonetheless, we can see that they are both present in the film and account for a good deal of our interest in it. Even in our most intimate relationships, we do not always fully understand how other human beings experience their world because they bring to that experience frames of reference derived from membership in social groups other than ones to which we belong. Although Angie and Flipper come together for a while, they do so for very different reasons. Had *Jungle Fever* been willing to acknowledge the complexity of its own story, it would have been an even more interesting and compelling film.

Notes

1. All quotations from *Jungle Fever* are from my transcription of the film's sound track.

2. Jack Kroll, Vern E. Smith, and Andrew Murr, "Spiking a Fever," *Newsweek,* June 10, 1991, p. 46. This issue of *Newsweek* featured a picture of Spike Lee on the cover.

3. Kroll et al., "Spiking a Fever," p. 45.

4. That *Jungle Fever* has an important relationship to *Guess Who's Coming to Dinner* can be seen, for example, from the fact that Kroll et al. begin "Spiking a Fever" with a discussion of *Guess Who's Coming to Dinner.*

5. Lee, quoted in Kroll et al., "Spiking a Fever," p. 46.

6. Malcolm X, *By Any Means Necessary* (New York: Pathfinder Press, 1970), p. 9.

7. The African Americans shown in this film are either affluent—like Flipper's family and their friends—or members of the underclass—like his brother, Gator. The film thus reflects a growing polarization of the African American community into these two classes. For a general discussion of the significance of this, see William Julius Wilson, *The Declining Significance of Race* (Chicago: University of Chicago Press, 1980).

8. Kenneth B. Clark, "Contemporary Sophisticated Racism," in *The Declining Significance of Race? A Dialogue Among Black and White Social Scientists,* Joseph R. Washington Jr., ed. (Philadelphia: n.p., 1979), pp. 100–101.

9. Gunnar Myrdal, *An American Dilemma: The Negro Problem and Modern Democracy* (New York: Harper and Row, 1944), p. lxxi.

10. Booker T. Washington, *The Future of the American Negro* (Boston: Small, Maynard and Company, 1899), p. 233.

11. E. U. Essien-Udom, *Black Nationalism: A Search for an Identity in America* (Chicago and London: University of Chicago Press, 1962), p. 37.

12. Malcolm X, *By Any Means*, p. 9.

13. Elijah Muhammad, *Herald-Dispatch* (Los Angeles), November 21, 1959, pp. 3 and 10. Quoted in Essien-Udom, *Black Nationalism*, pp. 164–165.

14. The quotation is from 1 Corinthians 7: 2.

15. Spike Lee's second feature film, *School Daze* (1988), a musical set in a Southern black college, satirizes this very obsession.

16. Here, Lee is mobilizing the claim that absent black fathers are a serious problem with ghetto life. Two of his recent films—*Get on the Bus* (1997) and *He Got Game* (1998)—develop this theme further.

17. The film contains two scenes that explicitly call attention to this aspect of her desire. The first one occurs during one of the intimate take-out dinners that the two of them have after work as a prelude to their affair. When Flipper confronts Angie by claiming that she was fascinated by his dark skin, she denies it, but then admits that she was looking at it. In the second one, as the two of them stroll through an amusement park, she asks him whether it is true that black men do not like to "go down" on women. Both times, the film clearly calls attention to the presence of a sexual mythology as playing a role in Angie's view of Flipper.

18. One of the few reviewers of the film to notice this point is Bert Cardullo. See his "Law of the Jungle," *Hudson Review*, 44 (1991–1992): pp. 639–647.

19. Quoted in Brian D. Johnson, "Sex at the Color Bar: Spike Lee Dissects Inter-racial Romance," *Macleans*, June 17, 1991, p. 55.

20. I take the term "morality tale" from Douglas Kellner's analysis of Lee's films. See his "Spike Lee's Morality Tales," in *Philosophy and Film*, Cynthia A. Freeland and Thomas E. Wartenberg, eds.(New York and London: Routledge, 1995), pp. 201–217.

21. Kroll et al., "Spiking a Fever," p. 45.

22. It may be that Angie's being from the working class is an important factor in Flipper's deciding to pursue her. The film does not really provide evidence for or against this.

23. For a discussion of this problem, see Arlie Russell Hochschild, *The Second Shift: Working Parents and the Revolution at Home* (New York: Viking, 1989).

8

Mississippi Masala

Love in a
Postcolonial World

Set in Greenwood, Mississippi, in the summer of 1990, Mira Nair's
Mississippi Masala (1991) tells the story of the romance between Mina
(Sarita Choudhury), a young Indian immigrant from Uganda, and
Demetrius (Denzel Washington), an African American and native
Mississippian. Because Mina's family was expelled from Uganda, exiled by
Idi Amin, as were all Ugandans of Asian descent, her father, Jay (Roshan
Seth), who wishes in any case for his daughter to marry within their im-
migrant enclave, adamantly opposes her liaison with a black man.
Although the film's narrative centers on Mina's relationship with
Demetrius, Jay's continuing obsession with their expulsion is an impor-
tant ancillary theme—as the film's wrenching sequence depicting the
family's departure from Uganda indicates.

Mississippi Masala's affirmation of a woman's right to choose her own
romantic partner rather than submit to the wishes of her parents links this
film to the tradition vindicating romantic love—traceable at least as far
back as *Romeo and Juliet*—that we saw animate the critique of racism in
Guess Who's Coming to Dinner. Indeed, because the Indian community in
Greenwood supports the traditional practice of arranged marriage, the
world portrayed in *Mississippi Masala* is actually closer in spirit to that of
Romeo and Juliet than is the world of *Guess Who's Coming to Dinner*.

But emphasizing the concerns that *Mississippi Masala* shares with *Guess
Who's Coming to Dinner* threatens to underplay its far more sophisticated
politics as well as its novel use of the narrative figure of transgressive love

to ground a more general investigation into problems of identity formation in postcolonial settings: How, in such settings, to resolve competing demands for loyalty from both the colonizing and the colonized cultures? In immigrant communities such as the one portrayed in the film, this quest for identity requires individuals to adjudicate between the claims of inherited nationality or ethnicity and those of the new homeland. The postcolonial must decide whether and how to maintain a sense of ethnic or national filiation in a society that asks, in more or less extreme fashion, for conformity to *its* practices.

In focusing on Mina's attempt to forge a romantic liaison with Demetrius, *Mississippi Masala* brings a feminist perspective to its depiction of the struggles facing this postcolonial, immigrant woman. Mina's quiet protofeminism suggests that the attempt to (re)constitute an Indian identity through fidelity to the traditional practice of arranged marriage—which, in the film, functions as a metonym for the more global attempt to maintain/create a "pure" Indian identity in exile—is a denial of the complex and conflictual character of her experience. The film insists that an authentically postcolonial identity cannot be derived from within the now-diminished horizons of traditional practice, ethnic or national, but requires that bursting of obsolete boundaries symbolized by the Mina-Demetrius couple.

Because the story of Mina's unlikely romance and the story of Jay's nostalgia and rage are intercut, many critics have castigated *Mississippi Masala* for lack of unity.[1] But a careful unpacking of the film's representational and narrative strategies reveals that, on the contrary, its argument proceeds through the development of a parallel between the predicaments of Indians in Uganda and in the United States: In both countries, Indian exclusivism has manifested itself in antiblack racist practices. The film urges Indian immigrants to reject these, despite the material benefits they confer, to find a way to live in solidarity with other postcolonial peoples of color.[2] In deploying the figure of the unlikely couple to interrogate attempts to develop a pure postcolonial ethnic identity, *Mississippi Masala* expands the possibilities of the genre as a vehicle for social criticism.

Before proceeding further, there is a terminological problem that needs to be acknowledged. I characterize the species of identity the Indian community wishes to (re)create in Greenwood as *ethnic*. There are two problems with this usage: First, that it may not accord with the self-ascription of the Indians in the film, who may think of themselves instead as (re)creating a *national* identity;[3] and second, that the film presents this mode of identity formation as parallel to that of African Americans, a designation that is at least ambiguously *racial*.[4] Despite my awareness of its inadequacies, the term "ethnicity" seems preferable to its alternatives—"nationality" or "race"—which pose even deeper problems in attempting to describe the issues raised by the film.

The Politics of Postcolonial Life

Mina's struggle to construct a postcolonial identity in the face of opposition from her family and from the larger immigrant community raises a momentous question: In the aftermath of colonialism, is it desirable or even possible for postcolonial peoples to maintain/recover a pure ethnic identity?[5]

Among the options the film dramatizes, affirming one's ethnic identity by submitting to a set of practices designed to (re)create authentic prelapsarian culture is quite explicitly rejected. And the film does this by satirizing the attempts of Greenwood's Indian immigrants to perpetuate traditional Indian practices, most notably that of arranged marriage, and by exposing the racism consequent upon those attempts. Indeed, it is this aspect of *Mississippi Masala* that has caused reviewers and film and social theorists alike to rebuke it for ethnic stereotyping.[6]

These criticisms prompt the questions: What makes a representation stereotypical? And why is this mode of representation problematic? As Homi Bhabha has argued, a social stereotype is not simply a negative image of a group:

> The stereotype is not a simplification because it is a false representation of a given reality . . . [but] because it is an arrested, fixated form of representation that, in denying the play of difference (that the negation through the Other permits), constitutes a problem for the *representation* of the subject in significations of psychic and social relations.[7]

In so far as I understand Bhabha's point, it is that stereotyping involves a simplification of a more complex, heterogeneous reality, one that involves multiple, shifting identities. In the case of the postcolonial, a stereotype would not acknowledge competing demands on allegiance, but would treat one claim—such as the desire to restore a pure ethnic identity—as exclusive and obligatory.

Now, there is a sense in which *Mississippi Masala* does traffic in stereotypes. Its portrayal of the immigrant Indian community in Greenwood is undoubtedly harsh and satiric. What its critics fail to recognize, however, is how this representational strategy serves the film's more comprehensive political critique of the postcolonial fantasy of a pure ethnicity. The film recognizes—indeed, it emphasizes—the difficulties facing postcolonial immigrants, but it knowingly ridicules this desire for ethnic purity as hopelessly out of touch with the realities of their children's lives. Postcolonial identities are inherently mixed or hybrid and the film portrays these children as sufficiently Westernized that the attempt to impose archaic, ethnically inflected practices such as arranged marriage can only lead to deep discontent and/or revolt. It is precisely to convey the unsatisfactory nature of this solution to the problem of postcolonial identity that the film resorts to caricature and stereotype.

The key metaphor the film proposes for understanding the situation of postcolonials is that of a *masala,* the pungent mix of spices ubiquitous in Indian cuisine. The Mississippi *masala* of the film's title is, in the first instance, Mina, for she is ethnically Indian, was born and spent her early life in Uganda, but is now American both in domicile and cultural allegiance. Indeed, at a crucial point in her relationship with Demetrius, Mina refers to herself as a *masala,* explaining to her puzzled partner that the blend of Indian, Ugandan, and American influences on her make her just such a spicy mixture. In the second instance, Greenwood's congeries of races, nationalities, and ethnicities make *it* a *masala.* From the film's point of view, the Indians living there deny this fact, segregating themselves from American culture and (re)creating their Indianness through traditional observance.

Mississippi Masala thus insists on the inescapably hybrid character of postcolonial immigrant experience. As a result, the film's use of stereotype does not automatically count as a defect, as its detractors assume, nor does it signal unconscious acceptance of a colonialist "discourse of the Other," but serves instead to debunk the colonized's counterdiscourse of an undefiled, recoverable origin.[8]

This perspective also allows us to see what is misplaced in bell hooks and Anuradha Dingwaney's complaint that the film adopts the colonizers' discourse, that is, that it fails to represent the viewpoints of postcolonials themselves.[9] Although critical of almost every aspect of the film, hooks and Dingwaney's deepest objection to *Mississippi Masala* is that its use of the romantic narrative renders it incapable of making a political statement, celebrating, instead, romantic love and the home.

Such criticism fails to recognize how its story of unlikely romance serves the film's complex political argument. That the film does have larger ambitions is recognized by E. Ann Kaplan in an essay that attempts to locate the film within a feminist filmmaking practice:

> Nair, then, is not simply writing a narrative about individuals who manage to find their personal happiness. She intends to indicate, to reference, larger perspectives regarding Third World nations, links between Africans and African Americans, decolonization in Africa and post-colonialism in America . . . [10]

Although she does not spell out the politics of the film, Kaplan does see that its love story is highly symbolic, for the romance between Mina and Demetrius tells us as much about the politics of postcolonialism as it does about them as individuals.

Further potential for critical discomfort with *Mississippi Masala* may lie with its harsh treatment of Indian immigrants—especially if one were to assume that the film is, or ought to be, striving for an even-handed depiction of Greenwood's Indian and African American communities. But this objection would ignore the film's focus on what it sees as problematic in Indian American traditionalism. The options that the film makes available to these immigrants are so portrayed as to support the film's condemnation of life choices that would evade the commonalities among postcolonial peoples. In maintaining their national traditions, Indians segregate themselves from other peoples of color, supporting, at best implicitly, the racism of American society. By contrast, the African American community acknowledges, with seriousness rather than cynicism, that in a white-dominated society, all postcolonials are in the same boat.[11]

The film's preference for the alternative of solidarity is thus clear. In many ways, this option may seem to involve assimilation, a rejection of traditional customs and practices in favor of those of the new homeland. And of course, assimilation is one path traditionally open to immigrants seeking a better life. But one of the unique features of *Mississippi Masala* is that it operates within an understanding of the restricted choices available to postcolonial Americans, be they descendants of enslaved Africans or Indians recently arrived from Africa or Asia. The racism of white Southern culture presents barriers to assimilation for either group. For the Indians, the film argues, there is an alternative to the creation of a stultifying, inward-turning, and defensive culture: acknowledgment that all postcolonial peoples—in the film's terms, all people of color—are in the same boat. Creating an identity based on this awareness allows for more flex- 'ible attitudes toward both the new homeland and other postcolonials.

Although the "f word" is not spoken once during the film, it is clear that this film reflects the feminist concerns of its female director. For example, Demetrius's respectful attitude toward Mina helps make her pursuit of solidarity with African Americans a means for realizing larger possibilities for herself.

Once we understand the options available to Mina in the United States, we can better understand her father's anger over his expulsion from Uganda. Jay is one of a group of Indians who benefited from their role in the administration of British colonialism. Although his father was a laborer brought to East Africa by the British to help build the railroad, Jay became a highly respected and powerful lawyer. Not surprisingly, he thought of himself as a Ugandan first—fully assimilated—and an Indian second. Hence, exile is truly traumatic for him.

Jay did not think of himself as an Indian, distinguished from his fellow Ugandans by virtue of this ethnicity. But the film reveals, if only gradually and mostly indirectly, through its examination of the Indian community in Greenwood, that Jay was simply wrong about this. In a flashback rather late in the film, the infamous dictator Idi Amin is shown on a television screen explaining why he has decreed that all Asians must leave Uganda. They have become rich while impoverishing the Africans, he charges. And despite the benefits Uganda has bestowed on them, they ungratefully cultivate a sense of their superiority. In evidence, he cites, in a remark the inclusion of which seems to signal the film's agenda, the Indians' "refus[al] to allow their daughters to marry Africans."[12]

By including this quasi-documentary element, *Mississippi Masala* not only indicates a certain sympathy with Amin's criticism of the Indians' exploitative role as well as with his condemnation of their hostility to exogamous marriage, but it also explains the significance of the film's focus on the romance between an Indian exile from Uganda and an African American from Greenwood. In exploring what Mina finds in her relationship to Demetrius and her father's opposition to it, the film intends a symbolic investigation of the history of Indian participation in Western colonialism. In Idi Amin's justification of his policy of expulsion, the film finds historical warrant for its emphasis on the issue of intermarriage, even as it remains critical of any search for a pure ethnic identity.

Thus, *Mississippi Masala*'s double narrative is not the defect that critics take it for, but a sign of the scope of its ambitions. The two narrative strands are mutually reinforcing: Perspectives developed in one shed light on concerns raised in the other. At the heart of both is the question of how postcolonials can construct identities that exempt them from complicity with colonialism itself.

The Failure of Ethnicity

The options available to Greenwood's Indian immigrants are vividly counterpointed through depictions of the traditional Indian marriage that opens the American section of the film on the one hand and the passionate romance that develops between Mina and Demetrius on the other. The marriage sequence takes place in August 1990, in Greenwood, Mississippi, where Jay and his family are settled after exile from Uganda and a stay of unspecified length in London. Their now-straitened circumstances contrast sharply with the opulence of their life in Uganda, where they lived in a beautiful house with breathtaking views, which the film represents, to the accompaniment of lush music, as a bucolic idyll. There Jay was an influential lawyer, a leader of the Indian community, whose views were sought by the foreign media. In Greenwood, they occupy two seedy rooms at the Monte Cristo Motel, whose owner, Anil (Ranjit Chowdhry), is a member of their extended family. While Jay spends his time obsessively pursuing his claim against the government of Uganda, his wife, Kinnu (Sharmila Tagore), supports the family by running a liquor shop. Mina herself works as a cleaning woman at the motel, presumably out of economic necessity rather than personal preference.

The Greenwood section of the film opens as preparations are under way for Anil's marriage to Chanda (Dipti Suthar). Their wedding furnishes a number of pretexts—most centrally, of course, around the issue of arranged marriage itself—for contrasting Mina's self-understanding with that of the other Indian immigrants. As in *Romeo and Juliet,* the question is whether parental or romantic preference should determine one's life's partner. *Mississippi Masala* employs a number of distinct narrative devices to make its case for romantic love. For example, as in other stories of transgressive relationships, the relative allure of the two male contenders is used to signify the relative validity of opposing principles of partner selection. Thus, Harry Patel (Ashok Lath) plays Demetrius's less winning foil, much as, in *Romeo and Juliet,* Paris does Romeo's. Harry, the favorite of Mina's parents, is a successful member of the immigrant community, the "good catch" so familiar to such dramas. Demetrius, of course, is the more attractive man, less uptight than humorless, self-important Harry, and someone with whom Mina connects much more directly.

Photo 8.1 An arranged marriage

A second of these narrative devices is the film's satirizing of arranged marriage. Horny Anil twice tries to make love to his new wife, but each attempt ends in failure (see Photo 8.1). The first time, Chanda inadvertently slaps Anil in the face; the second, already indifferent to his clumsy humping, she actually throws him off, complaining that he is hurting her. When Anil turns to the TV for solace, we see an ad that promises financial success, implying that his thwarted sexuality will only intensify his acquisitiveness. The film's satirical treatment of this assertion of Indian cultural practice in America treats Anil and Chanda's arranged marriage as a symbol of all that is wrongheaded in the turn toward a recovered traditionalism.[13]

If its ironic take on arranged marriage is one target of *Mississippi Masala*'s critique of Greenwood's Indian immigrant community, a second is its racism. India has its own light-skin/dark-skin fixation and Indians in America readily superimpose it on the U.S. racial hierarchy. This issue is raised during the wedding sequence when Kinnu reminds Mina that finding her a suitable husband has not been easy. In response, Mina tells her mother to accept the fact that she has a "darkie daughter," not a good catch by Indian standards.

This interesting and exciting young woman's wry evaluation of her marriageability is reinforced by two gossips (one of whom is played by Mira Nair, the film's director), who conclude that her chances of winding up with Harry Patel are slim: "You can be poor or you can be dark. But you can't be both poor and dark." If these busybodies are taken as representative of Indian attitudes generally, then differences in skin color and wealth would seem to be the only things that count when determining matrimonial suitability.

Mina departs the wedding with Harry, however, perhaps an indication that her mother's fondest wish may yet be fulfilled. Ironically, it instead results in the initiation of her relationship with Demetrius. Harry takes Mina to the Leopard Lounge, a disco at which the patrons are predominantly African American. After Demetrius asks Mina to dance and she accepts, a clearly annoyed Harry announces his intention to leave the club; later, Demetrius will drive her home.

Mina is clearly more at ease at the disco than at the wedding. Thus, as soon as she enters the club, she has a friendly exchange with an African American woman. Significantly, we have been shown no similar encounters with Indians. Perhaps, the African American community will allow Mina to be appreciated as an individual, rather than be condescended to for her dark skin color and her family's poverty.

Mina's desire to escape from the context of Indian immigrant life is presented by the film, then, as a refusal to accept these damaging measures of her worth and the limitations they imply. Instead, she insists on a relationship with a man of her choice, one who finds her attractive and interesting. And it is Greenwood's African American community, not her own Indian enclave, that offers her the chance to enlarge her sense of herself.

Two Communities, Two Responses

The differences that divide *Mississippi Masala*'s unlikely couple provoke different responses in the Indian and African American communities, and, in this film's judgment, to the discredit of the former.

Mina's is a bourgeois family, even though expulsion and dispossession have impoverished it. From her family's point of view, its current economic difficulty is not an accurate indicator of Mina's social status. The family experiences itself through its own history, a perception expressed by Jay's oft-stated desire that she pursue her education. He will have failed as a father, he tells her, if she does no more with her life than clean toilets.

Demetrius comes from a poor, but hardworking, African American family. His elderly father, Williben (Joe Seneca), works as a waiter in a restaurant. (Mrs. Morgan [Karen Pinkston], Williben's employer, is one of the few white characters who appear in the film. Her demeaning attitude toward Williben implies the ever-present context of white racism in which this story unfolds.)[14] From Demetrius's Aunt Rose (Yvette Hawkins), who seems keen that Mina hook up with Demetrius, we learn that he gave up a scholarship to Jackson State to care for his widowed father. Having chosen to remain in Greenwood, Demetrius has started his own carpet cleaning company, servicing many of the motels owned by the Indians in Mina's extended group, including the one in which she lives and works.

Demetrius is represented as hardworking and morally responsible, the sort of black man celebrated in black nationalist discourse, and the film underscores his exceptional character by playing up the contrast between him and the other young black men portrayed in the film. First, there is Dexter (Tico Wells), Demetrius's younger brother, whom the ambitious Demetrius repeatedly upbraids for his shiftlessness. Tyrone (Charles S. Dutton), Demetrius's business partner, although equally committed to their undertaking, serves to emphasize another important aspect of Demetrius's character: his respect for women. Tyrone fits the stereotype of the sexually predacious black male, eager to bed Mina from the minute that he meets her. Somewhat improbably, Demetrius seems hardly to notice her beauty, a narrative ploy designed to demonstrate that he is not obsessed with sex.[15]

How, then, are we to characterize the differences dividing Mina and Demetrius? On the one hand, they both are struggling economically and they even do the same sort of work, for both are cleaners. On the other hand, there is the difference that Mina's situation is the result of her being declassed in consequence of her family's expulsion from Uganda. In this context, the similarity in economic status represents a problem, for Jay refuses to accept his reduced lower-class position as really his, and the lawsuit represents his attempt to return his family to their prior and, from his point of view, deserved place.

The difference that keeps the two characters apart is that Demetrius is African American, and Mina, Indian. *Mississippi Masala*'s presentation of why this difference makes a difference is unique among unlikely couple films in that it does not treat the attitudes of the partners' communities of origin as parallel. In both *Guess Who's Coming to Dinner* and *Jungle Fever*, the families of the unlikely partners are equally opposed to the couple. *Mississippi Masala* shows that although ethnic difference can be an obstacle for its unlikely couple, it need not be. For the African Americans who are Demetrius's family and friends, Mina is simply another person of color. As a result, not only is there no opposition to her relationship with him at all, there is even general support for their forming a couple. Mina's dark skin establishes their kinship as people of color oppressed by whites.

This is made clear when Demetrius invites Mina to a barbecue celebrating Williben's birthday to make his former partner, Alicia LeShay (Natalie Oliver), jealous.[16] Asked to explain why there are Indians in Africa, Mina responds that they were brought there by the British to build the railroads. This prompts Tyrone and Dexter to draw the analogy between the presence of the Indians in Africa and the presence of Africans in America: Both groups were uprooted by imperialist powers and transported by sea to perform forced labor. Coming from Africa, the ancestral home of black Americans, even gives Mina a certain cachet among Demetrius's friends and family, for, of course, they have never been to their lands of origin.

This scene demonstrates how the complex histories of two postcolonial peoples allows them to discover that their differences can be something other than absolute barriers. Indeed, the criss-crossing identities acknowledged by the characters in this scene emblematize the potential for solidarity between these groups.

On the other hand, Mina's family and friends respond to their liaison with hostility, for to them Demetrius is clearly an inappropriate partner for her. The reasons for this are various. First, there is the fundamental fact that Demetrius is not an Indian, and as we have seen, Mina's family copes with exile by ghettoizing itself. Clinging defensively to their identification as Indians, Mina's relatives insist that Mina do the same. And this self-evidently entails that only another Indian immigrant would make her a suitable husband.

The fact that Demetrius is African American and poor reinforces Indian opposition to his relationship with Mina. Jay is a snob who looks down on menial labor, and his ignorance of the situation of blacks in America—shared by the immigrant community in general—causes him to severely underestimate Demetrius. Rather than appreciate that Demetrius's ownership of his own firm is an indication of his ambition, Jay sees only the menial nature of the work he does. The audience knows this young man's aspirations to a college education were thwarted by his sense of responsibility to his family—hence his profession is really a symbol of his moral virtue—but Jay dismisses him as unworthy to be his son-in-law.

Because, as we have seen, India has suffered from its own fixation with skin tone, the film suggests that Greenwood's Indian immigrants are susceptible to American race thinking. As a result, black Americans seem to them inherently inferior to Indians, and so on grounds of race, Demetrius is automatically excluded as a partner for Mina.

A final reason for the Indians' opposition to the couple has to do with the course that the relationship takes. When the fact that Mina and Demetrius are sleeping together becomes a public scandal, her family takes steps to separate them. Although this affair has followed the more-or-less typical pattern for Americans, to the traditional Indians, Mina's sexual activity has brought shame on herself and her family.

How different Mina's attitude is from that of her parents is emphasized in a scene that comes shortly after her affair with Demetrius has been discovered and made public. When Mina announces her love for Demetrius, her parents respond in ways that reflect their determination to maintain their Indian way of life. Thus, Mina's mother objects, "You call this love, when all you've done is bring down such shame on our heads." Kinnu's reproach—that her daughter's feelings for Demetrius could not be love because the relationship violates Indian norms governing courtship—suggests that her mother has a very different understanding of what love means. For Mina, whose conception of love is the one prevalent in American society, love is what she feels for Demetrius no matter what society has to say about it.[17]

The difference in their attitudes is underscored when Kinnu questions her about how Demetrius's family feels. "This is America, Mom," Mina says, "nobody cares." To Mina, her mother is simply living in the past, holding on to cultural values irrelevant in the American context. Her mother's response—"We care, your father and I. If we don't care, who will?"—indicates just how different an understanding of the role of family she has from the one Mina has absorbed in her adopted country.

This exchange neatly encapsulates the dilemma that immigrants of any origin face in their new homeland. Themselves products of different cultural traditions, they want their children to maintain the practices they value and accept. But their children are necessarily more attuned to their surroundings and so their ancestors' cultural patterns are no longer attractive and compelling. These children long to be fully a part of the culture their parents view warily. Through its enumeration of the dilemmas facing Greenwood's Indian immigrants, *Mississippi Masala* thus conveys the fundamental challenge of the postcolonial situation: to construct a meaningful identity that rejects the spurious allure of a pure native culture, undefiled by colonial penetration.

Romance in Solidarity

The contrast between Anil's loveless marriage to Chanda and Mina's romantically inspired relationship with Demetrius emerges very clearly in the scene in which the latter make love in a Biloxi motel. The camera seems to luxuriate on their intertwined bodies as they enact their passion for one another (see Photo 8.2). This is an pivotal episode, for at the same time that it marks the lovers' commitment to one another, it also results in their exposure and the scandal that seems to portend an end to their relationship.

For *Mississippi Masala*, the erotically charged relationship between Mina and Demetrius is of far greater emotional significance for its partners than the arranged marriage of Anil and Chanda is to them. The public consummation of that marriage emphasizes its social nature as a ritual celebrated out of fidelity to traditional Indian norms. Its contrast with the furtive encounter between Mina and Demetrius—the significance of whose relationship must remain hidden—could not be more stark. Indeed, once their relationship is publicly known, its very existence is threatened, for it goes against the norms of the Indian community (as well as, apparently, those of the white community).

There now follows a remarkable montage sequence in which almost all of the elements of Greenwood's social *masala* unite in their condemnation of Mina and Demetrius's relationship. The first scene in the sequence is an encore appearance of the two gossips from Anil's wedding. When one expresses delighted indignation at what Mina has done—"Can you imagine! Dropping Harry Patel for a black!"—the other vows to send her daughters back to India lest they too take up with black men. In the second scene of the sequence, as Anil hangs up on Demetrius, who has phoned for Mina, we realize that her extended family is going to do its best to keep them apart. Next, an older white man, whose accent identifies him as working class, laughs into a phone, as he jokes to one of the Indians, "Are ya' all having nigger trouble?" Then, after a shot of Demetrius's partner, Tyrone, staring through a locked door with a "closed" sign, Mrs. Morgan, Williben's employer, who had helped secure an auto

Photo 8.2 The passion of romantic love

loan for Demetrius, promises to call the bank to retract her support. In quick succession, we then see one of the Indians on the phone with Demetrius insisting, "There's nothing I can do. I've already hired someone else"; Alicia on the phone with Demetrius, scolding him for taking up with an Indian woman—there is no shortage of available black women in Greenwood; someone from the local chamber of commerce informing Demetrius that his membership has been revoked; and, in the final scene in the montage, Demetrius slamming down the phone in anger and frustration. This montage of phone conversations brilliantly evokes the array of social forces working to defeat the lovers. Not only can they not contact one another, but Demetrius has become a pariah. He is clearly being punished for forgetting his "place."

After a number of longer scenes in which the reprisals against him develop to a sort of crescendo, Demetrius comes to the motel to talk with Mina. Jay intercepts him, and with help from one of his fellow Indians, turns him away, for he has "caused enough trouble." In the ensuing confrontation, two different cultures meet head on. Demetrius challenges Jay: "So, you think that I ain't good enough for your daughter?" Although he does not fully understand the cultural context that makes his relationship with Mina so deeply troubling to her community, he is aware that her father rejects him because he is black and uneducated.

For his part, Jay responds in the expected manner, citing "my responsibility as her father. . . . Once, I was just like you two. I thought I could change the world. But the world is not so quick to change." He continues, "I don't want her to go through the same struggles that I did." Jay cannot help but assimilate Mina's situation in Greenwood to his in Kampala, invoking his sense of betrayal by the Ugandans, a wound as present to him as ever. And implicit is his belief that Mina too will experience betrayal if she seeks to establish an intimate relationship with someone who is not of her own ethnicity, as he did when, at the moment of departure, his boyhood friend, Okelo (Konga Mbandu), turned on him, repeating the slogan, "Africa is for Africans, black Africans." To spare her that betrayal, he intends to drive Demetrius away.

But Demetrius sees Jay's speech as so much evasion and when he counters, "As soon as you got here you started acting white," latent African American hostility to the Indian immigrants finally surfaces. Demetrius does more than simply reiterate the charge that the Indians have adopted white America's racial attitudes; he asserts that despite similarities in their postcolonial predicament, Indian immigrants act in concert with whites to maintain the oppression of African Americans.

Demetrius has ample grounds for his bitterness: Although he has made the payments on his van for nearly two years, the bank has canceled his loan. With impeccable logic, the bank's white president has pointed out that since Demetrius has lost most of his local clients—who happen to be the very Indians who own the town's motels—his ability to continue to make his payments is very much in doubt and so the bank must foreclose.

Demetrius is thus the victim of a series of coordinated actions undertaken by both Indian immigrants and white businesspeople, and the film treats this de facto alliance as symbolic of the general role that Indian immigrants play in relation to other postcolonial peoples. By aligning themselves with white domination, the Indians become agents, in this case, of the oppression of the African Americans.[18] And here we are meant to recall the situation of Uganda and the retribution enacted on its Indian immigrant community. Demetrius's undoing contextualizes Idi Amin's decision to expel Uganda's Asian citizens: "Africa is for Africans, black Africans."

Not only has his love affair been disrupted, but Demetrius's financial situation is now desperate. Despite all his efforts over the past two years, his business is in danger of failing. Rather than face "this shit," Tyrone has left town, headed back to Los Angeles and a job driving a bus, abandoning his friend and business partner.

Demetrius and Mina's attempt to transgress the barriers of self-imposed cultural isolation the immigrant Indian community has erected for itself results in an outbreak of racial/ethnic enmity between these two postcolonial groups. As in other films featuring interracial romance, parental and familial opposition to its unlikely couple threaten a tragic end. Not only will intergroup hostility intensify, but the ties that bind Mina to her extended family may break as a result of the pressures put on them by her father's opposition to her romance.

But despite the presence in *Mississippi Masala* of so many of the usual elements of unlikely couple narratives—and in the face of much harsh and dismissive criticism—the innovative way these elements are used to explore the options for acculturation available to immigrants in a new country deserve respect. The dilemma facing the immigrant Indian community is that the very desire to maintain its traditional culture may result not only in the destruction of family, the basis of such culture, but also implicate these immigrants in the exploitation of other postcolonial groups in their new homeland.

Two Reconciliations

Mississippi Masala ends with two important reconciliations, both affirming the film's political vision of postcolonial solidarity. In the first, Mina decides to pursue her relationship with Demetrius, even though this threatens an irreparable break with her father. In the second, returning to Uganda to pursue his lawsuit, Jay discovers that he has been wrong to oppose Mina's relationship with Demetrius.

Both narrative strands are the result of Jay's receipt of a letter declaring that he will finally have his day in court. Since the family has been thrown out of the Monte Cristo—yet another expulsion!—as a result of a suit that Demetrius has filed against Anil, Jay decides that the best thing for the entire family is to move back to Uganda.

For Mina, this is an extremity, and not simply because it means that her separation from Demetrius will be irrevocable. We have been shown how Mina chafes against the limitations of the immigrant Indian ghetto. For her restless protofeminism, returning to Uganda would mean the elimination of the one cultural possibility she sees as offering her the hope of creating an acceptable life for herself, namely, affiliation with the African American community and its practices. This is what her relationship with Demetrius symbolizes to her and what she fears would be foreclosed to her by returning to Uganda.

Faced with this prospect, Mina acts decisively, taking Anil's car and hunting down Demetrius—who has decided to leave Greenwood too—ostensibly to say good-bye. Initially cool to her overture, Demetrius's anger soon overtakes him: She is the agent of his ruin. Now provoked, she accuses him of having initiated their relationship to make Alicia jealous. He admits this, ruefully acknowledging, "I never thought that I would fall in love with you." At this point, Mina asks to go with him and the two then decide to become partners. They head off into the unknown in an attempt to save Demetrius's van and, thus, his business.

Mina's entry into partnership with Demetrius seals the choice that she has made about how to live her life, in effect rejecting the Indian posture of ethnic superiority to affiliate instead with black Americans, a people like her own, that has suffered the devastating effects of European colonialism. And her choice epitomizes the film's case that in the postcolonial world, the options are stark: Either solidarity among the colonized or complicity with the colonizer.

One problem remains: Mina's reconciliation with Demetrius comes at the cost of her relationship to her father. When she calls to explain her choice to her parents, her father refuses to talk with her. Her challenge to his patriarchal authority is too much for him and so he rejects her. Like Capulet and Matt Drayton, this male patriarch cannot acknowledge his daughter's right to make decisions for herself.

The film's final sequence is once again set in Uganda, where Jay has returned to pursue his lawsuit and where he finally confronts his past. Jay's journey begins with his discovery that his childhood friend, Okelo, is dead. At the school at which Okelo worked, Jay is told by one of Okelo's fellow teachers that he simply disappeared around 1972, during "all the trouble." Shaken, Jay now realizes that Okelo's death may well have resulted from his, Okelo's, efforts to free Jay from jail. Thus, Jay's bitterness over his dead friend's imagined betrayal was itself a betrayal of their friendship.

Jay next returns to the house in Kampala, only to find it in ruins, animals now grazing on its once carefully tended grounds. We are meant to see that Jay's desire to return to Kampala is nothing but fantasy, based on his memory of what things once were like, and a refusal to face that everything has changed. There is no longer the grand house in Kampala in which he might live, just as there is no longer the friend to whom he can apologize.

Writing to Kinnu, Jay explains what he has learned. He tells her that Mina was right when she upbraided him for not saying good-bye to Okelo. More centrally, he tells her that he has learned that "home is where the heart is and my heart is with you." This comment recalls Matt Drayton's paean to the primacy of love in human life. But unlike *Guess Who's Coming to Dinner, Mississippi Masala* retains its politicized understanding of love: In the final scene of the film, as Jay watches some dancing black Ugandans, a black baby reaches out to him and he hugs it, his embrace symbolically affirming the principle of solidarity.

Employing many aspects of narrative structure common to unlikely couple dramas from *Romeo and Juliet* to *Guess Who's Coming to Dinner, Mississippi Masala* uses its setting among immigrant Indians in the southern United States nevertheless to make a distinctive political statement. Its vision of an affiliation between blacks and immigrant Indians is registered and validated as the love of Mina and Demetrius wins through despite the obstacles it faces. As in *Romeo and Juliet,* a crucial aspect of that vision is the rejection of arranged marriage in favor of romantic partner choice: in the context of this film, an agenda requiring that instead of withdrawing into a pure Indian ethnicity, Greenwood's Indian immigrants acknowledge that the circumstances under which they have to live have many significant similarities to those of the black Americans living there.

Notes

1. See, for example, the reviews by Cecelie S. Barry, *Cineaste,* 19:2–3 (1992–1993): pp. 66–67, and Erika Surat Andersen, *Film Quarterly,* 46:4 (1993): pp. 23–26.

2. The film's narrative strategy can be challenged on two grounds: First, the experience of African Americans is discontinuous with that of many postcolonials in that their connections to their own African roots were systematically destroyed; second, African Americans may not see themselves as postcolonials because they identify themselves as Americans despite the myriad injustices to which this country has subjected their people.

3. It is not clear what it means for Indians to think of themselves as sharing a national identity, given all the significant differences that divide the population, such as religion, caste, etc.

4. I remind the reader that the term "race," despite its evident problems, seems necessary as a way of characterizing the situation of African Americans. See footnote 1, Chapter 6.

5. I see the tension I outline as applying beyond the case of the Indians presented in the film, extending, for example, to my own situation as a first generation German-Jewish American. My analysis bears similarity to Werner Sollors's distinction between consent and descent identities in *Beyond Ethnicity: Consent and Descent in American Culture* (New York and Oxford, UK: Oxford University Press, 1986).

6. Two examples of reviews that criticize the film's use of stereotypes are those by Cecelie S. Barry and Erika Surat Andersen cited in footnote 1, above.

7. Homi K. Bhabha, "The Other Question: Difference, Discrimination, and the Discourse of Colonialism," in *Black British Cultural Studies: A Reader*, Houston A. Baker, Manthia Diawara, and Ruth H. Lindeborg, eds. (Chicago and London: University of Chicago Press, 1996), p. 98.

8. At a formal level, the film's structure manifests the hybridity it attributes to the identity of postcolonial people. Its African sequence is filmed in a more avant-garde manner, denying its viewers easy access to its narrative, whereas its American sequences are filmed in typical Hollywood style, with clearly identifiable transitions.

9. The article by bell hooks and Anuradha Dingwaney is titled simply "Mississippi Masala," *Z Magazine*, July/August 1992, pp. 41–43.

10. E. Ann Kaplan, *Looking for the Other: Feminism, Film, and the Imperial Gaze* (New York and London: Routledge, 1997), p. 177.

11. This is emphasized when Demetrius brings Mina home to a family celebration, an incident I discuss later in this chapter.

12. Since Idi Amin occupied for a time the American media's designated "crazed dictator" slot, a role later to be filled by Mu'ammar Gadhafi and, more recently, Saddam Hussein, the film's sympathetic presentation of him is startling. Amin's policy of expulsion smacks of the very sort of drive for a pure ethnicity, and to much more destructive effect, than that the film criticizes in the Indian community. Nonetheless, the film validates Amin's characterization of the problem.

This and all subsequent quotations from the film are from my transcription of the film's sound track.

13. The practices that establish the identity of the members of the Indian community are not necessarily practices that were actually brought from India or practiced by the immigrants there. What is crucial is that they regard the practices as ones that Indians should follow.

14. One unique feature of this film is that whites are only present peripherally. The central characters are African, African American, and Indian immigrants.

15. *Mississippi Masala*'s exceptionalization of Demetrius shows that it too, no less than *Guess Who's Coming to Dinner*, worries that viewers will respond to a

black male on the basis of negative stereotype. The film is thus liable to the criticism that it reinforces the very same clichés by the various strategies it uses to distance Demetrius from them.

16. It is not clear whether Alicia was Demetrius's girlfriend or wife. Although Williben tells her, much to Demetrius's displeasure, that she will always be a member of the family, there is no further discussion that disambiguates her status.

17. Mina's view of love is typically Western; love is seen as located in two individuals with no regard for how it affects others.

18. I use the term "align" in a slightly different sense than I did in *The Forms of Power: From Domination to Transformation* (Philadelphia: Temple University Press, 1990), chap. 7. Its usage here has important implications for understanding how power works.

9
Ali:
Fear Eats the Soul
The Privileges of "Race"

Each of the films discussed in the three preceding chapters employs a narrative of interracial romance to critically explore race relations in American society. Inevitably, all raise questions about the viability of integrationist strategies as a response to historic injustice, and each invests its hopes in a specific political program—two, *Guess Who's Coming to Dinner* and *Mississippi Masala*, in integration; the third, *Jungle Fever*, in separatism.

Like these, Rainer Werner Fassbinder's *Angst essen Seele auf* (*Ali: Fear Eats the Soul*, 1974) examines the nature of racism. *Ali's* undertaking transcends the familiar assumptions about racism that dominate the other films, however. Although numerous acts of individual race prejudice are depicted—as is true, too, of both *Guess Who's Coming to Dinner* and *Jungle Fever*—this film goes beyond these to the more profound question of racism's persistence. It is the film's attempt to document an answer to this that makes it a uniquely probing unlikely couple film.

This being understood, critics' complaints about the film's lack of concern with the conditions of *Gastarbeiter* (guest workers) in Germany—of whom its male lead is one—recede to irrelevance. The forms of prejudice shown in *Ali*, like those in *Guess Who's Coming to Dinner*, are not all that extreme. And unlike the more "realistic" *Jungle Fever*, no one is physically attacked or threatened in any way: no lynching, intimidation, or other acts of violence, systematic or otherwise, against Turks, Vietnamese, or black Africans. In the context of German history (or U.S. history, for that matter), the behavior depicted in the film is simply not that extreme.

But all this is simply beside the point, for *Ali* is less concerned with moralizing about the injustice of racism than with understanding its intractability, its resistance to efforts to eliminate it. What Fassbinder's film shows is that racial hierarchy is produced/maintained by a network of unacknowledged social privilege that "racial superiors" enjoy in exchange for their participation in practices of racial domination and subordination.

This analysis, which is represented through the changing relational dynamic in *Ali's* interracial unlikely couple, explains racism's persistence: The benefits of racial privilege contaminate even the most well intentioned. However other films of interracial romance resolve their unlikely relationships, they suppose that in the face of racism, individuals can hope to make a difference.[1] *Ali's* pessimistic assessment is that racial hierarchy is so deeply imbedded that this supposition is hopelessly naïve.

Although the focus of the present chapter is on *Ali's* exploration of racism, it will also call attention to Fassbinder's use of nonnaturalistic techniques. Whereas the other films considered in this study are essentially naturalistic, *Ali* employs various devices that call attention to its constructed nature.[2] These have been the subject of a great deal of discussion and are of much interest among film theorists, but I discuss them only as they serve to advance Fassbinder's narrative objectives.[3]

In placing *Ali* alongside three American films dealing with racism, I take the "German (Aryan)-foreigner" dichotomy in Germany to parallel the "white-black" dichotomy in the United States. Since the former appears to be a distinction in nationality rather than race, it may seem that I confuse the two. For almost two centuries, however, German nationalism has articulated itself within a racialized discourse in which "purity" has notoriously figured. As a consequence, members of other races are seen as posing a threat to the integrity of the German nation. For this reason, I hold that it makes sense to interpret *Ali's* concerns as continuous with the preoccupations of the American films, even as the film surpasses their more limited understandings.

Creating the Couple

Crucial to *Ali's* narrative strategy is its depiction of a relationship that provides deep and heartfelt satisfactions to its two unlikely lovers. Only because of this can the difficulties that result from the couple's racial makeup be made to bear the significance the film assigns them.

It is the very implausibility of Ali (El Hedi ben Salem), a handsome young, Moroccan *Gastarbeiter*,[4] finding Emmy Kurowski (Brigette Mira), an elderly, somewhat homely German *Putzfrau* (cleaning woman), a suitable sexual and romantic partner that leads to their first encounter. On her way home from work, a sudden rainstorm forces Emmy to seek shelter in a bar catering to Moroccan guest workers. From the very first shot after the title sequence, Emmy's social isolation is emphasized. Thus, we see her enter the Asphalt Pub in a long shot taken from the end of the bar farthest from the door, where all the other patrons are clustered. A reverse shot now shows Ali, a friend, and the owner of the bar coolly gazing at this surprising customer. A great deal of Fassbinder criticism is devoted to the importance of the "gaze" in this film.[5] In the present context, the gazes directed at Emmy register her presence as unwelcome and signal her to keep her distance. This way of representing the hostile reaction of the bar's familiars to Emmy presages the film's later and repeated use of the gaze to communicate social disapproval of the film's unlikely relationship.

When Barbara (Barbara Valentin), the Asphalt Pub's owner, approaches to take her order, Emmy apologizes for her presence, alluding to the rain and to the "strange music" that she hears whenever she walks by. Pressed to order, Emmy's discomfort is evident:

BARBARA: What do you want to drink?
EMMY: What's the usual?
BARBARA: Everyone drinks what they like. Perhaps, a beer or a cola?
EMMY: Yes. That's fine.
BARBARA: What then?
EMMY: Cola, please.[6]

Told she can drink whatever she likes, she still has trouble expressing her own desire. Evidently, her inclination is to conform to whatever others are doing, as if to deflect their attention by blending into their context.

Although Emmy feels alien in the bar, Ali, a guest worker, seems much more at home in this environment. As he and his friend lean in at the bar, he is even propositioned by a German woman (Katharina Herberg) who patronizes the place. He declines her sexual advance—"Prick broke," he tells her—but this is clearly his milieu. The Asphalt Pub provides a social space in which this foreigner can feel at home, or at any rate, more at home than the native Emmy.

The very first scene marks Ali and Emmy as a very unlikely duo, and this in two ways—race and age. First, Emmy and Ali are members of different "races." As suggested above, the trope of race has been important to German identity since at least the early nineteenth century.[7] The idea of a pure *Volk* (people) plays a role in Germany analogous, in important ways to that played by "whiteness" in the United States. In the name of "Germanness" or "Aryanness," members of different social groups have been persecuted, the Holocaust being the most horrific result of this racialized thinking. For want of a better term, we can classify Emmy as a "true" German, that is, a member of the dominant race. (Her family name is Kurowski; she married a Pole after the war. Her Germanness is already compromised by this, as her neighbors are quick to point out once they have seen her with Ali.) As a Moroccan guest worker, a *Schwarzer* (black), Ali is treated as less than human by most of the Germans with whom he has contact.

The second category separating Ali and Emmy is age. By every social assumption, the dowdy, fiftyish Emmy is an unlikely object of youthful male desire. Ali is young and sexually attractive, as the bar patron's come-on makes evident. One of the ways in which sexism functions is to make a sexual relationship between an "older" woman and a "younger" man socially inappropriate. For Emmy to become Ali's lover, she must claim for herself desires that her world would regard as obscene in a woman of her age. On the other hand, to her fellow Germans, the basis of Emmy's relationship with Ali can only be sexual, for how else to explain her interest in a *Gastarbeiter*?[8]

Ironically, Ali first approaches Emmy in the bar as a sort of joke. The woman whose sexual overture Ali has just turned down maliciously suggests that he ask "the old lady" to dance. When he does so, Emmy is somewhat bewildered. She protests that she has not danced in a long time, but he persists—"Sitting alone not good," he tells her—and, characteristically, she agrees.

"Prick broke," "Sitting alone not good"—Ali's language sets him apart from the film's other characters. Like many guest workers, he speaks German in short, staccato sentences in which there are neither articles nor conjugated verbs. It is difficult to capture the full impact of these sentences in English, which lacks the inflections of the German.[9] For example, the film's title is drawn from one of Ali's sayings: *Angst essen Seele auf.* A more literal translation is "Fear Eat Up Soul." Despite his limited command of the formal rules of German—even to a certain extent because of it—Ali's language is striking in its directness. When he says to Emmy, "Sitting alone not good," he is able both to express empathy for her situation and to cut through the ways in which correct speech maintains social boundaries even as it fosters other types of communication.[10] Unlike Emmy, who often resorts to banalities, his language is notable for the immediacy of its perception and the clarity of its judgment.

When Emmy leaves the bar, Ali accompanies her home. Waiting for the rain to let up, they stand in the entryway of her apartment building and talk. During their conversation, it becomes even clearer that Emmy's life is empty of significance. When Ali asks her what type of work she does, Emmy confesses that she is embarrassed to tell people she is a cleaning woman because they ridicule her for it. "Not Ali," he responds understandingly. She warms to him, admitting how nice it is to have someone to talk to, for she is alone most of the time. When Ali tells her that in Morocco families live together, so that mothers do not wind up alone, Emmy wistfully repeats the cliché, "Other countries, other customs."

This interchange underlines Emmy's social isolation and her feelings of inconsequence. As if in a mirror, Ali's own subordinate social position allows him to recognize her as a person. The intimacy the two are able to establish, and that neither otherwise enjoys, is based on a mutual need to be fully acknowledged by another.

Emboldened, Emmy decides to invite Ali upstairs. As they sip brandy, the two continue to open up to one another. It seems that Emmy has little understanding of the situation of guest workers, for she is surprised to hear that Ali and his comrades are forced to live six men to a room. From this perspective, her own modest two-bedroom apartment seems luxurious. Ali informs her that Arabs are treated in Germany as if they were not human. This recalls an earlier reference to the racism of his German fellow workers. While describing his work to Emmy, he had told her that Germans refuse to associate with Arabs: "German master, Arab dog." In the face of constant humiliation, he now tells her, it is better not to think—"No think, much good"—for thinking only leads to futile preoccupation with how awful one's situation is.

To spare Ali a long, late-night tram ride home, Emmy makes up a bed for him. Unable to sleep, he goes to her room to talk. There, he confesses that he too is alone much of the time and that his life consists mostly of work and drink, "Maybe German right: Arab not person." Emmy comforts him with the reassurance that Germans are wrong. Ali responds to her acknowledgment by caressing her arm and the camera fades as they begin to have sex.

The relationship that now develops between Ali and Emmy quickens both their lives. We know that Emmy's work provides her with no satisfaction and that she has little contact with her children—or with anyone else for that matter. As an older woman who no longer fits the norms of sexual attractiveness, she is more or less abject. For his part, Ali, "Arab dog," fills his life with work, drink, and periodic casual sex.

The coupling of their two lives now endows the experience of each with significance. In part, this is because they provide one another with emotional support. More important, despite their marginal social positions, each can feel like a human being because, through the couple, they receive acknowledgment from one another. Ironically, it is their marginality that allows them to come together, trumping the important social differences between them.

If we limit our attention to the manner in which the love between Ali and Emmy is developed, we find a now-familiar picture: As long as they are off by themselves, they seem untroubled by the social differences between them. Unlike the interracial romance Spike Lee depicted in his *Jungle Fever*, the attraction these two have for one another has nothing to do with the allure of an exoticized, forbidden Other. Ali and Emmy are simply two people who have managed to open themselves to one another in the way we call love.

Thus, as the first part of the film ends, the two unlikely lovers seem able to shape a mutually satisfying life together. Although it is repeatedly made clear that this couple is viewed by others as an affront, their bond promises to surmount the difficulties they will encounter. We shall see, however, that this promise cannot withstand the pressures placed on it. Emmy and Ali are not as isolated as they feel—immersed in a deeply racist society, they will be denied the Disneyesque "forever after" mocked by *Jungle Fever*'s Flipper Purify.

Exploring Racial Privilege

If the first third of the film depicts how these two marginal characters come to provide one another with unaccustomed self-esteem and emotional security, the next section exposes the now publicly identifiable couple in almost clinical fashion to the racism of their social environment. Fassbinder's aim is to demonstrate that Emmy's status as a "true" German endows her with privileges of which she is completely unaware. He proceeds by indirection, however: By virtue of her relationship with Ali, she forfeits that privilege and comes to be treated as if she were herself a racial Other. Totally unprepared for this ordeal of rejection, by the end of this section of the film, she breaks down in grief.

The lesson of this painful sequence of episodes is that even the least members of the "master race" enjoy racial privilege—that is, a set of advantages that accrue because of membership in a racially superior caste. That there is such privilege is generally not understood by those who enjoy it, since they do not experience its workings as unusual. Rather, in ways imperceptible to them, it structures their very assumptions about who they are and how they deserve to be treated. As a result, the loss of that privilege is registered existentially as the dissolution of their own selves.

The subtleties of racial privilege can be illustrated by the well-known disparity between the experience of black and white shoppers in the United States. Well-dressed white American shoppers are rarely accorded a second look by suspicious clerks, whereas well-dressed blacks, whose skin color is taken to signify a propensity to shoplift, are accustomed to intense and sometimes hostile scrutiny.[11] The latter experience is generally understood as indicative of prejudice, but the relaxed attitude toward white patrons is less often identified as part of the same phenomenon. It is, therefore, necessary to insist that privileging white skin—or in this case, German nationality—is every bit as racist as demeaning black.

Particularly striking in this middle section of *Ali* is its showing that even Emmy—an older woman lacking education or skills, the widow of a Pole—has unwittingly benefited from racial privilege. Fassbinder's demonstration proceeds in systematic fashion, examining the damage done to each of four sets of relationships in Emmy's life—with her family members, her coworkers, her fellow apartment dwellers, and her local grocer—as a result of her relationship with Ali.

The seriousness of Emmy's transgression is immediately brought home at the small family gathering at which she has planned to announce her marriage. When she presents Ali to her children, the results are nothing less than catastrophic: One son, Bruno (Peter Gauhe), kicks in her TV; the second, Albert (Karl Scheydt), calls her a whore; to her daughter, Krista (Irm Hermann), the situation is "piggish." As they leave in scandalized disgust, what was to have been a joyous occasion ends with Emmy weeping.

The audience had been warned there would be trouble—the first time Emmy and Ali ascended the stairs together to her apartment, her neighbors had cast racial aspersions on them both. But this bit of unpleasantness had not conveyed the depth of these prejudices, which overwhelm even family ties.

A second incident occurs in the local grocery when Ali asks for some margarine in perfectly understandable German, only to have Herr Angermayer (Walter Sedlmayr), its proprietor, pretend not to understand his foreigner's syntax. Subsequently confronted by Emmy, the shop owner denies her charge of prejudice and throws her out. He would rather not have her as a customer than serve her foreigner lover.

As we have seen, Emmy's neighbors are scandalized by her relationship with Ali. Of course, they gossip among themselves, but more egregiously, they not only attempt to have her evicted by informing the landlord that she has someone living with her and call the police when Ali has a few friends in, they also generally make life in the building miserable for the two of them.

Finally, Emmy's colleagues shun her when they find out she is married to Ali. That these cleaning women were prejudiced against foreigners became evident on the day after Emmy and Ali slept together. Presumably to test the waters, Emmy raised the subject of relationships between German women and guest workers, and the response was unanimous and clear: Any woman who would consort with one of "them" is a whore. One of her coworkers, Paula Borchert (Gusti Kreissl), adds that no one speaks to a woman in her building who is married to a guest worker. When Emmy says, "Maybe she needs no one else if he speaks to her," Paula responds with a line that foreshadows Emmy's own fate: "No one can live without others. No one, Emmy."

Thus, it is no surprise that after Paula visits the apartment and meets Ali, her fellow workers freeze Emmy out, treating her as a pariah.[12] This scene ends with a shot of Emmy standing on the staircase of the building in which she works, looking out the window. She is shot from outside the building, framed by the building's geometry, and this shot is held motionless for several seconds, interrupting the flow of the narrative. Both features—the use of architecture as a framing device and the stationary camera that lingers on its subject—are typical of Fassbinder's technique in this film, here providing viewers a visual correlate of Emmy's isolation and dejection.[13]

Emmy's world reacts with disgust to her relationship with Ali. Thus, in this sequence of episodes, the film straightforwardly addresses those stereotypes of the black male sexuality that *Guess Who's Coming to Dinner* tries so hard to circumvent. Instead of evasion, Fassbinder directly confronts racism's sexual demonology: Ali, *this* black man, is in love with an aging German *Putzfrau!* As a result, the audience is less invested in erotic fantasies about on-screen events and so is able to see that the depth of animosity this couple brings out in others can only be accounted for psychodynamically—as a defensive reaction against unacknowledgeable desire. Emmy can only be viewed as a whore by others who project their own recognition of Ali's sexually desirability onto her and then condemn her for acting on it, even though that is not the ground of her relationship with him.

When Emmy and Ali subsequently go to an outdoor café and find themselves once more the object of hostile gazes, this time of the entire staff, Emmy once again breaks down (see Photo 9.1). Clearly, she had no idea what she was getting herself into. Unaware of her own investment in racial privilege, she could not anticipate how costly her transgression would be. As a result, she is only able to see herself as an isolated target of the hatred of others, the very sort of experience that when they first met, Ali had told her about as characteristic of his own life.

Love Versus Privilege

The third and final part of *Ali*—up to the apparent reconciliation between Ali and Emmy and his subsequent collapse and hospitalization—has puzzled viewers and critics alike. All the characters appear to have reversed their behavior: Those whose prejudice led them to reject Emmy now make up to her; she, in turn, begins to bully Ali and humiliate him in front of others; and Ali, who had earlier rejected Barbara's advances, now turns to her for solace. What are we to make of all this?

Critics who have focused only on the supporting cast attribute their changed behavior to their recognition that Emmy was actually very useful to them: The grocer needs her business, her son needs a baby-sitter, a neighbor wants to use her storage locker, and her coworkers need her support in securing a promised raise. Typical is Judith Mayne's reading of the significance of this reversal: "Social behavior is seen as the function of basic economic motivation. 'Prejudice' is no longer indulged when child care service is necessary or when groceries have to be sold."[14] According to this interpretation, the narrative now turns on the truism that when it is economically advantageous to discriminate, people will do so; and when their interests require them to veil their prejudice, they will behave accordingly.

This emphasis on the motivations of the film's secondary characters ignores the relation between their changed behavior toward Emmy and the emergence of difficulties between her and Ali, however. Burns and Lamb,

Photo 9.1 Emmy and Ali as the object of others' gaze

who do make this connection, argue that the rappr ochement between Emmy and her fellow Germans allows issues intrinsic to the couple to surface. Thus, in their view, the racist surround that seemed the source of their trouble really brought Emmy and Ali together, covering up otherwise serious incompatibilities.[15] In this interpretation, the significance of this reversal lies in its depiction of the ways in which obstacles external to a couple can create a false sense of connection between the partners.

Burns and Lamb are right to connect these narrative strands, but their analysis fails to correctly situate the significance of Emmy's increasingly racist behavior toward Ali. This change, on which, if I am right, the whole point of Fassbinder's inquiry into the persistence of racism rests, is puzzling—for although she has admitted to having been in the Nazi party as a young woman, Emmy has up to now shown no evidence that she harbors racist sentiments.

The first incident in which Emmy's changed attitude toward Ali is revealed occurs when Frau Ellis (Anita Buchler), a neighbor, asks if she can store some things in Emmy's cellar. Frau Ellis's willingness to approach

Emmy is the first signal to her that people may be willing to overlook her breach of the norms of racial etiquette. (The audience has already seen, in an incident of which Emmy herself is unaware, the grocer's wife urge him to make up with Emmy to regain her business.) Emmy agrees to Frau Ellis's request and promises that Ali will help move her things. Emmy returns to her apartment and, in essence, commands Ali to provide the help she has just promised. Since, as far as he knows, the neighbors are racists who have done everything imaginable to get him thrown out of the apartment, this seems inexplicable to him. Offering no explanation, Emmy acts as if Frau Ellis has been their friend all along, curtly ordering Ali to move things to the cellar.

Although this incident signals a change in Emmy's attitude toward Ali—albeit rather subtly—a later incident makes things clearer. Ali has asked Emmy to make couscous for him, but instead of responding to this expression of his homesickness, she proceeds to lecture him. First of all, she does not like couscous—as if that were a reason to deny his request—and anyhow, he needs to become used to things German. The idea that foreigners should trade in their ways—couscous for *Kartoffel*—is, of course, one frequently brandished by racists. The introduction of alternative practices into Germany sullies the purity of the *Volk*. Emmy's refusal smacks of this attitude. How different from the wistful, "Other countries, other customs," with which Emmy earlier met Ali's description of the multigenerational Moroccan household.

The issue here is not, of course, whether Emmy will make couscous for Ali, but the attitude behind Emmy's response: that Moroccan customs have nothing to offer Germany. Instead of allowing Ali a space in which to bring his own cultural background into his life in Germany, Emmy demands that he reject his heritage and conform to German practice. The film here asserts that the politics of integration is covertly one of assimilation, demanding that others reject their own culture in favor of that of the dominant group.[16] In light of Emmy's own mixed status as the wife of a Pole, her assertion of the superiority of German practices is deeply ironic.

The most shocking example of Emmy's collusive embrace of racism occurs when her two German coworkers visit her home. Two events contribute to their renewed acceptance of Emmy as one of them. First, after their other coworker had been fired for stealing, she was replaced by a Yugoslav. Yolanda (Helga Ballhaus) is the group's new scapegoat, the Other whose exclusion affirms their superiority, so that Emmy no longer need occupy this position. Second, the women have not received the pay raise due them and they require Emmy's participation as they plan to get what they think they are owed. Grateful for their approach, Emmy invites her two German colleagues, Paula and Hedwis (Margit Symd), to her apartment to discuss strategy.

Earlier, when Paula had been there, she had met Ali and this had led to Emmy's ostracism. This time, Emmy submits Ali to their Orientalizing gazes. The scene opens with a shot of Ali taken from behind Emmy and her coworkers. Paula comments, "He's so good looking, Emmy. Really. And so clean." This encourages Emmy to laud her husband's cleanliness in terms that transform him into an object of prurient curiosity. When Ali's build is remarked on, Emmy has him flex his biceps for her coworkers to examine. Fingering his bunched muscles, they circle around him, marveling at the softness of his skin (see Photo 9.2).

Doubly disturbing about this awful scene is how willingly Emmy demeans Ali in exchange for her colleagues' envious approval. In effect, she treats her relationship with him as if it were the purely sexual one the others fantasize. Emmy further demeans Ali by talking about him as if he were not there, as if he could not understand what was being said.

Stung, Ali breaks through the circle to escape the women, prompting one to ask what is wrong. "He has his moods," Emmy responds, "that's his foreign mentality." This last comment shows how fundamentally Emmy has changed. Emmy has just acquired some standing with her colleagues, who now admit they find the young and muscular Ali attractive. But their price for their acceptance is his humiliation—he is a moody foreigner, irrational, unlike "true" Germans who merit respect—a humiliation that Emmy willingly enacts.

Emmy's precipitous fall into racism is difficult to interpret because Fassbinder does not allow us access to the subjectivity of his characters. Rather, through a variety of cinematic techniques—such as the extended still shots that break up the flow of the narrative and the rather blank faces of the actors as they deliver their lines—we are denied sympathetic identification with their interior lives.[17]

Nonetheless, once we recall how Emmy has suffered as a result of her racial demotion, her behavior is readily understood. Her colleagues' renewed acceptance has allowed Emmy to experience racial privilege once again, with her racist treatment of Ali the price of her return ticket. It is as if she now understands what enjoying the privileges associated with being German requires. Prejudice and privilege are but two sides of the same racist coin. In principle, alternatives were open to Emmy. For example,

Photo 9.2 Ali on display

she could have turned to Yolanda and made common cause with her. Instead, rather than opt for solidarity with a fellow victim of her colleagues' racism, Emmy seems only too glad to win back for herself the racial privilege—and the self—she has lost.

Precise psychological explanations of Emmy's behavior are not important to Fassbinder. His interest is in showing how racial privilege works.[18] Once Emmy has experienced what it is like to be treated as racially Other, how it feels to be a foreigner in Germany, she is prepared to assume the cruel responsibilities such privilege entails.

Dismissed and disdained, Emmy and Ali were attracted to one another out of a shared need for acknowledgment. Because of their isolation, they could think of themselves as two loveless atoms come together to forge a common life. The film reveals the illusory nature of this belief. Like all human beings, Emmy and Ali are social individuals, their identities bound up in a complex web of relationships. Emmy—whose changing attitudes toward Ali are, after all, the real focus of this film—is not an individual who is incidentally German; her Germanness constitutes much of who she thinks she is, although she is not fully aware of this, even at the end of the film. *Ali* is a study of the impact of Emmy's social identity on her feelings and attitudes.

The striking aspect of Fassbinder's study of racial privilege, then, is its demonstration that even as socially marginal a German as Emmy is accorded significant racial privilege. Although it might seem that both Ali and Emmy are so marginal as to preclude a power differential between them, racial privilege is too deeply implicated in Emmy's existence for this to be true. The nature of the privileges she enjoys emerges from the contrast between Emmy's treatment before she became involved with Ali and her treatment subsequently. Fassbinder's cynical analysis is that awareness of racial privilege, rather than promoting solidarity with the oppressed, actually reinforces racism. The weakness of Emmy's character lies in her hunger for acceptance, a hunger that results in her acquiescence in social injustice. Emmy, who could not even order a drink in the Asphalt Pub without first knowing "the usual," cannot be expected to react to her ostracism with sympathy for the oppressed.

The ending of *Ali: Fear Eats the Soul* could be read as an attempt to deny the starkness of this conclusion. Emmy and Ali seem headed for reconciliation when he collapses, for they have danced together once again and acknowledged their love. In the hospital, Emmy plays the dutiful wife, sitting by the bed of the stricken Ali, waiting for him to get better.[19]

But for this reading to be plausible, the love that Emmy has for Ali would have to be shown to be stronger than her need for recognition by her fellow Germans. This is just what the film has shown not to be true. Emmy has tacitly accepted the exchange demanded of her: that she treat Ali as inferior if she expects the privileges due a "true" German. Although the consequence of her doing so is the loss of Ali, the film has not shown that, in practice, there is another option for her, a way for her to maintain her loving relationship with Ali in the face of the loss of her racial privilege.

As a result, *Ali* does not view its unlikely couple as presaging a possible future free of racism. The structures of racial hierarchy are too deeply implicated in the fabric of the self to be overcome by romantic love. Without explicit political commitments—unlike *Jungle Fever,* for example—*Ali*'s bleak inquiry into the existential realities of race privilege constitutes a devastating critique of the easy assumptions of films like *Guess Who's Coming to Dinner.*

A Final Problem

Ali's analysis of racial privilege is certainly impressive. It is tempting, therefore, to generalize its narrative into an account of the character of racists as lacking the psychic resources to withstand the pressures exerted by the withdrawal of racial privilege. Unfortunately, the film employs narrative and representational strategies that make such a generalization difficult to justify.

To show that racial privilege is a pervasive aspect of the existence of all "pure" Germans, the film adopts the narrative strategy of showing that even a seemingly powerless and marginal German enjoys racial privileges that a foreigner lacks. As we have seen, to make this point, the film employs a narrative in which the loss of her privilege causes Emmy to invert her way of interacting with Ali, accepting the terms of exchange offered by her fellow Germans: We will treat you as a fellow German so long as you show us that you understand that Ali is not. To make this reversal convincing, the film relies on a representational strategy of presenting Emmy as lacking self-confidence, as relying on others' opinions rather than her own views. This is the reason, for example, for the cola incident early in the film; it shows that Emmy lacks a strong self and is thus very susceptible to how others view her.

But although this representational strategy makes the narrative of Emmy's transformation plausible—and thus enables the film to show in stark relief the dynamics of racial privilege—it also limits the generality not so much of its analysis of racial privilege but of its explanation of what causes a person to accede to its pressure. Although Emmy is shown to lack the psychic resources that would enable her to bear her ostracism, say, by allowing her to conceive of herself as doing so in an heroic attempt to overcome the racism of German society, the film includes important elements that limit the generality of this analysis.

First, Fassbinder uses a variety of techniques that undercut the audience's tendency to identify with Emmy. In addition to the representational strategy of having her be an older, unattractive woman, the film keeps the audience psychologically distant from her by not revealing much of what she feels. As a result, audience members can see the analysis of Emmy's character as so specific that it does not explain why racism is such a pervasive feature of German society. They can distance the film's analysis by believing that racism infects only those with defective character structure, unlike themselves.

Second, the film includes narrative elements that suggest that Germans other than those in Emmy's milieu do not share its racist attitudes: The landlord's son, Herr Gruber (Marquard Bohm) chastises Emmy's neighbors for the way they have acted and the police are apologetic as they act on the neighbors' complaints. The inclusion of these episodes is unfortunate, for it suggests that people of a higher social status—owners and officials—do not share the racist attitudes of those in Emmy's environment. Again, this limits the generality of the film's explanation of why racism persists.

Thus, Fassbinder's *Ali*, despite its remarkable achievement in portraying the dynamics of racial privilege, finds itself in some of the same binds as the other unlikely couple films we have discussed. Its use of certain narrative and representative strategies to accomplish its goal undercuts its ability to achieve it. At the same time that *Ali* pushes the interracial unlikely couple film to new heights, it reveals the tensions inherent in the genre.

Notes

1. Despite its acknowledgment of the persistence of white racism, *Jungle Fever* has no analysis of that fact. Because the film offers Flipper a course of action that it endorses, its outlook is actually more optimistic. *Ali* is unique in its refusal to name a correct way of dealing with the reality of racism.

2. *Jungle Fever* does employ nonnaturalistic techniques, albeit in a less coherent way than *Ali*. Stylistic flourishes, they rarely advance the film's narrative line.

3. See, for example, Judith Mayne, "Fassbinder's *Ali: Fear Eats the Soul* and Spectatorship," in *Close Viewings: An Anthology of New Film Criticism*, Peter Lehman, ed. (Tallahassee: Florida State University Press, 1990), pp. 353–369, and Kaja Silverman, "Fassbinder and Lacan: A Reconsideration of Gaze, Look and Image," *Camera Obscura*, 19 (January 1989): pp. 54–83.

4. In U.S. terms, a German *Gastarbeiter* stands somewhere between a migrant worker and an illegal alien. Legally resident in Germany, they are nonetheless not German citizens and their children, even if born in Germany, are not entitled to citizenship. The situation of *Gastarbeiter* leads to many problems, but these are not central to *Ali*. Although at the time most guest workers were from Turkey, the film displaces this origin to take advantage of El Hedi ben Salem, who is Moroccan. Ali is actually the character's nickname. His real name parallels that of the actor: El Hedi ben Salem M'Barek Mohammed Mustapha.

5. See the essays mentioned in footnote 3, above.

6. In transcribing quotations from *Ali*, I generally follow the translations given in the subtitles. I occasionally change them, however, to improve their fidelity to the spoken German.

7. For an influential formulation of the issue of the purity of the German race, see Nietzsche's *Genealogy of Morals*, in *Basic Writings of Nietzsche*, Walter Kaufmann, ed. and tr. (New York: Modern Library, 1968). The extent to which Nietzsche's philosophy is contaminated by racism has been much debated.

8. *Ali*'s representative strategy is the inverse of that of *Guess Who's Coming to Dinner*. Not only do both characters come from the bottom segments of society,

but the black male's sexual attractiveness is emphasized by the film. The film thus courts racist reactions to the depiction of a sensual black male on the screen. I leave to the side the question of how Fassbinder's homosexuality may have affected this strategy. For an interesting study of the film that considers the question of homosexuality in relation to Ali, see Kaja Silverman, *Male Subjectivity at the Margins* (New York and London: Routledge, 1992), pp. 125–156.

9. Tonto, the Lone Ranger's sidekick in the radio and, then, the TV series, is a character who speaks English with something like the truncation of Ali's German, albeit without his perspicacity.

10. The difference between Ali's directness and normal German is pointed up in the sequence in which Emmy visits her daughter and son-in-law, who barely communicate despite their mastery of the rules of proper German.

11. Patricia Williams has written eloquently about personal experiences she has had of this sort in her *The Alchemy of Race and Rights* (Cambridge, MA: Harvard University Press, 1991).

12. The attitudes of her colleagues are conditioned by more than simple national chauvinism. Emmy's first marriage had already tainted the purity of her Germanness, so the hostility that her relationship with Ali causes must be the result of a more serious transgression.

13. The different meanings that these extended shots without action have in the film are discussed by Rob Burns and Stephen Lamb, "Social Reality and Stylization in *Fear Eats the Soul*: Fassbinder's Study in Prejudice," *New German Studies,* 9:3 (Autumn 1981): pp. 203 ff.

14. Judith Mayne, "Fassbinder's *Ali*," p. 364. A similar point is made by Burns and Lamb, "Social Reality and Stylization," p. 198.

15. Burns and Lamb, "Social Reality and Stylization," p. 196.

16. *Ali* thus views integration in a very different light from *Mississippi Masala.*

17. Fassbinder's technique derives from Brecht's conception of an epic theater. See *Brecht on Theatre: The Development of an Aesthetic,* John Willett, ed. and tr. (New York: Hill and Wang, 1964), pp. 33–42.

18. This leaves out of consideration an important aspect of racism, viz., how it inscribes itself onto the fantasy lives of human beings. This is a dimension of racism's tenacity that lies outside the ken of this film, but that we saw investigated by *Jungle Fever.*

19. Critics from Laura Mulvey on have pointed to the similarity between *Ali* and Douglas Sirk's *All That Heaven Allows* (1955). Although I believe that emphasis on these similarities has diverted attention from the distinctiveness of Fassbinder's study of racial privilege, their endings are similar. Fassbinder is not content with an upbeat conclusion, however, adding the doctor's verdict that Ali will never recover, for his illness will recur every six months until he dies. Fassbinder himself calls this an "absolutely authentic bit of guestworker-reality breaking in." See his *The Anarchy of the Imagination,* Michael Töteberg and Leo A. Lensing, eds. (Baltimore: Johns Hopkins University Press, 1992), p. 13.

Part Three

Sexual Orientation

10
Desert Hearts
Betting on Lesbian Love

The films considered in preceding chapters feature couples whose unlikeliness stems primarily from their cross-class and interracial makeup; their heterosexual character is one respect in which these couples are likely, that is, socially appropriate. This might suggest that for the genre as a whole, the normative status of heterosexuality is taken for granted—that romantic couples are necessarily composed of a man and a woman—a premise that would warrant the charge of heterosexism, the illicit privileging of heterosexuality as the only acceptable sexual orientation. The films that I turn to in this chapter and the next—*Desert Hearts* and *The Crying Game*, respectively—by using the romances of their nonheterosexual couples to show that the injuries inflicted by heterosexism are as profound as those caused by class, race, and gender hierarchy, incidentally clear the genre of this charge.

Set in the confining atmosphere of 1950s Nevada, Donna Deitch's 1986 film, *Desert Hearts*—the subject of this chapter—tells the story of a transgressive love affair between two women: twenty-five-year-old Cay Rivvers (Patricia Charbonneau), who works as a change girl in a casino, and Vivian Bell (Helen Shaver), a professor of English literature at Columbia University who has come to Nevada to get a divorce. Cay was thrown out of art school for her lesbianism, and she now pursues her interest in sculpting in her spare time, grudgingly reconciled to the safer, albeit less fulfilling, life she leads among Reno's gamblers and casino employees.[1] To meet Nevada's residency requirement, Vivian has established herself on the ranch run by Cay's stepmother, Frances Parker (Audra Lindley).[2] As Vivian tells her lawyer early in the film, she is seeking a divorce because, at age thirty-five, she is tired of living dishonestly: "I want to be free of who I've been."[3] Unlike Cay, Vivian has achieved a great deal, but at the cost of her own happiness. Her desire to lead a more emotionally satisfying life is tempered, however, by her fear of the consequences of striking out on her own.

Following what we now recognize as the standard logic of the unlikely couple film, *Desert Hearts* presents romantic union as the solution to the problems facing these two women: Each can encourage the other to express that part of herself she has denied. All that stands in the way is Vivian's reluctance to publicly identify herself as lesbian. Most of the film concerns Cay's resolute campaign to get Vivian to acknowledge her lesbianism and, along with it, her need for Cay. Although the younger woman suffers from a last-minute case of the jitters when confronted with the possibility of success, Vivian's internal resistance is the real obstacle this couple needs to overcome.

At the same time, as we have reason to expect, the story of these two unlikely partners advances a critique of sexual hierarchy—for *Desert Hearts* intends the story of Cay and Vivian as a challenge to heterosexuality's normative status, a demonstration that there is a plurality of valid expressions of human sexual desire.[4] The film's brief for this position is developed through the contrast between what Cay's and Vivian's lives can be when supported by their love for one another and the sadness and desperation they otherwise suffer.

At the narrative level, then, *Desert Hearts* depicts how the existence of the "closet"—the consignment of homosexuality to a space of acknowledged invisibility—exacts deep psychic costs to those both within and without it.[5] In the case of Vivian, who is living in the closet, her sacrifice of emotional fulfillment is clearly attributable to the dynamics of heterosexism and homophobia; as for Cay, living out of the closet, her "deviance" has deprived her of opportunity to develop her artistic talents.

But *Desert Hearts*'s significance as an unlikely couple film transcends its extension of the genre to the subject of homosexuality: Hoping to reach a wide audience, yet keenly aware of the prejudices of many of its members, the film designs a set of representational strategies to deflect homophobic responses to its depiction of lesbian lovemaking. Of considerable interest, then, is the manner in which the film simultaneously presents a love story with which lesbian viewers can identify while developing ways to keep straight viewers from reacting negatively to its graphic portrayal of lesbian sex.

"If You Don't Play, You Can't Win"

Unlike the cross-class films—such as *It Happened One Night*—that its transformation narrative resembles, *Desert Hearts* involves a quite direct program of seduction. Cay realizes almost immediately that Vivian can provide her with the love she both desires and needs, and this sets her on a course of action designed to push Vivian to reciprocal acknowledgment of her need for Cay. Because of Vivian's reluctance to come out, or even to acknowledge her lesbianism to herself, Cay must proceed cautiously, encouraging Vivian's developing self-acceptance without spooking her. For Cay, however, each step is also a gamble staked on her dream.

In asserting the necessity of risk, *Desert Hearts* transforms its Nevada setting from an interesting locale, suitable because of its contrast with New York, into its central metaphor for living out one's desire. This use of gambling as metaphor is made explicit in the scene in which Vivian enters the casino where Cay works, sporting a new, red cowgirl shirt that Cay has helped her pick out. The transformation in her appearance marks the first step in Vivian's rejection of her old self, whose customary tailored suits made her look old, unattractive, and emotionally pinched. In the casino, she encounters a woman (played by Donna Deitch, the film's director) who has just won a large jackpot playing the slots. As Vivian looks on, the woman tells her, "If you don't play, you can't win." In their different ways, both Vivian and Cay have sought to control their lives by reducing their exposure to the opprobrium of the straight world.[6]

In the very next sequence, the metaphor is extended further, as Vivian finds herself, at the behest of a gambler, rolling the dice at a craps table. Reluctantly, she has given in to his repeated entreaties. When she actually wins, her excitement and pleasure convey how costly her avoidance of risk has been. Once she is induced to overcome her inhibitions, gambling—or at least, winning—proves to be exhilarating. The question now suggests itself: Will she be persuaded to overcome her fears of lesbianism and allow herself to risk being with Cay?

The film's answer is that to get Vivian to decide to play *this* game, Cay herself has to place a number of calculated bets. And, as in this vignette, Vivian ultimately enjoys playing so much that she takes the final step— and before Cay is quite ready.

Finally, the metaphoric claim for the necessity of gambling can be extended self-reflexively to *Desert Hearts* itself. Faced with the likelihood of homophobic reactions to its depiction of lesbianism, the film slowly allows itself to take bigger and bigger risks in its representation of lesbian love. At the same time that it tells the story of these two gay women in the repressive atmosphere of 1950s Nevada, *Desert Hearts* reveals its own concern with the repressiveness of popular cinema in the 1980s and, like its characters, decides that it can only achieve its aims by making a large wager.

Disarming Homophobia

Prior to 1980, there was, unsurprisingly, no cinematic tradition of depicting homosexual sexual relationships in a positive light.[7] Homosexuality has been—and continues to be, despite some recent attempts to change this[8]—a controversial topic for mainstream filmmaking. Stephen Farber explains:

> Before 1961, the Production Code, Hollywood's censorship ordinance, forbade any hint of "sex perversion." When the code was finally revised to allow discreet treatment of homosexuality, the first movies on the subject—*Advise and Consent* and *The Children's Hour*—depicted gays as repressed and miserably unhappy.[9]

In the 1970s and 1980s, films began to be made that focused on gay couples without stigmatization. Only after the gay liberation movement had secured recognition, at least in a certain segment of the population, that a homosexual orientation was not a perversion was it possible to make popular films depicting gay relationships as nonpathological.

Still, lesbianism was largely absent from mainstream film. *Desert Hearts* marks a new determination to bring it before popular audiences.[10] Consequently, although financed entirely by Deitch's own efforts, the film possesses Hollywood-like features—for example, its transformation narrative and country music sound track—presumably to reassure skittish heterosexuals in its audience.[11] At the same time, the film wants to give lesbians positive images of lesbian romance and sexuality.

As a result, *Desert Hearts* had to develop narrative and representational strategies that would deflect, insofar as possible, homophobic responses to its depictions of queer couples. The quandary confronting Deitch was much like that facing makers of the interracial unlikely couple films of the late 1960s and the 1970s, who were forced to disarm negative stereotypes of black male sexuality—for example, *Guess Who's Coming to Dinner,* by desexualizing its male protagonist, and *Ali: Fear Eats the Soul,* by exhibiting the vicious stupidity of those stereotypes. As we shall see, *Desert Hearts* devises strategies of its own designed to ensure that its audience responds to the on-screen representation of lesbianism in a positive manner.

One such strategy involves deploying characters who react homophobically to the film's unlikely couple, characters whose animosity is revealed to be based on their own unrequited desire for one of the partners, Cay. In thus tainting their motivations, the film seeks to enlist its audience's sympathy for the couple.

Frances, Cay's stepmother, is the first of two characters whom the film invests with this homophobic response. Many heterosexual unlikely couple films feature a parent of the female partner—usually the father—who presents a serious obstacle to the couple, but Frances's opposition to her stepdaughter's relationship is different from that of these patriarchs, for, as suggested above, it is motivated by her unacknowledged attraction to Cay.[12]

That this is the source of Frances's hostility to the couple emerges in a scene that takes place one night when Cay encounters Vivian in the ranch house kitchen. Anxious not to awaken Frances, the two quietly search for something to eat and drink. As they do so, a deep bond develops between them because of Cay's solicitude for the fragile and suffering Vivian: Cay alone acknowledges Vivian's courage in seeking a divorce. Their attempts at quiet are unavailing, however—Frances calls down to Cay, asking her to bring up a Coke. The older woman has been drinking, and when she asks to be held, Cay hesitates. For her part, Frances is critical of Cay, who is wearing only a shirt, admonishing her to dress more appropriately in front of Vivian. As Cay reluctantly cradles her stepmother in her arms, Frances reveals that she may be forced to sell the ranch. But, she assures Cay, she will buy another place where the two of them may live, and she will even help Cay return to art school.

Many features of this scene establish Frances's repressed sexual attraction to Cay. Cay's state of undress is discomfiting, not on Vivian's behalf, but because Frances is aroused by it; her desire to be held is the only socially acceptable form her yearning can take. Finally, Frances's fantasy of the two of them alone together—Did she simply forget the existence of her son, Walter (Alex McArthur)?—expresses the real nature of her impermissible wish.

Frances's thwarted desire is also the best explanation of her overreaction when Vivian and Cay return to the ranch together the morning after the wedding of Cay's good friend, Silver (Andra Akers): Frances humiliates

Vivian by throwing her off the ranch and nearly precipitates the very break with Cay she fears. Although she claims to be acting out of moral revulsion at lesbianism, it is her fear of losing Cay to Vivian that unhinges her.

The same mechanism underlies Frances's repeated emphasis on the cross-class nature of the couple. Early on, she warns Vivian to stay away from Cay—"It's just that she doesn't have anything in common with a person of your caliber"—and she later cautions Cay that Vivian will hurt her because Vivian's superior class position precludes her having a committed relationship with a working-class woman.[13] The truth is that Frances's hostility to Vivian is attributable to her realization that Vivian's class position as an intellectual promises Cay's ambitions as an artist the supportive environment Frances cannot provide no matter how hard she tries.

Desert Hearts's revelation that Frances's homophobic reaction to the Cay-Vivian couple has its unacknowledged origin in her thwarted desire for Cay is meant to preempt a similar reaction by its audience members. Insofar as they accept the film's critical depiction of Frances, they should find it difficult to simply endorse whatever negative reactions they themselves might have to its lesbian lovers.

In analogous fashion, Darrell (Dean Butler), Cay's boss, represents heterosexual male disapproval, and for the same reason: As a result of a brief affair, Darrell has fallen in love with Cay and continues to pursue her despite her repeated protestations that she is a lesbian who stupidly allowed herself "to get attracted by his attraction" for her. Cay consistently turns down his rather forceful attempts to rekindle their romance, but Darrell just as steadfastly refuses to accept Cay's "No."

Darrell stubbornly believes he, and not Vivian, should be Cay's partner, and he makes a number of attempts to come between the two women. After one particularly obnoxious effort, he comments to Silver, "Cay's stepping way out of her range with that woman." Like Frances, Darrell takes exception to the couple because he is attracted to Cay, and again like Frances, he expresses his frustration by denigrating the couple's cross-class makeup as well as its lesbianism.

Desert Hearts's representational strategy, then, is to use both Darrell, a heterosexual male character, and Frances, an apparently heterosexual female one, to problematize for the audience its own possible homophobic reactions to the couple. Because the film presents these two unsuccessful suitors' homophobia as a displacement of their sexual attraction to Cay, it expects its audience to distance itself from their censorious reactions to the couple.

Corollary to this strategy is the inclusion of Cay's friend Silver, whose positive attitude toward the couple can model the response that the film intends for its audience. Like Darrell and Frances, Silver too is working class, but unlike them she is happily in love and her wedding plays an important role in the film. Silver, the film argues, can be supportive of Cay and undisturbed by Cay's sexual orientation because she is not personally threatened by lesbianism. The film goes out of its way to depict Silver's untroubled acceptance of Cay despite the difference in their sexual orientations, even showing them taking a bubble bath together—while Joe (Antony Ponzini), Silver's fiancé, makes them dinner—with no suggestion that the women's physical intimacy is a problem for any of them. Thus, by contrasting the attitude of someone who is emotionally fulfilled to the attitudes of two deeply unhappy characters, *Desert Hearts* attempts to foreclose the possibility of a homophobic response to the couple on the part of heterosexual viewers.

Desert Hearts's depiction of Darrell's and Frances's sexual insecurity as the cause of their opposition to lesbian couples could be taken for a general claim about the sources of homophobia. The film would then be seen to offer an analysis of why the opposition to such couples is so strident, claiming that this vehemence provides an outlet for frustrated sexual drives. But even if it is granted that such an account is unsatisfactory—as I think it must be—the film's inclusion of these homophobic characters illustrates its awareness of the complexities of representing lesbian love in a still largely hostile society.

Representing Lesbian Love

The focus of *Desert Hearts*'s narrative is Cay's bold yet cautiously implemented seduction/transformation of Vivian, aimed at getting her to publicly acknowledge her lesbianism. Cay's cagey strategy of progressively upping the ante parallels that of the film itself as it gradually seduces its audience into accepting its representation of lesbian lovemaking. It, too, paves a way—in this case, for its unconventional portrayal of lesbian sex—with a series of less risky gambits. But in the end, like Cay, it can only achieve its goal through the calculated strategy of shedding its inhibitions and confronting the issue directly.

To have a successful career, Vivian has walled herself off from her own emotions, and although she finally has initiated divorce proceedings out of her dissatisfaction with her marriage, the resultant feelings overwhelm her. Vivian seems unaccustomed to coping with disruptions of her calm,

Photo 10.1 Cay transforming Vivian

professorial routines. Only slowly will she allow Cay to free her of the many ways she has stifled her desires.

Vivian's transformation is first adumbrated through the safe choice of altering her attire and coiffure. When we first see her, her severe appearance—her suits, her tightly controlled hairstyle—accentuates her primness. Moreover, she is shot in sharp focus and in washed-out gray tones to the same effect. Cay's first step in transforming Vivian involves helping her buy some Western clothes. With boots, jeans, and a red Western shirt, all set off by a modish, new hairstyle allowing her long hair to flow more freely, Vivian soon cuts a very different figure from the drone who descended the train in Reno (see Photo 10.1). Again, the effect is technically heightened, this time by the film's use of softened lighting and richer color. With a little help from her newfound friend, a different Vivian is emerging, one expressive of those appetites the repressed academic had for so long kept in check.

Although the first stage of Vivian's transformation is represented in safe terms, avoiding any direct depiction of lesbian sex, things soon take a

Photo 10.2 Lesbian passion

more carnal turn, when on the morning after Silver's wedding, Vivian and Cay go to Lake Tahoe to watch the sunrise. As the sun ascends over the mountains, Cay tells Vivian that she is gay. The professor takes this opportunity to explain why they cannot be a couple but she cannot quite get the words out; then, an abrupt jump cut reveals a drenched Vivian sitting in the car to escape the rain, with Cay standing outside, banging on the window. When Vivian responds by rolling down the window, Cay begins to nuzzle her and, then, slowly the hesitant Vivian allows herself to share in a deep, passionate kiss (see Photo 10.2). Suddenly, Vivian breaks off the kiss and shakily rolls the window back up. Cay reenters the car, clearly very excited, for to her the kiss they have exchanged symbolizes Vivian's openness to a lesbian relationship. Vivian immediately retreats, however, telling Cay, "I don't know where that came from. It's back where it belongs and I don't want to talk about it anymore."

Both Cay and the film have taken a calculated risk with this next step in their respective seduction scenarios. Cay has gambled that Vivian has progressed sufficiently far in understanding the real nature of her sexuality that she now needs only further encouragement for their relationship to be consummated. Vivian's reaction seems to bode ill for Cay's project, but we shall see that it only reinforces Cay's determination to stake all on its success.

Desert Hearts has also taken a calculated gamble in its representation of lesbian sexuality. Counting on the rapport it has established with its audience, it now frankly depicts an on-screen kiss between two women—by way of comparison, recall *Guess Who's Coming to Dinner*'s timid depiction of an interracial kiss contained by a taxi's rearview mirror (see Photo 6.1).

Cay's gamble has succeeded in freeing Vivian's lesbianism from its closet, even if only for a moment, but it has seemingly disastrous consequences for the couple. In the scene to which I have already referred, Frances, claiming to be appalled by their disappearance and what it signifies, summarily throws Vivian off the ranch, as if that will end the relationship. Instead, it seals Cay's resolve to leave the ranch as well and to embark on her—and the film's—riskiest stratagem yet.

Meanwhile, Vivian settles into a nondescript hotel, deeply unhappy about what has transpired: Publicly humiliated for her still-incipient lesbianism, she is also miserable because she fears she has lost Cay. The film conveys her sense of loss through one of its standard, but highly ironic, techniques: using an overtly heterosexual country song to convey Vivian's lesbian heartbreak. On the one hand, this strategy functions to normalize lesbianism, for the audience is asked to see that despite the differences between the song's heterosexist assumptions and the lesbian reality, the emotional situations are identical.[14] On the other hand, the humorous disparity between the song's heterosexual scenario and the film's lesbian one breaks the audience's suspension of disbelief, calling its attention to the film's clever construction and, implicitly, to the artlessness of conventional romantic narratives. Shot in slow motion, Vivian showers as Jim Reeves plaintively sings "He'll Have to Go," a song in which a jilted lover begs his betrayer to tell the man next to her in bed to leave. Despite the inappositeness of its content, the loneliness and desperation of the song convey Vivian's emotions.[15]

Things come to a head when Cay appears at Vivian's hotel door. A reluctant Vivian lets her in, but only to explain why their encounter at Lake Tahoe did not really mean anything. She talks of being "a respected scholar"—as if that were adequate grounds for denying her lesbianism—and of their kiss being "a moment's indiscretion and a fleeting lapse of judgment"—words that seek to contain the implications of what has transpired between them. Undeterred, Cay decides that circumstances require a final gamble: Behind Vivian's back and off-screen, she simply disrobes and sits waiting in bed with her breasts exposed. When Vivian finally notices her, she is shocked by Cay's directness and tries to get her to leave. But Cay will not be put off and, eventually, she prevails: Vivian accepts Cay's wager and an extended scene of lovemaking follows.

Cay's gamble is paralleled by the film's risk of an extended on-screen depiction of lesbian lovemaking. The chance it takes is that this sequence will either provoke heterosexual viewers to react homophobically or else be experienced by them as titillation. To forestall either possibility, the film's visual representation of lesbian sex departs from the classical heterosexual models that *Desert Hearts* has otherwise followed, accentuating the film's claim about the differences between lesbian and heterosexual love. Following on a conversation photographed in typical, and typically paced, shot/reverse shot manner, the lovemaking between Cay and Vivian is filmed either in close-up or at medium range with only minimal editing. The sequence begins with an extended medium shot of the two kissing. When Vivian breathlessly reacts with the rather stock exclamation that she never felt this way before, Cay removes Vivian's robe and the film cuts of a close-up of another kiss. Cay then moves her lips to Vivian's breast, followed by Vivian's descending to Cay's, in a reversal of position. Next comes a medium shot during which they both reach orgasm, the intensity of this moment now emphasized by rather frequent cuts. After a final kiss, the scene fades to black.

Technically interesting features of this scene include prolonged shots with little cutting or camera movement, except for an occasional pan. Although the two lovers are quite passionate, the scene has none of the speed and desperation we have come to expect of Hollywood representations of heterosexual intercourse. Instead, the editing conveys a sense that protracted lovemaking is necessary to the two women's sexual fulfillment. In addition to these visual techniques, the absence of music on the sound track heightens the immediacy of the sexual imagery. Instead of the building crescendos that normally cue the audience in to the rush of sexual passion—but also distract its attention from the visual images—*Desert Hearts* insistently foregrounds its visual presentation of lesbian lovemaking.

This scene is a high-stakes gamble indeed: To show its lesbian couple making love is to risk the possibility that it will titillate some heterosexual viewers and alienate others, thereby subverting the film's effectiveness as social critique.[16] A more risk-averse strategy would have involved some hugs, a few chaste kisses, and lots of dialogue emphasizing the couple's grand passion, the option Stanley Kramer chose for *Guess Who's Coming to Dinner*. In keeping with its message of "If you don't play, you can't win" and its commitment to normalizing lesbianism, *Desert Hearts* takes the bolder course.

The relaxed pace of the lovemaking, the subdued camera work, and the unobtrusive editing make viewing this scene very different from watching two women go at it in a porno film intended for men. There are no long shots inviting male viewers to fantasize their presence into the scene—the two women occupy almost all of the screen space, and unrevealingly at that.

On the other hand, it must be recognized that for lesbian audiences, this scene offers images never before available in mainstream film. Although *Desert Hearts* is not a Hollywood film, its high production values imply that it was made with hopes of commercial success and wide distribution. Nonetheless, its daring inclusion of lesbian lovemaking allows gay women to see on-screen a form of sexuality they can—although some might not—identify with. It certainly marks a significant expansion of what can be seen at the local multiplex on a Saturday night.

More remains before the couple can be assured of its future—Vivian falters once again before finally accepting her lesbianism and Cay has to face her fear of failure in New York—but both Cay and her creators have staked their limit. As the film proceeds to neatly wrap up the loose ends of its narrative, the audience's hope for this couple is that now that they have learned to play the game, their payout will be worth the gamble.

The Problem of Class

In this chapter, I have argued that *Desert Hearts* employs several interesting and innovative narrative and representational strategies aimed at depathologizing lesbianism. And as we have seen, its project of normalizing lesbian sexuality is served by some equally innovative filming. Although the use of these techniques has not been generally recognized by its critics, their significance justifies the judgment that *Desert Hearts* is an important contribution to a posthomophobic cinema.[17]

On the other hand, the film's representation of class—an issue I have so far avoided—invites a rather different assessment. Discussing the film's depiction of homophobia through the Frances and Darrell characters, I claimed that their negative emphasis on the couple's cross-class composition was a displacement of their real anxiety over its lesbianism. The film's overall portrayals of class cannot be so easily accounted for. Instead, we need to acknowledge that *Desert Hearts* represents working-class figures as generally incapable of the emotional depth it attributes to upper-middle-class intellectuals. For all its sensitivity to the injuries inflicted by heterosexual normativity, its representations of class difference are content with cliché.

This condescension to the working class is present even in the film's depiction of one of Cay's lesbian partners, Gwen (Gwen Welles). Early in the film, while taking Gwen home after a night together, Cay offers Vivian a lift into town to meet her lawyer. When Cay switches from a country station playing "Be Bop a Lula" sung by Gene Vincent to a classical one playing what Vivian identifies as Prokofiev's "Suite for Three Horns," Gwen attacks Cay for putting on airs to attract Vivian. Vivian resolves the conflict by switching back to the country station.

What is problematic here is that even this lesbian is presented as shallow, unable to give Cay what she needs, because she is working class and therefore incapable of understanding serious art. *Desert Hearts* posits a chain of equivalences similar to the one we saw *White Palace* criticize: Gwen = country music = working class = superficial; Vivian = classical music = upper class = deep. Although it is easy to see that the film invokes these equivalences to encode the alternatives available to Cay, in so doing it appears to endorse the class prejudices expressed by both Darrell and Frances. To supply Cay with a partner who can provide her with opportunities to develop her artistic talents, the film's representational strategy adopts, perhaps unreflectively, the overt class bias Frances and Darrell have expressed.

Despite this failing, *Desert Hearts* convincingly affirms the power of love to surmount barriers of class and sexual orientation. In so doing, it both condemns those heterosexist norms that continue to regulate the gender composition of romantic couples and contributes, in some measure, to their weakening.

Notes

1. Although the film's narrative identifies Cay as a sculptor, when we see her bungalow on the ranch, she seems to be a potter.

2. Legally, Frances is not Cay's stepmother, since she was not married to Cay's father, Walter. Nevertheless, she assumes the role of mother to Cay.

3. All quotations from *Desert Hearts* are from my transcription of the film's soundtrack.

4. In *History of Sexuality: Volume 1, An Introduction,* Robert Hurley, tr. (New York: Pantheon Books, 1978), Michel Foucault argues that defining human sexuality in terms of the sex of one's partner choice is a recent development and that sexual liberation involves factors more than depathologizing same-sex couples.

5. In the Introduction to *Epistemology of the Closet* (Berkeley: University of California Press, 1990), Eve Kosofsky Sedgwick eloquently argues that the closet, i.e., the need to conceal/reveal homosexuality, is a fundamental characteristic of Western culture. Sedgwick also emphasizes other forms of "sexual deviance" besides homosexuality, but these are beyond the scope of this discussion. In this connection, however, it might be worth explicitly acknowledging that Cay has been sexually active with both men and women.

6. Deitch acknowledges the importance of this metaphor to the film. She claims that she "was really drawn to the central metaphor" of Jane Rule's novel, *Desert of the Heart* (Tallahassee: Naiad Press, 1964), on which the film was based. See Michele Kort, "Independent Filmmaker Donna Deitch Controls her Whole Show," *MS,* November 1985, p. 66.

7. The history of depictions of homosexuality is discussed in Vito Russo's groundbreaking work, *The Celluloid Closet: Homosexuality in the Movies* (New York: Harper and Row, 1981 and 1987).

8. Recent films that attempt this include *Heavenly Creatures* (1994), *When Night Is Falling* (1995), and *High Art* (1998).

9. Quoted by Stanley Kauffmann in a negative review of *Desert Hearts* titled "Harsh Contradictions," *The New Republic,* May 12, 1986, pp. 24–26.

10. *Desert Hearts* is not the first popular narrative film to show lesbian lovemaking. *Personal Best* (1982) was, but in a very different way. Vito Russo's criticism, in *The Celluloid Closet,* of *Desert Hearts*'s depiction for the presence of "the steamy erotic sequences between women that heterosexual men have traditionally enjoyed" (p. 278) does not acknowledge the innovative way in which these sequences are filmed.

11. The difficulty of financing the film is discussed by Jackie Stacey in her article "'If You Don't Play, You Can't Win': *Desert Hearts* and the Lesbian Romance Film," in *Immortal, Invisible: Lesbians and the Moving Image,* Tamsin Wilson, ed. (London and New York: Routledge, 1995), pp. 92–114.

12. Jackie Stacey notes *Desert Hearts*'s use of this convention of romance films. But she does not see Frances's sexual attraction to Cay. See "'If You Don't Play . . . ,'" especially, p. 100.

13. This interesting suggestion parallels a standard view of how upper-class men treat working-class women—fine for sexual dalliances, but not for committed relationships, a theme explored in *White Palace.*

14. The film has been criticized for this equation. See, for example, Christine Holmlund, "When Is a Lesbian Not a Lesbian?: The Lesbian Continuum and the Mainstream Femme Film," *Camera Obscura,* 25–26 (1991): pp. 145–178.

15. Jackie Stacey calls attention to the film's strategy of disruption but fails to see how this might give rise to feelings of discomfort in an audience expecting a straightforward romantic narrative. As a result, her criticism of the film for its lack of emotional engagement seems off base. See her, "'If You Don't Play . . . ,'" pp. 106, 109.

16. In a generally critical discussion of the film's politics, *"Desert Hearts," The Independent,* 10:6 (July 1987): p. 17, Mandy Merck claims that the film places women viewers in the typically male, voyeuristic position of "actively desiring her [the woman's] seduction and identifying with her seducer." Merck sees Cay's seduction of Vivian as morally problematic rather than as the bold strategy I claim it to be.

17. *My Beautiful Launderette* (1985), another film that falls in this category, represents male homosexuality as a deviant type of couple formation, but in the context of ethnic as well as class difference.

11

The Crying Game

Loving in Ignorance

The conflict between the romantic and social perspectives that character-izes the unlikely couple film is predicated on the significance accorded hi-erarchic orderings of class, race, gender, and sexual orientation. From the social perspective, partners are unsuited to one another when one comes from a dominant, the other from a subordinate, group.[1] Although most of the films I have discussed are critical of the social perspective's valoriza-tion of a privileged term over a denigrated one, their criticism does not target hierarchical ordering itself.

Neil Jordan's *The Crying Game* (1992) sets its sights on this very issue—its goal, to destabilize such schemes of ordering by showing that they do not adequately capture—indeed they deform—the reality of human expe-rience. The film attempts to realize its ambitions by showing how an un-acceptable certitude in the soundness of the set of political distinctions—foremost among them, British/Irish, oppressor/oppressed—that governs the terrorist practice of an Irish Republican Army (IRA) cell results in ni-hilistic violence. The meanings of these distinctions, the film asserts, vary from context to context.

The Crying Game's basic narrative strategy is to use the story of a pair of unlikely couples—or more accurately, perhaps, of an unlikely triangle—to demonstrate that human beings can overcome the social divisions that separate them to arrive at an essential commonality. Among the obstacles capable of elimination are race; ethnicity; and, most significantly for the film, sexual orientation. The social perspective treats such obstacles to ro-mance as insuperable; the film shows us that there are redemptive possi-bilities for human connection more powerful still.

In what we might call its "metaphysics"—its understanding of how, at bottom, things are—these possibilities are related to a further distinction, one that *The Crying Game* endorses as unconditionally valid, between "frogs" and "scorpions." The politics of the IRA are represented as akin to the compulsions of the scorpion in Aesop's fable, who after stinging the frog bearing him across a river—even though that ensures his own death—explains that he did it because it was in his nature to do so.[2] The gullible frog had been led to his death through his empathy with the scorpion's difficulties. This distinction between those who exploit the empathy of others and those who empathize is the one distinction the film claims to be resistant to destabilization, and is the one that explains the connection of the unlikely partners, for they are all three frogs.[3]

The film's ingenious narrative destabilizes ethnic and racial hierarchies with seeming ease. There is one dichotomy, however—that between heterosexuality and homosexuality—that seems resistant: Even if we accept the idea that sexual orientation is a social construction, there seems no easy way to challenge one's understanding of one's own sexual orientation. But this is just what the narrative of *The Crying Game* proposes in its story of the relationship of an IRA terrorist, Fergus Hennessy (Stephen Rea), to two black men: Jody (Forest Whitaker), the British soldier taken hostage, and Dil (Jaye Davidson), a transvestite who was Jody's lover.[4]

Destabilizing Sexuality

To understand how *The Crying Game* proceeds, we need to recall how the unlikely couple film deploys its narrative of transgressive romance for purposes of social critique. As we have seen time after time, the genre's basic narrative strategy is to use its audience's empathy for its subject couple to subvert the hold of certain dominant norms, and this entails that the transgressive lovers be sufficiently appealing to motivate outrage toward the society that would proscribe their romance. What the films need, then, are representational strategies that allow their audiences to form positive attachments to their unlikely couples (or at least, to one of the partners).

Again, as I have repeatedly remarked, the pervasive hold of negative stereotypes presents a problem for films seeking to counter invidious distinctions of class, race, gender, and sexual orientation. Because some—perhaps many—in their audiences will be captives of such stereotypes, films that target these distinctions must set about defusing anticipated negative viewer response.

To further its agenda of destabilizing the "hetero/homo" distinction, *The Crying Game* chooses the radical course of problematizing those assumptions about sexual desire that underlie that distinction. Rather than attempting to minimize homophobic responses by sanitizing its depiction of homosexuality, the film limits its audience's knowledge to allow the crucial revelation of Dil's sex to undermine viewers' faith in their own sexual certainties.

The Crying Game, then, challenges its audience's faith in the homo/hetero distinction, less by trying to valorize a form of "deviant" sexuality—the strategy I attributed to *Desert Hearts*—than by showing that human sexuality is too complex and fluid to be neatly captured by these two, hierarchized categories—indeed, that human sexuality cannot be understood in the terms normally taken to define it.

Owing largely to the work of feminist theorists, the sex-gender distinction has become central to current discussions of human sexuality. Adopting their practice, I use the term "sex" here to refer to that division of the species into male and female based on certain physical characteristics. Although recent research indicates that the human species is not sexually dimorphic, that there are other possibilities for the distribution of sexual characteristics than those represented by the standard two sexes, our understanding of human sexuality is still generally predicated on the idea that the presence of either a penis or a vagina is determinative.[5] The term "gender" is then be reserved for distinctions made on the basis of certain practices, clearly socially determined—such as wearing or not wearing dresses and makeup—constitutive of femininity and masculinity.

Unless it is assumed that gender is exhaustively determined by biological sex, discriminating sex from gender complicates the assumption that there are just two sexual orientations—hetero- and homosexuality.[6] Particularly confounding are transvestites, or cross-dressers, biological males who enact femininity or biological females who enact masculinity. Although transvestites can be either hetero- or homosexual, it is the existence of homosexual transvestites that destabilizes a binarized understanding of sexual orientation—since, for example, a male transvestite can be the desired sexual object of a homosexual man. One aim of *The Crying Game* is to show that the hetero/homo dichotomy does not do justice to those vagaries of human sexual desire to which the existence of transvestism attests.[7] Thus, central to the film's strategy of destabilization is its claim that in the realm of human sexuality, things are not as immutable as our categories make it seem. Sex, gender, and sexuality are more various and shifting than the language we use to conceptualize their natures.

Other social hierarchies targeted by *The Crying Game* are destabilized more conventionally, in a succession of episodes depicting the developing friendship between Fergus and Jody. But with sexuality, a more complex narrative strategy seems required to convince viewers that *their* sexual desire is less simple than they may have thought. Thus, the film leads its predominantly straight audience into actually sharing Fergus's experience of destabilization.

A Strategy of Deception

The Crying Game's narrative strategy involves deceiving its viewers about the significance of what is transpiring on-screen. In this way, the film hopes to get male viewers to see a male transvestite as sexually desirable and female viewers to identify with her, at once undermining both male and female viewers' assumptions about sexuality and securing the film's metaphysical views. Of course, since most viewers would deny that they could even have such experiences, they must be tricked into them.

It is generally true that one's experience of a film depends heavily on one's social status and cultural attitudes. With *The Crying Game,* however, there is an additional factor that affects its reception: whether viewers recognize that Dil is part of the transvestite bar scene in London. Those who know or suspect that Dil is a gay transvestite will not experience *The Crying Game* as intended.[8] That is, since they will not be ignorant in the specific way the film requires, the revelation at its center will not come as a surprise conveying an important truth. So, in what follows, I assume a naïve viewer whose point of view the film's narrative strategy privileges.[9]

Thus, *The Crying Game* attempts to place its viewers in an epistemic position in which they, like Fergus, are deceived about Dil's sex. This strategy makes *The Crying Game* unique among the unlikely couple films I have discussed, for with the others, the audience always possesses more knowledge than do the characters. Often, this is true if for no other reason than that the audience is aware before the partners are that the partners really do belong together. The disjunction between the audience's knowledge and that of the characters is one source of tension in these films' narratives. For example, if we watch *It Happened One Night* with some suspense, it is because we wonder whether, or at least how, the characters will be brought to acknowledge the love *we* know they really share.

The Crying Game intends its (naïve) viewers to assume, along with Fergus, that the person with whom he is falling in love is biologically female, that Dil's enacted gender identity is congruent with her biological sex. Once that bait is taken, the audience's sense that if this couple is unlikely, it is because Fergus is at least partially responsible for the death of Jody, Dil's former partner, is mistaken. (I ignore, for the moment, how Dil's race affects the couple's unlikeliness.) Caught up in the dynamics of Fergus's developing feelings for Dil and how those feelings relate to his guilt over Jody's death, the viewer tends to miss cues that suggest that there is more (or at least, "Other") to Dil than meets the eye.[10]

This technique is notably associated with the tradition of film noir, a genre in which the viewer characteristically shares an epistemic position of ignorance, if not one of error, with that character responsible for uncovering the truth.[11] Films in which the "punch" comes from the revelation that the perpetrator is not the character the audience has been induced to suspect must mislead.[12]

A straightforward example of *The Crying Game*'s use of this narrative strategy is the opening, country fair sequence that culminates in Jody's abduction. We see a white woman, Jude (Miranda Richardson), and a black man, Jody, on their way to what appears will be a casual sexual encounter. When Jody tries to kiss her, Jude suggests they move away from the crowded fair to a more secluded spot. No sooner are they alone, however, than a gunman—Fergus—suddenly appears to attack Jody and free Jude from his embrace. What seemed a simple pickup turns out to be a carefully staged IRA hostage taking.

The audience has been in virtually the same epistemic position as Jody, the character who seems to be propelling the narrative. Neither he nor we initially suspect that more is happening than appears on the surface.[13] But the film pulls the epistemic rug out from under his, and our, feet by revealing a level of significance of which he, and we, have been unaware. Once we understand that we have witnessed a political kidnapping, we retrospectively reinterpret what we have seen: Jude's attraction to this black man was feigned—she later reveals herself to have been repulsed by his touch—in order to lure him into a trap.

From the film's opening moments, then, the audience experiences surprise and shock. Had viewers' knowledge not been thus limited, had they known all along they were witnessing a ruse in aid of a hostage taking, they might have been repulsed by Fergus's violence, or they might have enjoyed seeing the IRA execute an action, but they would not have been surprised by any of it. Instead, the audience is caught up in what appears to be an interracial liaison only to be shocked by the discovery of what is actually transpiring.

Destabilizing Difference

In the next, hostage sequence of the film, the development of a friendship between Jody and Fergus initiates the film's assault on received social hierarchies. But by placing Fergus's relationship with Jody in the context of an unfolding terrorist plot, the intense hostage drama serves to direct the audience's focus elsewhere. As a result, intimations of homoeroticism go unremarked. Nonetheless, because it has witnessed Fergus's pleasure in a male friendship that transgresses "normal" bounds, the audience is being subtly prepared for the possibility of a homosexual relationship.

From the beginning of Jody's captivity, Fergus manifests both empathy for and curiosity about him. When Jody is first brought to the cell's hideout, Fergus orders Jude to give him tea. Unlike the other terrorists, who understand the need to see Jody as no more than a bargaining chip, Fergus sees him as a human being, to be treated as humanely as possible in the circumstances. It is this nascent sympathy that Jody sets out to cultivate to save his own life.

As Fergus watches over Jody, the relationship between the two men grows. First, Fergus gets permission from the cell's leader, Peter Maguirre (Adrian Dunbar), to grant Jody's request to remove the uncomfortable burlap hood he has been forced to wear. Of course, the hood is intended to conceal the terrorists' identities should they actually succeed in exchanging Jody for an IRA leader held by the British. But since Jody has already seen both Jude and Fergus, this precaution makes little sense: As Jody jokes to Fergus, there is no point to keeping the hood on him since he had already seen, "You're the handsome one."[14] Although this remark clearly has homoerotic overtones, the viewer tends to hear it simply as a joke intended to foster their growing intimacy. When Fergus finally removes the hood, Jody wisecracks that there was only one thing he was mistaken about: "You're no pin-up" (Jordan, *Reader,* p. 187). Fergus as pinup, that is, as an object of Jody's sexual desire, is a surprising idea and a possible tip-off to Jody's sexual orientation.[15] But again, in the context of the hostage narrative, the naïve viewer hears it as only another joke, a throwaway remark.

The sequence comes closer to revealing Jody's sexual orientation when he shows Fergus a picture of Dil. Jody has been reflecting on the irony of having been trapped by a female, although neither Fergus nor the viewer is aware of precisely where the irony lies. He tells Fergus that he believes he will be killed because it is not in the terrorists' nature to let him go. The irony of his situation, he now explains, is that he wound up as a hostage because he fell for Jude's seduction routine even though he was not really attracted to her: "I didn't even fancy her . . . She's not my type" (Jordan, *Reader*, p. 189). By way of explanation, he asks Fergus to take his wallet and look at a photograph. After glancing at a snapshot of Jody in a cricketer's outfit, Fergus finds a picture of him with what appears to be an attractive black woman. In the ensuing dialogue, the two men share an erotic fantasy:

> FERGUS: She'd be anyone's type.
> JODY: Don't think of it, fucker.
> FERGUS: Why not?
> JODY: She's mine. Anyway, she wouldn't suit you . . .
> FERGUS: She your wife?
> JODY: Suppose you could say that. (Jordan, *Reader*, p. 190)

The naïve viewer watching this exchange is, like Fergus, ignorant of Jody's sexual orientation and Dil's sex. Two men are apparently engaged in a familiar pattern, establishing, but controlling, their affection for one another through their mutual attraction to a woman both see as desirable. It is only later, once Dil's sex has been revealed, that the viewer can understand exactly what Jody meant by warning Fergus off.

The question of Jody's race will have been on the viewer's mind for some time, but becomes explicit in the narrative only when Jude expresses her feelings of repulsion at being touched by this black man. Indeed, her crudely racist reaction taints the entire IRA team and is part of the film's strategy of undermining sympathy for their political stance. As Jody points out, in Northern Ireland—"the one place in the world where they call you nigger to your face" (Jordan, *Reader*, p. 191)—the use of a black man to represent British power is particularly inappropriate. Despite his being a soldier enforcing British colonial rule in Northern Ireland, one would expect the IRA to treat a black male from Antigua as a fellow victim of British colonialism, rather than as a surrogate for the Crown.[16] In kidnapping a black ex-colonial, the terrorists show themselves prisoners of inflexible political categories that cannot accommodate real-world complexities, in this case the complexities Jody's hybrid identity represents.[17]

The conversation between Jody and Fergus that most explicitly points up the problematic nature of reductive distinctions concerns the respective merits of cricket and hurling, sports associated with their different nationalities: In Antigua—Jody's birthplace—"cricket's a black man's game," he tells Fergus, not the game of the English upper class (Jordan, *Reader*, p. 191). Although the context of this interchange is distant from the film's political concerns, it makes the relevant point: The terrorists accept an inflexible set of categories that ignore the shifting meanings things acquire. But as Jody suggests, meanings depend on context.

The highly symbolic scene in which the allowable limits of Jody and Fergus's heterosexual friendship are transgressed—when Fergus is forced to help Jody urinate—occurs in such a way as to cause the viewer to miss its significance. Fergus actually removes Jody's penis from his pants because Jody cannot do so since he is handcuffed. When Fergus is reluctant to touch Jody's penis again to put it back, Jody delivers a line that will later prove highly ironic, "It's only a piece of meat," and jokes that it has no major communicable diseases (Jordan, *Reader*, p. 193).

The homoerotic overtones to this scene are clear, for Fergus has now, probably for the first time in his life, handled another man's penis. Fergus's squeamishness might be amusing, but this act marks how far the intimacy between these two men has developed. Fergus is willing to do things that disgust or embarrass him to spare Jody pain or humiliation, a willingness that distinguishes him from his fellow terrorists.

This scene exemplifies the nature of the boundaries that establish the sorts of intimacies appropriate between heterosexual males. The developing friendship between Fergus and Jody demonstrates that unlike his comrades, Fergus is neither racist nor ideologically rigid: Indeed, his growing rapport with Jody causes him to waver in his political commitments. Nonetheless, Fergus's reluctance to touch Jody's penis reflects his masculine anxiety. Since Jody clearly needs Fergus to remove his penis from his pants and then replace it in them, and since Fergus has come to befriend him, why does this act cause Fergus such discomfort? The film suggests that because of their homophobia, heterosexual males operate under certain taboos, observing the rigid boundary that confirms their identity as masculine and heterosexual. It is not, of course, that homosexuals usually behave as Fergus does in this scene, but that certain body parts acquire an aura of taboo for other males because they are associated with homosexual practices. Mutually objectifying women, talking sports—these are appropriate male things to do; touching another man's penis simply is not.

True to form, however, the film once again deflects our attention from the homoerotic implications of this scene as Jody and Fergus laugh about the incident. When Jody empathizes with Fergus's discomfort, Fergus dryly replies, "The pleasure was all mine" (Jordan, *Reader*, p. 194). So what if Jody needed help urinating? No need to make a fuss about it!

But by this time, Peter has become concerned about the relationship that has developed between Fergus and Jody, and he orders Fergus to replace the noxious hood. When Fergus reluctantly obeys, Jody once again commiserates with him: "Y'see there's two kinds of people. Those who give and those who take" (Jordan, *Reader*, p. 196). It is at this point that Jody—only his mouth now exposed—recounts Aesop's fable of the scorpion and the frog.

Instead of all the differences that society takes to be significant—class, race, ethnicity, sex, gender, and so forth—the fable presents the one distinction the film treats as unqualifiedly valid. Jody interprets this distinction between frogs and scorpions as one between those who give and those who take, but a more revealing characterization of the difference is as that between those who empathize with the situation of others and those who exploit others because they do not. The frog in the fable dies because it responds to the scorpion's need and tries to help it. The scorpion attributes its vicious, and ultimately self-destructive, behavior to its unchangeable nature, but its real difference from its benefactor is that it is unable to care about the creature who cares about it.

The Crying Game argues that social divisions such as class, race, ethnicity, and sexual orientation can be transcended by empathetic understanding. The only difference that cannot be so overcome, according to the film, is the presence/absence of this fundamental capacity. Again, the film's strategy is to demonstrate the instability of all these other differences—while depicting Fergus's gradual acceptance of his own froglike nature.

It is worth noting the oddity of the film's metaphysics. Few would accept a distinction between the empathetic and the exploitative as both irreducible and stable, let alone endorse a critique of terrorism based on it. Yet in the dizzying world of *The Crying Game*, it provides the audience with a comforting sense of certainty.

As if to illustrate the lesson of the fable, Jude now reappears, adjusts the hood to cover Jody's mouth, then cruelly smashes him across the face with her gun. When she leaves and Fergus exposes Jody's bloody mouth, the doomed hostage comments, "Women are trouble. . . . Dil wasn't trouble. No trouble at all," once again hinting at Dil's "real" nature (Jordan,

Reader, 199). Jody then asks Fergus to find Dil after his, Jody's, death to see if she is all right.

The test of Fergus's nature will be his willingness to execute Jody. But true to form, the film does not resolve this issue. When Fergus is ordered to kill him, Jody makes a run for it, thinking that Fergus will not shoot him in the back. As Fergus chases him, Jody runs out onto a road and, in another horrific scene, is run over by an armored vehicle. The British have figured out where Jody was being held and have mounted an all-out assault that seems aimed more at killing the IRA terrorists than at freeing their captive.

The audience is barely allowed time to reflect on Jody's horrible death and the Brits' display of force. Again, the effect of the action narrative is to deflect our attention from what we have seen develop between Fergus and Jody: a homoerotic bond rooted in an empathy that transcends the social differences between them.

Unveiling Difference

In many ways, the dramatic as well as the conceptual climax of the film, although not its narrative closure, occurs when Fergus discovers Dil's biological sex. This revelation comes during the sequence in London in which Fergus has found Dil and fallen in love with her. The naïve viewer has continued to share the limitations of Fergus's epistemic position and so is just as shocked by the revelation of Dil's sex as Fergus is, having experienced, along with him, Dil's stunning enactment of femininity (see Photo 11.1). From the point of view of its sexual politics, this is the goal of *The Crying Game*'s narrative strategy of deception, for, as I have already suggested, it aims at destabilizing the audience's assumptions about sexuality.

After the disastrous outcome to the hostage taking, Fergus has bolted to London and assumed a new identity. Working at a construction site overlooking a cricket field, which gives him ample opportunity to think about Jody, to honor his promise to seek out Dil, Fergus finds the hair salon in which she works and lets her cut his hair. He then follows her to the Metro, the bar that she and Jody frequented together. After a brief conversation mediated by Col (Jim Broadbent), the bartender, they are interrupted by Dave (Ralph Brown), who assaults Dil and forces her to leave the bar with him. Fergus follows them to Dil's apartment, where he sees their shadows on the shades as they appear to have sex. When Fergus returns home, he dreams of Jody bowling in his cricket whites.

Drawn back to the Metro sometime later, Col greets him as a regular and is about to reveal Dil's "secret" to him when he is interrupted by Dil

Photo 11.1 Dil as the object of male desire

herself, who performs a torchy lip-synch version of the song "The Crying Game," during which Fergus is transfixed by her image.

Subsequently, as Dil and Fergus talk, they are once again interrupted by Dave. And once again, Dil leaves with him, but this time, when Dave pauses in an alley to hit her, Fergus intervenes and beats Dave up, thereby taking on the role of Dil's protector. In part, Fergus assumes this role out of guilt. His feeling of responsibility for Dil grows stronger as he realizes that she had entered into a masochistic relationship with Dave after Jody's death.[18] But he also is attracted to her, an attraction always mediated by his awareness of Jody as her former partner.

The revelation of Dil's sex comes during a scene in which Dil and Fergus prepare to make love. Dil had controlled their first sexual encounter by diverting Fergus's hand as it moved to her crotch and fellating him. During that scene, the film emphasized the complexity of Fergus's desire for Dil: He registers Jody's photograph as she descends to his penis and his orgasm follows a fantasy in which Jody bowls a cricket ball. Having come, Fergus questions Dil about Jody and her feelings for him, concerned that her actions were a betrayal of that relationship.

This suggests that Fergus's interest in Dil is conditioned by his feelings about Jody. His guilt over Jody's death is an obvious reason for his concern about her. But his sexual interest in Dil—the object of Jody's desire— serves to maintain a homoerotic connection to the dead man.

Their second sexual encounter proves that Fergus will not get what he bargained for. He and Dil have just returned to her apartment from the Metro, where he told her that he would look after her. Dil changes into a red negligee in her bathroom, and as Fergus removes it, the camera pans

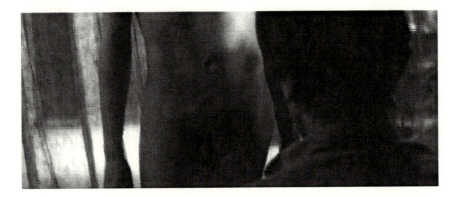

Photo 11.2 Fergus's "discovery"

from her face down her body: a shot taken from his point of view exposing first a flat chest and then a penis, both of which profoundly shock
Fergus and, along with him, the naïve viewer (see Photo 11.2). Disgusted,
Fergus hits Dil as she tries to reach out to him and then runs to the bathroom to vomit repeatedly, a scene we witness in a long shot taken from
Dil's point of view (see Photo 11.3). A dejected Dil insists that she was
not purposely misleading him, but thought he "knew."

   This scene became the most famous one in the film and contains the
revelation of the "secret" that the reviewers both obsessively alluded to
and compliantly kept.[19] It is also the pivot about which the film's narrative
turns. Once Fergus learns that Dil is sexed male, that the woman he has
been coming to love and with whom he has had a sexual encounter is really biologically male, his homophobic anxiety causes him quite literally to
retch. Whatever issues might have been raised by Dil's race and her relationship with Jody are simply overwhelmed by this discovery.

   Eschewing *Desert Hearts*'s strategy of rendering homosexual desire as
wholesome, *The Crying Game* intends nothing less than the subversion of
the hetero/homo distinction itself. As the audience shares Fergus's epistemic position, it, like Fergus, accepts Dil as a suitable object of male (het-
ero) sexual desire. But with that disturbing glimpse of Dil's penis, naïve
viewers have been confronted with a male enacting a sexually attractive
woman, one whose performance of fellatio they may have found erotic. I
refer to this as a destabilizing experience for it challenges the taken-for-
granted congruence of biological sex and social gender that lies at the ba-

Photo 11.3 Fergus's revulsion/Dil's despair

sis of the assumed binarism of sexual orientation. Especially for hetero-sexual males, who generally refuse to admit the possibility of being sexu-ally attracted to other males, this revelation can be deeply troubling, for the film confronts them with just that "appalling" possibility. For hetero-sexual females, the shock may be as great, for they have seen a male, not a female like themselves, as an object of male desire. In either case, for the naïve viewer, the adequacy of the framework through which he or she has conceived sexuality has been placed in question.

Male viewers are confronted with the further possibility that at least certain elements of a form of male homosexuality are not all that foreign to the structure of their own sexual desire, for now they too have experi-enced, albeit in ignorance, desire for a male transvestite. By getting these naïve—homophobic?—viewers to realize that they themselves can be sub-ject to the very desires and feelings that structure certain homosexual practices, *The Crying Game* argues that those desires are perverse only if all desire is.[20]

In a brief discussion of the film, Marjorie Garber confirms this analysis. After reporting that many men of her acquaintance insisted that a body double had been used in the revelation scene, Garber interprets this "dis-avowal" in the following terms: "They had come to desire that which, once they 'knew' what it was, they 'knew' they didn't desire it."[21] Rather than acknowledge that they were sexually aroused by a male, these men denied the evidence of their senses. The destabilizing nature of the revela-tion need not be disavowed or denied, but as I have been arguing, can change one's understanding of one's own sexual desire.

In pushing for such a reassessment, *The Crying Game* exposes how our conscious desires are structured by socially constituted assumptions about sexual propriety. Only because Fergus (and the naïve viewer) sees Dil as an appropriate object of male desire do his (and, possibly, their) sexual feelings for her develop. The revelation of her real sex causes Fergus's revulsion, his own desire no longer consistent with his view of what is acceptable. Only in ignorance of Dil's "nature" can Fergus love her unproblematically.

In this scene, *The Crying Game* moves beyond standard representations of desire and its regulation according to categories of social acceptability. In many unlikely couple narratives, the difference that disqualifies romance is apparent to both the two partners and the audience. In others, that difference may be concealed from one of the partners. But only in *The Crying Game* are the grounds of unlikeliness concealed from one partner, whom we follow, as well as the audience, allowing both to have experiences that being fully knowledgeable would preclude. In depicting a love the transgressive character of which eludes the very categories with which we attempt to understand it, *The Crying Game* radically extends the critical potential of the unlikely couple film.

Overcoming Difference

The revelation of Dil's sex precipitates a crisis for *The Crying Game*'s unlikely couple, for Fergus's heterosexuality should preclude romance with a male transvestite. The film cannot leave things this way, however, without denying its own metaphysical view. Fergus's relationship with Jody showed him that empathy for another could transcend some differences taken to be significant—ethnicity and race; his relationship with Dil challenges him to extend his empathy across a divide that initially seems unbridgeable. But to sustain its view that the only insurmountable difference is that between scorpions and frogs, Fergus must find the capacity to love across that divide as well.

And indeed, in the final sequences of the film, Dil and Fergus move toward a kind of love with which both can be at least partially satisfied. Although this is neither the traditional upbeat ending of many unlikely couple films nor a clearly tragic one, it does support the film's claim that empathy can overcome the socially determined categories that both structure and contain the possibilities of human connection, sexual and otherwise.

But as we have learned to expect from this film, the narrative does not develop in straightforward linear fashion. For as Dil and Fergus attempt to reconstitute their relationship, the IRA is determined that Fergus will carry out a political assassination as penance for his desertion. Once again, *The Crying Game* deflects our attention from its sexual politics by recontextualizing its unlikely couple story in the ongoing action narrative.

Miraculously, Jude and Peter, too, have escaped the destruction of their hideout and are angry with Fergus for having "fucked up" (Jordan, *Reader,* p. 240). Instead of simply killing him, however, they decide to send him on a suicide mission, with the threat to harm Dil if he does not agree. Fergus's reaction shows how far he has evolved, for his main concern now is to keep Dil—an innocent like Jody—from harm at the hands of the IRA. Being Dil's protector, willing to sacrifice his life for hers, is his final acknowledgment that this failed scorpion has accepted his frog nature.

One of the more intriguing plot twists then follows, as Fergus disguises Dil as a man(!), thus aligning her sex and her gender. To re-mark her as masculine, he returns to the beauty salon where she works and proceeds to give her a short haircut, thus replaying their initial encounter in inverted form. He then takes Dil back to her apartment where he has her dress in Jody's cricket outfit.

Whereas Fergus has himself come to occupy Jody's place as Dil's "gentle man," Dil has now been physically transformed into a parody of Jody, a parody for Dil now looks like a woman in drag.[22] There is more to her feminine gender identity than simply her long hair, makeup, and woman's clothing. Fergus's efforts to transform Dil's gender simply do not succeed, for her way of holding herself and her body language are enactments of a feminine identity. Her gender, even granting its social constitution, is more than skin deep, residing in a body that resists being camouflaged.[23]

It is to this transformed Dil, who is in a euphoric state, having taken a lot of drugs to combat an unspecified blood disease—AIDS lurking?—that Fergus is able to confide his previous identity as a terrorist and his role in Jody's death. Because she is drunk and has taken mood-altering drugs, at this time Dil is unable to fully react to Fergus's revelations. The film then uses parallel editing to intercut two narrative lines. In the first, on the morning after Fergus's confession, Dil reacts by tying Fergus to the bed and threatening him with his own gun as he struggles to free himself—if he misses his rendezvous with Peter and Jude, Dil will be in danger. Interspersed with this sequence are shots of Jude dressing, this time preparing to play the femme fatale. At the end of this double sequence, the two "women" in Fergus's life are both armed and angry.

The assassination plot is resolved first: Peter realizes that Fergus is not going to show up on time, takes his place, and is killed by his victim's bodyguard. When Jude flees the scene, we know that she will come after Fergus for yet another fuckup. Meanwhile, Dil still holds Fergus captive. Threatening him, she demands that he declare his love for her. Interestingly, Fergus's coerced declaration seems genuine: Although Dil has forced him into it, his affirmation is sincere.

Once Fergus assures the doubtful Dil that he will never leave her, Jude appears, gun in hand, ready to kill Fergus for having once again let down the cause. Instinctively, Dil fires to protect Fergus and, as she continues to shoot Jude, she realizes that this is the woman who used "her tits and that cute little ass" to trap Jody (Jordan, *Reader*, p. 265). The scene ends as Fergus (whom Dil had earlier untied) stops the stunned Dil from turning her gun on herself, hustles her out of the apartment, and replaces her fingerprints on the gun with his own. The police arrive and we realize that Fergus will give himself up as Jude's murderer.

As many critics have pointed out, this sequence epitomizes the film's strategy of pitting its one biological woman against a transvestite, and to the advantage of the latter. [24] Indeed, Jude is the most poisonous character in the entire film: It is as if transvestites—feminine males—can be accorded sympathetic treatment only if biological females are represented negatively. To reject society's claim that transvestites are not real women, the film endorses Jody's earlier characterization of female women as trouble. The film seems able to accord males a space in which gender assumptions can be destabilized only by vilifying biological females. From the point of view of Fergus's evolution, however, this sequence shows how thoroughly he has changed: Having made a clear choice to protect his unlikely partner, he betrays his former allies, selflessly taking on Dil's punishment, perhaps to assuage his guilt.

The Politics of Redemption

The final scene of the film is a sort of coda that inverts the powerful guard-prisoner image of its hostage sequence. Fergus, the former IRA terrorist, is now a prisoner in a British jail. Sitting opposite him is Dil, for whose crime he has been punished.[25] Dil, who appears dressed as a woman once again and who now plays the devoted wife, seems to have regained her former self-assurance. When she asks Fergus why he has chosen to take the rap for her, he responds, "As the man said, it's in my nature," and he then retells the fable of the scorpion and the frog (Jordan, *Reader*, p. 267). As Fergus recites the tale, the camera does a long reverse tracking shot to the rear of the visiting room, always keeping Fergus and Dil in sight. Fergus's recitation is accompanied by Lyle Lovett's rendition of Tammy Wynette's hit song, "Stand By Your Man," a song and performance that are multiply ironic in this context, parodying yet celebrating Dil's allegiance to Fergus and providing a feeling of emotional closure for the audience.

The Crying Game is an unusual unlikely couple film, just as Dil and Fergus are an unusual unlikely couple at the film's end. First, the film is not simply a romance, but a hybrid narrative that unfolds its transformation narrative in the context of an action film. Throughout, that narrative repeatedly drives the romantic story into the background. In addition, unusually for an unlikely couple film, there is no single couple that fully dominates the narrative. Thus, Jody and Dil are a couple, although we never see them together except in photographs. Fergus and Dil—despite their difficulties in adjusting their needs to one another—are a romantic couple too, as Dil reminds Fergus, misleadingly quoting the first five words of John 15: 13: "Greater love hath no man than this, that a man lay down his life for his friends." But Jody and Fergus are also an unlikely couple, at least in an extended sense of that term, and it is Jody who first starts Fergus down the developmental path that culminates in his relationship with Dil. Finally, our understanding of this as an unlikely couple film is further complicated by Jody's ambiguous significance for Fergus, in whose desire for Dil he is repeatedly implicated.[26] The presence of these overlapping emotional relationships keeps the film from fitting neatly into those narrative patterns that assume a couple constituted by a single, unambiguous, although possibly conflicted, desire.

Yet, to see this film as an unlikely couple film allows us to appreciate the transformation narrative through which the film asserts the power of empathy to transcend social difference. Although the film suggests that a redemptive love cannot easily be found, the Fergus we see sitting opposite Dil is expiating his guilt by taking on the punishment that should be hers. This ethic of suffering for others provides Fergus with a sense of integrity that his terrorist politics could not. Although the final image of Fergus and Dil is a far cry from, say, that of Edward and Vivian on the fire escape in *Pretty Woman,* the film asks its audience to see Fergus and Dil as having achieved a type of love that overcomes the difference in their sexual orientations and even grants them a degree of wholeness and peace.

The film ends without definite narrative closure—we do not know, for example, exactly what will happen to Fergus or how his relationship with Dil will develop—but Fergus has maintained his empathy with Dil, overcoming the homophobia at the core of his heterosexual identity. Although the film refuses to define the precise nature of Dil and Fergus's relationship, he has accepted the role of her protector, even though his repeated admonitions that she not use such terms of endearment as "love" or "darling" imply that he does not want her to consider him her lover. On the other hand, Dil's devotion to him suggests that she sees them as a couple because she believes that Fergus's actions are motivated by love, even if that love cannot be easily sexualized.

This refusal to finally disambiguate Fergus and Dil's relationship accords with the film's strategy of destabilization. By withholding an easy description of the pair—not quite lovers yet also not simply friends—the film forces viewers to maintain their awareness that sexuality exceeds the grasp of the hetero/homo dichotomy.

Earlier, I mentioned that *The Crying Game* has been criticized for its denigration of biological females. The film has also been reproved by a number of reviewers and film theorists for racism, most tellingly for its use of blacks as vehicles for the spiritual enlightenment of a white male.[27] Without denying the validity of these criticisms, and without wishing to endorse the film's own Aesopian metaphysics, I want to stress the achievement of its strategy of destabilization. Particularly because of its innovative use of aspects of the noir tradition, *The Crying Game* invests the figure of the unlikely couple with an interest and complexity beyond most of the earlier films we have considered. It demonstrates the resilience and significance of this narrative figure by providing its audience with transgressive experiences of attraction and desire, thereby calling into question our confidence that we know what difference means.

Notes

1. This characterization poses problems for films about homosexual couples. If one of the partners is ambivalent about his or her sexual orientation, as is the case in *Desert Hearts* and *The Crying Game*, this characterization does apply.

2. Although this fable stems from Aesop, *The Crying Game* takes it from Orson Welles's *Mr. Arkadin* (1955).

3. In an otherwise insightful article, "The Scorpion and the Frog: Agency and Identity in Neil Jordan's *The Crying Game*," *Camera Obscura,* 35 (May 1995): pp. 25–51, Amy Zilliax fails to see this parable as a source of the film's metaphysics.

4. The film's problematizing of sexual categories causes difficulty in finding appropriate language to describe it. Thus, should Dil be referred to as "he" or "she"? I choose the latter, out of deference to her own gender choice, but note my discomfort with having to choose either.

5. For a brief discussion of the problems with such assumptions, see Anne Fausto Sterling, "How Many Sexes Are There?" *New York Times,* March 12, 1993, p. 15.

6. To simplify matters, in this chapter I repeatedly ignore the possibility of bisexuality.

7. *The Crying Game* makes it difficult to determine whether Dil is a transvestite or a transsexual, i.e., someone who "perceives his or her gender identity as incongruous with the anatomical reality and actively seeks to resolve the conflict through sex-reassignment surgery" (Deborah Heller Feinbloom, *Transvestites and Transsexuals: Mixed Views* [n.p.: Delacourte Press, 1976], p. 24). I simplify by characterizing Dil as a transvestite.

8. This is not to say that they might not enjoy the film or find its political standpoint convincing, only that the narrative of the film is not structured with them primarily in mind.

9. Maurice Yacowar also discusses the film's "implication of the viewer in its dynamics" in "Neil Jordan's Viewing Game," *Queen's Quarterly,* 100:2 (1993): pp. 457–464. He fails to discuss how the viewer is misled by the film, however.

10. When the film was first shown, it was a sign of great sophistication to claim that one had not been fooled by the film, that one knew from the outset that Dil was a cross-dresser. Did this reflect a discomfort felt at the violation of the audience's assumption of epistemic superiority?

11. Film noir tends to use this "trick" often. In *Sea of Love,* for example, the audience is made to share the Al Pacino character's epistemic position and is startled to find out that it is mistaken in so doing. See Nick Pappas's discussion of *Sea of Love* in *Philosophy and Film,* Cynthia A. Freeland and Thomas E. Wartenberg, eds. (New York and London: Routledge, 1995), pp. 109–125. Other recent films that rely on this device include *The Usual Suspects* (1997), *The Spanish Prisoner* (1998), and *In the Company of Men* (1997).

12. The many more complexities of the noir genre continue to fascinate film theorists. See, for example, Richard Dyer's analysis in his *The Matter of Images* (New York and London: Routledge, 1993), pp. 52–72. Dyer's discussion of the labyrinthine structure of noir films fails, however, to note this important epistemic characteristic of the genre.

13. The audience is given some visual clues—of which Jody is unaware—that prepare it for the subsequent reversal. There are repeated shots of Fergus and of

Jude looking for or at him. Nonetheless, it is only after the kidnapping has taken place that the audience acquires a context for placing these clues.

14. Neil Jordan, *A Neil Jordan Reader* (New York: Vintage, 1993), p. 185. All future references to this work will be given parenthetically.

15. Jody's interest in Jude might make some readers uncomfortable applying the label "gay" to him. Since he claims that Dil is his type, I take him to be implicitly characterizing himself as gay. But the film's destabilizing strategy includes the recognition that there are hybrid forms of sexuality, that a gay male can find a female desirable and pursue her. The film wants us to see that sexual desire and sexuality are not as rigid as terms such as "gay," "straight," and "bisexual" make it seem.

16. Forest Whitaker is, of course, an American actor trying to play an Antiguan black. This odd casting choice is the result of marketing considerations that make it imperative to have some American "names" in a film destined for U.S. distribution.

17. The film makes no attempt to understand the political goals and tactics of the IRA, but only to discredit the terrorists for their cruelty.

18. In "*The Crying Game* and the Destabilization of Masculinity" (*Film and Philosophy*, 3 [1996]): pp. 176–185), Richard Gull emphasizes the importance of sadomasochistic games in the film's plot. Although highlighting an important aspect of the film, Gull's interpretation globalizes in a way that distorts other elements of the film's narrative.

19. The press reaction to the film is critically surveyed by Lola Young in "'Nothing Is as It Seems': Re-viewing *The Crying Game*," in *Me Jane: Masculinity, Movies, and Women*, Pat Kirkham and Janet Thumin, eds. (New York: St. Martin's Press, 1995), pp. 273–283.

20. Regardless of whether the naïve viewer identifies with Dil as an object of male desire or with Fergus's desire for her, the revelation of her sex disrupts the boundaries of their categories of gender and sexuality.

21. Marjorie Garber, *Vice Versa: Bisexuality and the Eroticism of Everyday Life* (New York: Simon and Schuster, 1995), p. 231.

22. Fergus has now transformed the object of his desire into a version of Jody, emphasizing once again that Fergus's attraction to Dil functions to maintain an erotic link to the dead man.

23. This failure suggests that the human body resists the destabilization for which the film argues. Zilliax makes this point in "The Scorpion and the Frog."

24. See, for example, Kristin Handler, "Sexing *The Crying Game*: Difference, Identity, Ethics," *Film Quarterly*, 47:3 (Spring 1994): pp. 31–42.

25. Although Dil claims that Fergus is serving time for her, the elaborate security arrangements suggest that he has been imprisoned as an IRA terrorist for the political assassination Peter carried out.

26. In *The Crying Game* (London: The British Film Institute, 1997), pp. 11–12, Jane Giles asserts that "the triangular relationship [is the] single most dominant theme in his [Jordan's] work."

27. This charge is made by, among others, bell hooks, "Seduction and Betrayal: *The Crying Game* Meets *The Bodyguard*," in *Outlaw Culture* (New York: Routledge, 1994), pp. 53–62; Alan A. Stone, "Review of *The Crying Game*," *Boston Review*, June/August 1993, pp. 25–27; and Kristin Handler, "Sexing *The Crying Game*."

12

Movie Romance and the Critique of Hierarchy

This study of a type of movie romance I dub the unlikely couple film has documented the reason for the genre's enduring attraction for filmmakers and its persisting appeal to audiences. Through my investigation of the narrative and representational strategies of ten significant instances of the genre, I have demonstrated its power to illuminate a broad range of social issues, most centrally those that bear on the legitimacy of social hierarchy. I have argued that the conflict between the romantic and social perspectives embodied in the narrative figure of the unlikely couple explains this preoccupation with practices that occlude democratic/egalitarian social relations. Thus, my interpretations have revealed that although often derided as mere entertainment, unlikely couple films can—and often do—deeply engage fundamental social and philosophic issues.

Narrative Film and Social Criticism

My claim for the unlikely couple film as a vehicle for social criticism is at odds with many of the most serious attempts to theorize the significance of mass cultural artifacts. Developed under the aegis of the Frankfurt School's dismissal of all forms of mass culture as regressive, important tendencies in academic film studies have treated popular narrative film as necessarily complicit with dominant social interests.[1] According to this view, film's potential to resist such interests is severely limited. Rather than criticize oppressive social relations, popular film shapes its consumers into subjects who willingly embrace their own subordination.

This general perspective has achieved particular prominence in film studies, albeit rather indirectly—for example, in Laura Mulvey's extraordinarily influential article, "Narrative Cinema and Visual Pleasure," which incorporates Lacanian psychoanalysis and feminist theory into her critique of the political effect of popular film.[2] Mulvey argues that viewers derive pleasure from narrative film by identifying either with male seducers or the female characters who serve merely as the objects of the males' desire. This endlessly repeated bifurcation of gender roles into active male heroes and passive female beauties, Mulvey argues, operates to reproduce patriarchy: Male viewers are invited to enjoy idealized versions of themselves while female viewers are offered only demeaned and demeaning selves with which to identify.

The reductiveness of Mulvey's argument can be—and has been, even by Mulvey herself[3]—met at a variety of different levels. One well-known line of criticism, developed by the practitioners of cultural studies, argues that Mulvey's Lacanian psychoanalytic perspective is too deterministic, treating audiences as fated to receive film along clearly established paths of identification. Viewers, it is argued contra Mulvey, can choose their own lines of affiliation with on-screen characters and are not constrained to respond to particular characters in predetermined ways. Thus, female viewers' identification with *Pretty Woman*'s sexy prostitute need not be masochistic, that is, as the object of male desire, but, as Hilary Radner argues, could stem from a perception of Vivian's role as a sexual entrepreneur whose desirability gives her power over men.[4] This strategy of "reading against the grain" conceives of the film audience as able to develop for itself interpretations of films that violate the filmmakers' expectations.[5]

Both perspectives offer important insights about the nature and reception of film, but neither is adequate to the interpretation of the politics of popular narrative. Although Mulvey and those influenced by the Frankfurt School attribute to film the power to completely structure audience response, practitioners of the cultural studies paradigm treat viewers as having nearly total freedom to construct interpretations to suit their own purposes. By focusing on the socially critical elements present in the narratives themselves, I attempt to steer a middle course, one that analyzes the "textual" meaning that viewers must incorporate into their more individualized, "contextual" responses to a film. The analyses I have offered in this book are guided by the judgment that film, a form of mass culture, is capable of sophisticated social criticism, a fact that needs to be taken into account in theoretical reflection on the nature of the medium.

My exploration of the narrative and representational strategies of the unlikely couple genre also suggests that the relationship of audiences to

on-screen characters is not as one sided as both of these theoretical perspectives conceive. It is doubtful that audiences of the films I have discussed uncritically identify with individual characters, either compliantly
or against the grain. Instead, because these characters are often as complex
and nuanced as the people who matter to viewers in their everyday lives,
viewers are asked to critically examine—not identify with—the masculinity and femininity of the characters. Consider, for example, Peter Warne
and Ellie Andrews, *It Happened One Night*'s unlikely partners. Although
there are attractive aspects to both, each must be educated to overcome a
form of pride. How is a viewer who simply identifies with Peter to appreciate some of the film's more memorable sequences—as when Ellie bests
Peter by getting them the lift he could not—or catch the significance of
Peter's humiliation as a takedown of his masculinist attitude of
superiority?

My approach to film thus involves neither its wholesale dismissal as
ideological nor its uncritical adulation as subversive. Although always desirous of exploring the social-critical reach of unlikely couple films, I have
also sought to register unevennesses, hesitations, retreats, and incoher-
ences. Throughout, my interpretations have insisted on close readings of
the individual films themselves, tracing the development of their critical
perspectives on class, race, gender, and sexual orientation.

Romance and Self-Development

A further challenge to my approach to the unlikely couple film comes
from second-wave feminism, which sees the celebration of the romantic
couple as an objectionable ideological prop for patriarchy. For example, in
her study of Hollywood romance, Virginia Wright Wexman characterizes
the project of such films as "modeling reified gender roles and romantic
attachments."[6] Although Wexman admits that many contemporary
Hollywood films no longer conform to this description—largely, she
thinks, because of changing sexual and gender norms in the broader society—she claims that popular narrative cinema's focus on romance provides models for the romantic practices of their audiences.

My examination of the unlikely couple film indicates some of the limitations of Wexman's view. First, although many of the films assume that
romance necessarily eventuates in marriage, the two homosexual unlikely
couple films we have investigated specifically challenge the normative status of heterosexuality. There is nothing about narrative cinema in general

or the unlikely couple film in particular that prohibits it from exploring nonheterosexual avenues.

That said, it is fair to acknowledge that unlikely couple films do endorse long-term, committed relationships, whether sanctioned in marriage or not. In part, this is because without such commitment, there would be little social tension to investigate. For this reason, the unlikely couple film cannot explore forms of sexual relationship alternative to the couple.

But the fact that the figure of the romantic couple serves to ground these films' critiques of social hierarchy casts doubt on Wexman's assertion that the films have supported what she calls reified forms of romantic relationship. Although the romances are central in these films, they are not simply models to which audiences are meant to aspire. And in any case, the relationships themselves do not conform to Wexman's characterization, for at least in films like *It Happened One Night,* the heterosexual relationship is deliberately founded on the male partner's rejection of his noxious masculinism.

A related critique of romance, albeit one that targets literature rather than film, is articulated by Vivian Gornick in her recent, widely acclaimed book, *The End of the Novel of Love.* Gornick claims that works that attribute transcendent power to romantic love—the power to endow the self with lasting coherence and purpose—are anachronistic, out of touch with contemporary developments, among them, although never explicitly acknowledged, feminism: "Romantic love now seems a yearning to dive down into feeling and come up magically changed, when what is required for the making of a self is the deliberate pursuit of consciousness."[7] Although Gornick's talk of a self as "made" or "achieved" is somewhat puzzling—Who or what, after all, is it that makes or achieves this self?—she is clearly suspicious of what we might call the central trope of the unlikely couple film—the profound, transformative potential of romantic love. She sees the crafting of a mature self as, of necessity, taking place in isolation from others: "For better or worse, that effort [of creating the self] is a solitary one, more akin to the art of making art than of making family."[8]

Gornick's one-sided emphasis seems to me to slight one of the main insights of the unlikely couple film: that self-development always occurs in a social context of some sort, even if that context posits the physical absence of others. Rejecting the individualism of the modern Western philosophic tradition—where all "action" takes place in isolated reflection in the thinker's study and not in, for example, families or the workplace[9]—the unlikely couple film celebrates the possibilities for accelerated self-development offered by romantic love. The partners in these films draw on the acknowledgment and support their unlikely unions provide to meet the challenges that threaten further growth and self-understanding.

But unlikely couple films do not simply offer the vague promise that romance will bring fulfillment; rather, their narratives take up these challenges and show how, specifically, the experience of romance helps one to meet them. In so doing, the unlikely couple film aligns itself with Hegel, one of whose paramount philosophic achievements, the establishment of the necessary and inherent sociality of the individual, he memorably rendered in the formula, "an I that is a We and a We that is an I."[10] Although the interpretations developed in previous chapters must stand as the main evidence for these claims, let me briefly rehearse some of the ways in which unlikely romance encourages—sometimes, indeed, forces—individual growth.

Some individuals, able to do only what they think others expect of them, may never yearn for something more; but others are torn between the ever-present lure of social conformity and a kind of barely submerged despair over the lack of meaning in their lives. In his magnum opus, *Being and Time*, Martin Heidegger refers to the phenomenon of the "they-self," that is, a self constituted by that anonymous mass, the "they," whose opinions are our own.[11] Although a number of characters in the films I have discussed experience this tension—Emmy in *Ali: Fear Eats the Soul*, who succumbs to the they; *Mississippi Masala*'s Mina, who does not—none confronts it more squarely than *White Palace*'s Max Baron. Only through his love for Nora and her withdrawal from him does the numb adman find the courage to reject the vapid conformism of his yuppie milieu.

A second threat to individual fulfillment is the illusion of a kind of radical self-sufficiency. I have characterized this belief as the failure to acknowledge one's finitude, one's dependence on others, and not just for the fulfillment of one's material needs. Perhaps no character exemplifies this failure more, despite his education and accomplishments, than *Pygmalion*'s Henry Higgins. Eliza Doolittle's love for Higgins awakens all her astonishing powers, but he is never able to accept his feelings for her, clinging instead to his sterile bachelorhood.

In showing that constraining social circumstances can be a significant obstacle to individual development, *Mississippi Masala* isolates a third threat to personal growth. Although Mina's submersion in her immigrant enclave threatens to choke off her aspirations to a wider field of experience, her unlikely relationship with Demetrius gives her the strength to challenge her father's authority and to break out of that confining milieu.

As we have seen, the unlikely couple genre also includes films that temper celebrations of the transformative power of unlikely romance by showing that other factors are necessary to individual development. In their different ways, both *Jungle Fever* and *Ali: Fear Eats the Soul* dispel the illusion that love is by itself sufficient to foster personal growth, that love is all you need. Most centrally, both films posit community with others as an important additional element in this process, something that a love relationship not only cannot provide by itself but in these instances jeopardizes.

My acknowledgment of the unlikely couple film's valorization of the importance of romantic love connects to claims that Stanley Cavell has made in connection with the genres he calls the comedy of remarriage and the melodrama of the unknown woman.[12] Cavell, too, stresses the importance of romance—indeed, in his view, of marriage—to human fulfillment. The difference is that for Cavell, the fundamental threat to successful romance is skepticism, individuals' inability to acknowledge fully the reality of other human beings, whereas unlikely couple films posit a range of threats stemming from the transgressive makeup of their couples. By contextualizing the threats to self-development in structures of social hierarchy, the unlikely couple film provides a more various and yet also more specific account of the power of romantic love.

Strategies of Critique

Throughout, I have emphasized that the unlikely couple film is fundamentally concerned with questions of the legitimacy of specific forms of social hierarchy—especially, of class, race, gender, and sexual orientation.[13] Indeed, I view this focus as the principal source of the genre's philosophic interest. At this point, I want to review in more systematic fashion the various forms of critiques advanced in the films I have examined.

The simplest strategy employed is that of inversion, valorizing the previously inferior term in a dichotomy while simultaneously denigrating the term earlier privileged. In the first essay in his *The Genealogy of Morals*, Nietzsche offers an example, arguing that our current moral scheme—which he calls "slave morality"—is the result of just such an inversion of a previous, "aristocratic" framework of valuation.[14] Behaviors that had been dismissed as bad by the earlier code are now endorsed by slave morality as good.

Despite my reservations about *White Palace*'s ending, it functions in just this way. Emblematic is the use to which the opposition highbrow opera/lowbrow country music is put. Max's turnaround in the final scene—in which the Oak Ridge Boys win out over *Gianni Schicchi*—seals the film's more general elevation of blue-collar authenticity over yuppie phoniness.

Desert Hearts also effects an inversion, in this case of sexual orientations. Although not fully and consistently pursued, the film repeatedly shows lesbianism to be less exploitative, more caring, than heterosexuality, especially in its contrasting depictions of Darrell's and Vivian's interest in Cay.

The primary problem with this strategy is the obvious one: It substitutes one hierarchy for another. As a result, although the initial, invidious, valorization is challenged, it only sets another hierarchy—one perhaps equally problematic—in its place.

A second approach to undermining the legitimacy of hierarchy may be likened to the philosophic technique of argument by counterexample. Calling attention to particular instances that violate assertions of generality, counterexamples demonstrate the invalidity of those general claims. The apocryphal story of Diogenes exhibiting a plucked chicken to defeat the proposed definition of the human being as a featherless biped illustrates the technique.

In *Pygmalion,* the British aristocracy's pretension that an inherent biological superiority justifies its privilege is undermined by the counterexample of the lowly flower girl who passes as a duchess. Eliza's ability to learn the manners and speech habits associated with aristocrats serves to demonstrate that their socialization, not their genetics, is responsible for their distinction.

The problem with this approach is that the counterexample may not be understood—or, perhaps, even intended—as a general indictment of hierarchy. Instead, the character presented in this way may be taken as exceptional, thus leaving hierarchy in place. Indeed, I have analyzed *Pretty Woman* as precisely this sort of response to *Pygmalion*'s ascent narrative.

Human beings in general have a difficult time reconciling themselves to the fact of their finitude, their mortality and necessary dependence on others, and a great deal of energy in Western culture has been expended in the attempt at its denial. Unlikely couple films make an interesting intervention in this regard: Because they connect social inequality to this anxiety, they illuminate the appeal of hierarchy to the privileged. For example, in *It Happened One Night* both Ellie's class position and Peter's gender induce postures of superiority that fuel such denials and that they must shed to acknowledge their need for each other.

Interracial unlikely couple films are noteworthy for their assumption that racial hierarchy is illegitimate. Their preoccupation is the question of how this hierarchy can be eliminated—their focus less on the question of legitimacy than on that of eradication. These films constitute an ongoing dialogue about whether integration is a viable strategy for attaining racial equality. We have seen how *Guess Who's Coming to Dinner* and *Jungle Fever* give their respective affirmative and negative answers to this question, their discordant assessments a function of their distinct social and historical contexts as well as the differing political commitments of their makers.

Mississippi Masala, although sharing *Guess Who's Coming to Dinner*'s commitment to integration, has a very different understanding of what is at issue. Its focus is the doomed attempt of a community of immigrants to maintain/construct a pure national identity in their new homes, an attempt that implicates them in the same kind of racist practices that had contributed to their displacement.

Ali: Fear Eats the Soul demonstrates the unlikely couple film's ability to address not only acts of individual prejudice but also structural aspects of racism. Its presentation of how Emmy's loss of privilege affects her attitude toward her unlikely partner is a brilliant examination of why racism is so resistant to projects for its elimination.

The final mode of critique mobilized by the genre is destabilization. To destabilize a hierarchic ordering is to show that it is inadequate to the reality it attempts to conceptualize. We first saw this possibility in connection with *King Kong,* a film that ultimately destabilizes the nature/culture (or animal/human) dichotomy that it initially posits. Kong's susceptibility to white (!) female beauty checks his uninhibited desire, as his developing tenderness for Ann Darrow humanizes him.

The initial sequences of *White Palace* pursue a more general strategy of destabilization by depicting the differences that divide its unlikely partners as unexpected sources of the couple's vitality. The obsessively neat Max and the equally compulsively messy Nora are not only not unsuited to one another, but, because they share similar experiences of tragic loss, actually connect at a level that escapes the social categories dominant in Max's yuppie milieu.

But only *The Crying Game* fully explores destabilization as a means of undermining social hierarchy. Its story of how a series of oppositions—of race, ethnicity, sexual orientation—can be overcome through empathy illustrates the inability of these exhaustive and antagonistic dichotomies to adequately conceptualize being human and the meaning of difference. More impressive still is the way the film actually guides what I have called naïve viewers through a destabilizing experience, and because they can only retrospectively understand the significance of feelings evoked by its characters, it is able to undermine surety about the categories with which we habitually conceive sexuality. Through these tactics, *The Crying Game* attempts to reach out to viewers who do not share its political perspective.

This survey of the strategies unlikely couple films undertake to subvert hierarchy demonstrates both the range of their social criticism and the seriousness of their intent. These popular narrative films are not simply vehicles for mass entertainment, although they are that; they are just as much an occasion for provoking collective reflection about the inequities of hierarchy and the possibilities for its elimination.

The Unlikely Couple Film as Mass Art

Throughout this study, I have noted how specific unlikely couple films compromise their narratives as a result of their concern about how depictions of certain characters might affect their audiences' responses. This raises the general question of how narrative film's status as a mass art form affects the nature of the genre.

This is a difficult question, the answer to which would require a great deal more attention than I can give it here. I would like to point out, however, that the unlikely couple film's status as a genre of a mass art form cuts both ways: Although it is tempting to treat film's need to appeal to a broad audience as incompatible with its status as art or its potential as critique, this very necessity also helps explain the genre's embrace of a socially critical, democratic perspective.

To begin, let me rehearse some of the effects that result from the requirement of appealing to a broad audience. One such is the demand that endings be uplifting, affirmative resolutions of whatever conflicts have been raised. The problem that this demand creates, especially when it is imposed on films by concerns about marketing, is that tacking on such feel-good endings may trivialize critical perspectives developed over ninety minutes or more. Both *Pygmalion* and *White Palace* suffer from such mutilation. And *Pretty Woman* was actually transformed from a critique of the ruthlessness of capitalism into an affirmation of the anachronistic family firm.

This is a significant problem, especially when studios require that films pass the test of audience response rather than aesthetic coherence. Perhaps all that can be said here is that many of the films I have discussed show that it is possible for films with positive narrative closure to address important issues.

Unlikely couple films are themselves concerned that their own transgressive depictions of unlikely love not elicit in their audiences the very prejudices they are trying to counter. This concern is present in most of the interracial unlikely couple films we examined. For example, *Guess Who's Coming to Dinner* and *Mississippi Masala* both exceptionalize their male partner to minimize the likelihood that their audiences will perceive them as sexual predators. In each case, there is a price to be paid: *Guess Who's Coming to Dinner*'s lack of realism is attributable directly to its one-dimensional exaltation of John Prentice, whereas *Mississippi Masala*'s Demetrius, a paragon, can be read as the exception that proves the rule as far as black males are concerned.

The films that deal most successfully with their audiences' susceptibility to noxious stereotypes are those that do not simply seek to preempt the problem through idealized representations but critically address them in their narratives. Thus, for example, both *White Palace*—with its concern to block the consignment of the working-class "dumb blonde" to the position of mistress-but-not-wife—and *Ali: Fear Eats the Soul*—with its portrayal of the crassness and stupidity of racial bigots—successfully confront stereotypes that might otherwise bedevil them.

A film's anticipation of issues stemming from its reception by a mass audience can thus be as much a spur to its socially critical perspective as a hindrance. It is a serious theoretical mistake to treat the mass status of the medium as simply an obstacle to film's claims as an art form. Indeed, the antihierarchic spirit of the unlikely couple film may owe as much to its desire to appeal to a broad audience as it does to any other single factor. And as the success of three unlikely couple films—*Good Will Hunting, As Good as It Gets,* and *Titanic*—at the 1998 Academy Awards, as well as one—*Shakespeare in Love*—at the 1999 Awards attests, explorations of issues of social hierarchy continue to interest filmmakers and draw in audiences.

A Parting Word

I began this study by analyzing a shot from *Some Like It Hot,* pointing out how a beguiling appearance may conceal a reality the depths of which can only be appreciated through sympathetic engagement. My intention for this study of the unlikely couple film parallels that discussion: I wanted to plumb the often overlooked depths of a series of films frequently taken to be merely diverting. I hope I have shown that these films offer their audiences much more than simple diversion: As well as engaging important philosophic issues, unlikely couple films present sophisticated social and political critiques of some of the central issues of their—and our—day. Their narratives embody a critical dialogue between a romantic perspective that privileges love above all else and a social perspective that claims realism in its favor. Our abiding interest in the outcome of that dialogue guarantees that the unlikely couple film will remain a significant genre of popular narrative film.

Notes

1. One important source for this view of mass art forms is the chapter on the culture industry in Max Horkheimer and Theodor W. Adorno's *Dialectic of Enlightenment* (New York: Continuum, 1982), pp. 120–167.

2. Originally published in *Screen,* 16:3 (Autumn 1975): pp. 6–18, this article has been widely anthologized.

3. See her "Afterthoughts on 'Visual Pleasure and Narrative Cinema' Inspired by *Duel in the Sun* (King Vidor, 1946)" in *Framework,* 15–17 (1981): pp. 12–15.

4. I discuss Radner's argument in Chapter 4.

5. Feminist film critics such as Claire Johnston have developed the concept of "reading against the grain." For a discussion of how such interpretations function, see Robert Lapsley and Michael Westlake, *Film Theory: An Introduction* (Manchester: Manchester University Press, 1988), pp. 27–31.

6. Virginia Wright Wexman, *Creating the Couple: Love, Marriage, and Hollywood Performance* (Princeton: Princeton University Press, 1993), p. 220.

7. Vivian Gornick, *The End of the Novel of Love* (Boston: Beacon Press, 1997), p. 162.

8. Gornick, *The End of the Novel of Love,* pp. 16–17.

9. For a philosophic exploration of these themes, see my "Descartes' Mood: The Question of Feminism in the Correspondence with Elisabeth," in *Feminist Approaches to Descartes,* Susan Bordo, ed. (State College: Pennsylvania State University Press, forthcoming).

10. This is one of the tasks that Hegel sets himself in his *Phenomenology of Mind,* A. V. Miller, tr. (Oxford, UK: Clarendon Press, 1977). That work can also be read as a dramatization of a variety of threats to the achievement of the self, threats progressively eliminated as an ever-richer individuality is developed.

11. Martin Heidegger, *Being and Time,* Joan Stambaugh, tr. (New York: State University of New York Press, 1996), pp. 107–122.

12. Cavell discusses these two genres in *Pursuits of Happiness: The Hollywood Comedy of Remarriage* (Cambridge, MA: Harvard University Press, 1981) and

Contesting Tears: The Hollywood Melodrama of the Unknown Woman (Chicago: University of Chicago Press, 1996).

13. Let me remind the reader that as I discussed in footnote 10 of Chapter 1, the unlikely couple film extends beyond these four types of hierarchy, but that I have limited myself to a consideration of these in this study.

14. Friedrich Nietzsche, *The Genealogy of Morals,* in *Basic Writings of Nietzsche,* Walter Kaufmann, ed. and tr. (New York: Modern Library, 1968), pp. 460–492.

Bibliography

Andersen, Erika Surat. 1993. "Review of *Mississippi Masala*." *Film Quarterly* 46:4, pp. 23–26.

Appiah, Kwame Anthony. 1992. *In My Father's House: Africa in the Philosophy of Culture*. Oxford, UK: Oxford University Press.

Barry, Cecelie S. 1992–1993. "*Mississippi Masala*." *Cineaste* 19:2–3, pp. 66–67.

Bhabha, Homi K. 1996. "The Other Question: Difference, Discrimination, and the Discourse of Colonialism." In Houston A. Baker, Manthia Diawara, and Ruth H. Lindeborg, eds., *Black British Cultural Studies: A Reader*, pp. 87–106. Chicago and London: University of Chicago Press.

Bogle, Donald. 1996. *Toms, Coons, Mulattos, Mammies, and Bucks: An Interpretive History of Blacks in American Films*. New York: Continuum.

Brecht, Bertold. 1964. *Brecht on Theatre: The Development of an Aesthetic*, John Willett, ed. and tr. New York: Hill and Wang.

Burns, Rob, and Stephen Lamb. 1981. "Social Reality and Stylization in *Fear Eats the Soul*: Fassbinder's Study in Prejudice." *New German Studies* 9:3 (Autumn), pp. 193–206.

Cardullo, Bert. 1991–1992. "Law of the Jungle." *Hudson Review* 44, pp. 639–647.

Carroll, Noël. 1990. "The Image of Women on Film: A Defense of a Paradigm." *The Journal of Aesthetics and Art Criticism* 48:4 (Fall), pp. 349–360.

_____. 1984. "*King Kong*: Ape and Essence." In Barry Keith Grant, ed., *Planks of Reason: Essays on the Horror Film*, pp. 215–244. Metuchen, NJ, and London: The Scarecrow Press.

Cavell, Stanley. 1996. *Contesting Tears: The Hollywood Melodrama of the Unknown Woman*. Chicago: University of Chicago Press.

_____. 1981. *Pursuits of Happiness: The Hollywood Comedy of Remarriage*. Cambridge, MA: Harvard University Press.

_____. 1979 *The World Viewed: Reflections on the Ontology of Film*. Cambridge, MA: Harvard University Press.

_____. 1969. *Must We Mean What We Say?* New York: Charles Scribner's Sons.

Chodorow, Nancy. 1978. *The Reproduction of Mothering: Psychoanalysis and the Sociology of Gender*. Berkeley: University of California Press.

Clark, Kenneth B. 1979. "Contemporary Sophisticated Racism." In Joseph R. Washington Jr., ed., *The Declining Significance of Race? A Dialogue Among Black and White Social Scientists*, pp. 99–105. Philadelphia: n.p.

Cripps, Thomas. 1993. *Making Movies Black: The Hollywood Message Movie from World War II to the Civil Rights Era*. New York and Oxford, UK: Oxford University Press.

DeMott, Benjamin. 1990. *The Imperial Middle: Why Americans Cannot Think Straight About Class*. New York: William Morrow and Co.

Douglas, Mary. 1966. *Purity and Danger*. New York and Washington, DC: Praeger.

Dyer, Richard. 1993. *The Matter of Images*. New York and London: Routledge.

_____. 1988. "Monroe and Sexuality." In Janet Todd, ed., *Women and Film*, pp. 69–96. New York: Holmes and Meier.

Essien-Udom, E. U. 1962. *Black Nationalism: A Search for an Identity in America*. Chicago and London: University of Chicago Press.

Fassbinder, Rainer Werner. 1992. *The Anarchy of the Imagination*, Michael Töteberg and Leo A. Lensing, eds. Baltimore: Johns Hopkins University Press.

Feinbloom, Deborah Heller. 1976. *Transvestites and Transsexuals: Mixed Views*. N.p.: Delacourte Press.

Foucault, Michel. 1978. *History of Sexuality: Volume 1, An Introduction*, tr. Robert Hurley. New York: Pantheon Books

Freud, Sigmund. 1962. *Civilization [Kultur] and its Discontents*, James Strachey, tr. and ed. New York: W. W. Norton.

Gainor, J. Ellen. 1991. *Shaw's Daughters: Dramatic and Narrative Constructions of Gender*. Ann Arbor, MI: University of Michigan Press.

Garber, Marjorie. 1995. *Vice Versa: Bisexuality and the Eroticism of Everyday Life*. New York: Simon and Schuster.

_____. 1992. *Vested Interests: Cross-Dressing and Cultural Anxiety*. New York: Routledge.

Gervasi, Tom. 1984. *America's War Machine: The Pursuit of Global Dominance*. New York: Grove Press.

Giles, Jane. 1997. *The Crying Game*. London: The British Film Institute.

Gill, Brendan. 1967. "Good Causes." *The New Yorker*, December 16, pp. 108–110.

Goldberg, David Theo. 1993. *Racist Culture: Philosophy and the Politics of Meaning*. Oxford, UK, and Cambridge, MA: Blackwell.

Gornick, Vivian. 1997. *The End of the Novel of Love*. Boston: Beacon Press.

Grimm, Jacob, and Wilhelm Grimm. 1944. *The Complete Grimm's Fairy Tales*. New York: Pantheon Books.

Grover, Ron. 1997. *The Disney Touch: Disney, ABC, and the Quest for the World's Greatest Media Empire*. Chicago: Irwin.

Gull, Richard. 1997. "*The Crying Game* and the Destabilization of Masculinity." *Film and Philosophy*, 3 (1996), pp. 176–185.

Handler, Kristin. 1994. "Sexing *The Crying Game*: Difference, Identity, Ethics." *Film Quarterly* 47:3 (Spring), pp. 31–42.

Hegel, G. W. F. 1977. *Phenomenology of Spirit,* A. V. Miller, tr. Oxford, UK: Oxford University Press.

Heidegger, Martin. 1996. *Being and Time,* Joan Stambaugh, tr. New York: State University of New York Press.

Hochschild, Arlie Russell. 1989. *The Second Shift: Working Parents and the Revolution at Home.* New York: Viking.

Holmlund, Christine. 1991. "When Is a Lesbian Not a Lesbian?: The Lesbian Continuum and the Mainstream Femme Film." *Camera Obscura* 25–26, pp. 145–178.

hooks, bell. 1994. *Outlaw Culture.* New York: Routledge.

hooks, bell, and Anuradha Dingwaney. 1992. "*Mississippi Masala.*" *Z Magazine,* July/August, pp. 41–43.

Horkheimer, Max, and Theodor W. Adorno. 1982. *Dialectic of Enlightenment.* New York: Continuum.

Ibsen, Henrik. 1985. *A Doll's House,* Michael Meyer, tr. London: Methuen.

Johnson, Brian D.. 1991. "Sex at the Color Bar: Spike Lee Dissects Inter-racial Romance." *Macleans,* June 17, p. 55.

Jordan, Neil. 1993. *A Neil Jordan Reader.* New York: Vintage.

Kael, Pauline. 1971. "Raising Kane." In *The Citizen Kane Book,* shooting script by Herman J. Mankiewicz and Orson Welles, notes on the script by Gary Carey, pp. 1–84. Boston: Little, Brown and Co.

Kant, Immanuel. 1987. *Critique of Judgment,* Werner S. Pluhar, tr. Indianapolis, IN, and Cambridge, MA: Hackett Publishers.

Kaplan, E. Ann. 1997. *Looking for the Other: Feminism, Film, and the Imperial Gaze.* New York and London: Routledge.

Kauffmann, Stanley. 1986. "Harsh Contradictions." *The New Republic,* May 12, pp. 24–26.

_____. 1967. "Recent Wars." *The New Republic,* December 16, pp. 19, 30.

Kellner, Douglas. 1995. "Spike Lee's Morality Tales." In Cynthia A. Freeland and Thomas E. Wartenberg, eds., *Philosophy and Film,* pp. 201–217. New York and London: Routledge.

Kort, Michele. 1985. "Independent Filmmaker Donna Deitch Controls her Whole Show." *MS,* November, p. 66.

Knight, Arthur. 1967. "The New Look." *Saturday Review,* December 16, p. 47.

Kramer, Stanley, with Thomas M. Coffey. 1997. *A Mad, Mad, Mad, Mad World: A Life in Hollywood.* New York: Harcourt Brace & Company.

Kroll, Jack, Vern E. Smith, and Andrew Murr. 1991. "Spiking a Fever." *Newsweek,* June 10, pp. 44–47.

Lapsley, Robert, and Michael Westlake. 1992. "From *Casablanca* to *Pretty Woman*: The Politics of Romance." *Screen* 33:1 (Spring), pp. 27–49.

_____. 1988. *Film Theory: An Introduction.* Manchester, UK: Manchester University Press.

Mayne, Judith. 1990. "Fassbinder's *Ali: Fear Eats the Soul* and Spectatorship." In Peter Lehman, ed., *Close Viewings: An Anthology of New Film Criticism*, pp. 353–369. Tallahassee: Florida State University Press.

Merck, Mandy. 1987. "*Desert Hearts.*" *The Independent* 10:6 (July), p. 17.

Morgenstern, Joseph. 1967. "Spence and Supergirl." *Newsweek,* December 25, pp. 70–77.

Mulvey, Laura. 1981. "Afterthoughts on 'Visual Pleasure and Narrative Cinema' Inspired by *Duel in the Sun* (King Vidor, 1946)." *Framework* 15–17, pp. 12–15.

———. 1975. "Visual Pleasure and Narrative Cinema." *Screen* 16:3 (Autumn), pp. 6–18.

Myrdal, Gunnar. 1944. *An American Dilemma: The Negro Problem and Modern Democracy.* New York: Harper and Row.

Neale, Steve. 1992. "The Big Romance or Something Wild?: Romantic Comedy Today." *Screen* 33:3 (Autumn), pp. 284–299.

Neale, Steve, and Frank Krutnik. 1990. *Popular Film and Television Comedy.* New York and London: Routledge.

Nietzsche, Friedrich. 1968. *Genealogy of Morals.* In *Basic Writings of Nietzsche,* Walter Kaufmann, ed. and tr. New York: Modern Library.

Noble, Lorraine, ed. 1936. *Four-Star Scripts.* New York: Doubleday, Doran and Co.

Ovid. 1955. *Metamorphoses,* Rolfe Humphries, tr. Bloomington: Indiana University Press.

Pappas, Nickolas. 1995. "Failures of Marriage in *Sea of Love* (The Love of Men, the Respect of Women)." In Cynthia A. Freeland and Thomas E. Wartenberg, eds., *Philosophy and Film,* pp. 109–125. New York and London: Routledge.

Plato. 1970. *The Symposium of Plato,* Suzy Q. Groden, tr. John A. Brentlinger, ed. Amherst: University of Massachusetts Press.

Radner, Hilary. 1993. "Pretty Is as Pretty Does: Free Enterprise and the Marriage Plot." In Jim Collins, Hilary Radner, and Ava Preacher Collins, eds., *Film Theory Goes to the Movies,* pp. 56–76. New York: Routledge.

Raskin, Robert. 1934. *It Happened One Night.* Hollywood, CA: Script City.

Riddell, Tom. 1985. "Concentration and Inefficiency in the Defense Sector: Policy Options." *Journal of Economic Issues* 19:2 (June), pp. 451–461.

Rowe, Kathleen. 1995. *The Unruly Woman: Gender and the Genres of Laughter.* Austin: University of Texas Press.

Rule, Jane. 1964. *Desert of the Heart.* Tallahassee, TN: Naiad Press.

Russo, Vito. 1987. *The Celluloid Closet: Homosexuality in the Movies.* New York: Harper and Row.

Sedgwick, Eve Kosofsky. 1990. *Epistemology of the Closet.* Berkeley: University of California Press.

Shakespeare, William. 1980. *Romeo and Juliet,* Brian Gibbons, ed. London and New York: Methuen.

Shaw, George Bernard. 1980. *The Collected Screenplays of Bernard Shaw,* Bernard F. Dukore, ed. Athens: University of Georgia Press.
_____. 1957. *Pygmalion.* London: Penguin Books.
Silverman, Kaja. 1992. *Male Subjectivity at the Margins.* New York and London: Routledge.
_____. 1989. "Fassbinder and Lacan: A Reconsideration of Gaze, Look and Image." *Camera Obscura* 19 (January), pp. 54–83.
Snead, James. 1994. *White Screens: Black Images.* New York and London: Routledge.
Sollors, Werner. 1986. *Beyond Ethnicity: Consent and Descent in American Culture.* New York and Oxford, UK: Oxford University Press.
Spelman, Elizabeth. 1991. *Inessential Other.* Boston: Beacon Press.
Spoto, Donald. 1978. *Stanley Kramer: Film Maker.* New York: G. P. Putnam's Sons.
Stacey, Jackie. 1995. "'If You Don't Play, You Can't Win': *Desert Hearts* and the Lesbian Romance Film." In Tamsin Wilson, ed., *Immortal, Invisible: Lesbians and the Moving Image,* pp. 92–114. London and New York: Routledge.
Sterling, Anne Fausto. 1993. "How Many Sexes Are There?" *New York Times,* March 12, p. 15.
Stone, Alan A. 1993. "Review of *The Crying Game.*" *Boston Review,* June/August, pp. 25–27.
Wartenberg, Thomas E. Forthcoming. "Descartes' Mood: The Question of Feminism in the Correspondence with Elisabeth." In Susan Bordo, ed., *Feminist Approaches to Descartes.* State College: Pennsylvania State University Press.
_____. Forthcoming. "Humanizing the Beast: *King Kong* and the Representation of Black Male Sexuality." In Daniel Bernardi, ed., *Classic Whiteness.* Minneapolis: University of Minnesota Press.
_____. 1998. "Romantic Love and the Feudal Household: *Romeo and Juliet* as Social Criticism." Unpublished manuscript.
_____. 1990. *The Forms of Power: From Domination to Transformation.* Philadelphia: Temple University Press.
Washington, Booker T. 1899. *The Future of the American Negro.* Boston: Small, Maynard and Company.
Wexman, Virginia Wright. 1993. *Creating the Couple: Love, Marriage, and Hollywood Performance.* Princeton: Princeton University Press.
White, Deborah Gray. 1985. *Ain't I a Woman? Female Slaves in the Plantation South.* New York and London: W. W. Norton & Co.
Williams, Patricia. 1991. *The Alchemy of Race and Rights.* Cambridge, MA: Harvard University Press.
Wilson, William Julius. 1980. *The Declining Significance of Race.* Chicago: University of Chicago Press.
X, Malcolm. 1970. *By Any Means Necessary.* New York: Pathfinder Press.

Yacowar, Maurice. 1993. "Neil Jordan's Viewing Game." *Queen's Quarterly* 100:2, pp. 457–464.

Young, Lola. 1995. "'Nothing Is as It Seems': Re-viewing *The Crying Game*." In Pat Kirkham and Janet Thumin, eds., *Me Jane: Masculinity, Movies, and Women*, pp. 273–285. New York: St. Martin's Press.

Zilliax, Amy. 1995. "The Scorpion and the Frog: Agency and Identity in Neil Jordan's *The Crying Game*." *Camera Obscura* 35 (May), pp. 25–51.

Index

CPSIA information can be obtained at www.ICGtesting.com
Printed in the USA
LVOW12s0743181214

419391LV00001B/7/P